Elementary
Survey Samplin

Elementary Survey Sampling

SECOND EDITION

RICHARD L. SCHEAFFER
University of Florida

WILLIAM MENDENHALL
University of Florida

LYMAN OTT
Merrell Research Center

Duxbury Press
North Scituate, Massachusetts

Library of Congress Cataloging in Publication Data

Scheaffer, Richard L.
   Elementary survey sampling.

   Authors' names in different order in earlier ed.
   Includes index.
   1. Sampling (Statistics) I. Mendenhall, William, joint author. II. Ott, Lyman, joint author. III. Title.
HA31.2.M45 1979   001.4'33   78-18866
ISBN 0-87872-170-3

DUXBURY PRESS
A Division of Wadsworth Publishing Company, Inc.
© 1979 by Wadsworth Publishing Company, Inc., Belmont, California 94002. All rights reserved. No part of this book may be reproduced, stored in a retrieval system, or transcribed, in any form or by any means, electronic, mechanical, photocopying, recording, or otherwise, without the prior written permission of the publisher, Duxbury Press, a division of Wadsworth Publishing Company, Inc., Belmont, California.

Elementary Survey Sampling was edited and prepared for composition by Carol Beal. Interior design was provided by Sandra Rigney. The cover was designed by Ann Washer.

Printed in the United States of America
  2 3 4 5 6 7 8 9 — 83 82 81 80 79

Contents

	Preface	*ix*
1.	Introduction	*1*
2.	A Review of Some Basic Concepts	*5*
2.1	Introduction	*5*
2.2	Describing a Set of Measurements	*6*
2.3	Probability	*7*
2.4	Expectations	*8*
2.5	Covariance and Correlation	*9*
2.6	Expectations of Linear Functions of Random Variables	*11*
2.7	Estimation	*12*
2.8	Summary	*15*
3.	Elements of the Sampling Problem	*19*
3.1	Introduction	*19*
3.2	Technical Terms	*20*

3.3	How to Select the Sample: The Design of the Sample Survey	*21*
3.4	Methods of Data Collection	*23*
3.5	Designing a Questionnaire	*26*
3.6	Summary	*28*

4. Simple Random Sampling *31*

4.1	Introduction	*31*
4.2	How to Draw a Simple Random Sample	*32*
4.3	Estimation of a Population Mean and Total	*34*
4.4	Selecting the Sample Size for Estimating Population Means and Totals	*42*
4.5	Estimation of a Population Proportion	*45*
4.6	Summary	*50*

5. Stratified Random Sampling *59*

5.1	Introduction	*59*
5.2	How to Draw a Stratified Random Sample	*60*
5.3	Estimation of a Population Mean and Total	*62*
5.4	Selecting the Sample Size for Estimating Population Means and Totals	*65*
5.5	Allocation of the Sample	*68*
5.6	Estimation of a Population Proportion	*76*
5.7	Selecting the Sample Size and Allocating the Sample to Estimate Proportions	*78*
5.8	Additional Comments on Stratified Sampling	*84*
5.9	An Optimal Rule for Choosing Strata	*88*
5.10	Summary	*89*

6. Ratio and Regression Estimation *99*

6.1	Introduction	*99*
6.2	Surveys That Require the Use of Ratio Estimators	*100*
6.3	Ratio Estimation Using Simple Random Sampling	*101*
6.4	Selecting the Sample Size	*110*
6.5	When to Use Ratio Estimation	*118*

6.6	Ratio Estimation in Stratified Random Sampling	*119*
6.7	Regression Estimation	*123*
6.8	Difference Estimation	*125*
6.9	Summary	*129*

7. Cluster Sampling *141*

7.1	Introduction	*141*
7.2	How to Draw a Cluster Sample	*142*
7.3	Estimation of a Population Mean and Total	*144*
7.4	Selecting the Sample Size for Estimating Population Means and Totals	*151*
7.5	Estimation of a Population Proportion	*155*
7.6	Selecting the Sample Size for Estimating Proportions	*158*
7.7	Cluster Sampling Combined with Stratification	*159*
7.8	Summary	*161*

8. Systematic Sampling *173*

8.1	Introduction	*173*
8.2	How to Draw a Systematic Sample	*175*
8.3	Estimation of a Population Mean and Total	*176*
8.4	Estimation of a Population Proportion	*182*
8.5	Selecting the Sample Size	*184*
8.6	Repeated Systematic Sampling	*187*
8.7	Summary	*190*

9. Two-Stage Cluster Sampling *201*

9.1	Introduction	*201*
9.2	How to Draw a Two-Stage Cluster Sample	*202*
9.3	Unbiased Estimation of a Population Mean and Total	*203*
9.4	Ratio Estimation of a Population Mean	*207*
9.5	Estimation of a Population Proportion	*209*
9.6	Summary	*212*

10. Sampling from Wildlife Populations — 217

- 10.1 Introduction — 217
- 10.2 Estimation of a Population Size Using Direct Sampling — 218
- 10.3 Estimation of a Population Size Using Inverse Sampling — 220
- 10.4 Choosing Sample Sizes for Direct and Inverse Sampling — 221
- 10.5 Summary — 225

11. Supplemental Topics — 229

- 11.1 Introduction — 229
- 11.2 Interpenetrating Subsamples — 229
- 11.3 Estimation of Means and Totals over Subpopulations — 232
- 11.4 Random Response Model — 237
- 11.5 Selecting the Number of Callbacks — 239
- 11.6 Summary — 241

12. Summary — 245

Appendix — 249

Answers — 271

Index — 277

Preface

Elementary Survey Sampling is an introductory text on the design and analysis of sample surveys intended for students of business, the social sciences, or natural resource management. The only prerequisite is an elementary course in statistics. The numerous examples, with solutions, also make it suitable for use as a supplemental text for higher-level courses.

Since it is written to appeal to students of limited mathematical background, the text emphasizes the practical aspects of survey problems. Each major chapter introduces a sample survey design or a possible estimation procedure by describing a pertinent practical problem and then explaining the suitability of the methodology proposed. This introduction is followed by the appropriate estimation procedures and a compact presentation of the formulas; then a practical example is worked out. The text is not entirely cookbook in nature. Explanations that appeal to the students' intuition are supplied to justify many of the formulas and to support the choice of particular sample survey designs. Examples and exercises have been selected from many fields of application. Answers, which are given for all exercises, may be subject to small rounding errors because of the complexity of some of the formulas.

The "Experiences with Real Data" sections found at the end of most chapters include suggestions on how the student can become involved with real sampling problems. These may be large or small projects, with some requiring computations to be handled by a computer, but we have

Preface

found such projects to be valuable learning experiences for students taking a sampling course. Working on a real project forces students to think about every aspect of the survey and causes them to realize that some ideas that sound simple in the textbook are not so easily carried out in practice.

The text includes a review of elementary concepts (chapters 1 and 2) and a description of terms pertinent to survey sampling, along with a discussion of the design of questionnaires and methods of data collection (chapter 3). Chapters 4, 5, 7, and 8 present the four most common sample survey designs—namely, simple random sampling, stratified random sampling, cluster sampling, and systematic sampling, respectively. Chapter 6 discusses ratio and regression estimation. The remaining chapters deal with two-stage cluster sampling, sampling of animal populations, and other specialized problems that occur in survey sampling.

There are several new and additional features incorporated into this second edition. The concepts of probability, probability distributions, and expectation are expanded, and a few simple numerical illustrations are included. This allows for the development of some elementary formulas later in the text. Numerical examples also illustrate the concept of confidence intervals and the fact that sample means tend to have normal distributions.

An approximately optimal rule for choosing strata is given in chapter 5, while chapter 6 includes new sections on regression and difference estimators. The concept of stratification is expanded to include ratio estimators and cluster sampling as well as a model for selecting callbacks from among nonrespondents.

In addition to the experiences with real data, described above, additional exercises have been included in most chapters for this second edition.

We wish to express our sincere appreciation to the many people who have helped in the preparation of this text. Particular thanks are due to the reviewers for their helpful comments during the preparation of this manuscript. Thanks are also due to Professor A. Hald for his kind permission to use the table of normal curve areas reprinted in the appendix. We are also deeply indebted to the typists who have given much of their time in preparing this text: Judith Donnelley, Mary Jackson, Catherine Kennedy, and Shirley Morley. Finally, we thank our families for assistance and encouragement throughout the duration of this project.

Richard L. Scheaffer
William Mendenhall
Lyman Ott

1.
Introduction

Introductory courses stress the fact that modern statistics is a theory of information with inference as its objective. The target of our curiosity is a set of measurements, a *population*, that exists in fact or could be generated by repeated experimentation. The medium of inference is the *sample*, which is a subset of measurements selected from the population. We wish to make an inference about the population based on the characteristics of the sample—or, equivalently, the information contained in the sample.

For example, suppose that a chain of department stores maintains customer charge accounts. The amount of money owed the company will vary from day to day as new charges are made and some accounts are paid. Indeed, the set of amounts due the company on a given day represents a population of measurements of considerable interest to the management. The population characteristic of interest is the total of all measurements in the population or, equivalently, the daily total credit load.

Keeping track of the daily total credit associated with charge accounts might seem to be a simple task for an electronic computer. However, the data must be updated daily, and this takes time. A simpler method for determining the total credit load associated with the charge accounts would be to randomly sample the population of accounts on a given day, estimate the average amount owed per account, and multiply by the number of accounts. In other words, we would employ a statistical estimator to make an inference about the population total. Elementary

1. Introduction

statistics tells us that this estimate can be made as accurate as we wish simply by increasing the sample size. The resulting estimate either would be accompanied by a bound on the error of estimation (Mendenhall, 1975, chapter 8) or would be expressed as a confidence interval. Thus information in the sample is used to make an inference about the population.

Many interesting examples of the practical uses of statistics in general and sampling in particular can be found in *Statistics: A Guide to the Unknown* (see the references at the end of this chapter). You might want to look at some of the methods and uses of opinion polling discussed in "Opinion Polling in a Democracy" by George Gallup and "Election Night on Television" by R. F. Link. Those interested in wildlife ecology should read "The Plight of the Whales" by D. G. Chapman. Find out how interrailroad and interairline billing is handled economically through sampling by reading "How Accountants Save Money by Sampling" by John Neter.

Since the objective of modern statistics is inference, you may question what particular aspect of statistics will be covered in a course on sample survey design. The answer to this is twofold. First, we will focus on the economics of purchasing a specific quantity of information. More specifically, how can we design sampling procedures that reduce the cost of a fixed quantity of information? Although introductory courses in statistics acknowledge the importance of this subject, they place major emphasis on basic concepts and on how to make inferences in specific situations *after* the data have been collected. The second distinguishing feature of our topic is that it is aimed at the particular types of sampling situations and inferential problems most frequently encountered in business, the social sciences, and natural resource management (timber, wildlife, and recreation) rather than in the physical sciences.

Even the terminology of the social scientist differs from that of the physical scientist. Social scientists conduct *surveys* to collect a sample, while physical scientists perform *experiments*. Thus we acknowledge that differences exist from one field of science to another in the nature of the populations and the manner in which a sample can be drawn. For example, populations of voters, financial accounts, or animals of a particular species may contain only a small number of elements. In contrast, the conceptual population of responses generated by measuring the yield of a chemical process is very large indeed. (You may recall that the properties of estimators and test statistics covered in most introductory courses assume that the population of interest is large relative to the sample.) Limitations placed on the sampling procedure also vary from one area of science to another. Sampling in the biological and physical sciences can frequently be performed under controlled experimental conditions. Such control is frequently impossible in the social sciences, business, and natural resource management. For example, a medical

1. Introduction

researcher might compare the growth of rats subjected to two different drugs. For this experiment the initial weights of the rats and the daily intake of food could be controlled to reduce unwanted variation in the experiment. In contrast, very few variables can be controlled in comparing the effect of two different television advertisements on sales for a given product; no control is possible when studying the effect of environmental conditions on the number of seals in the North Pacific Ocean.

In summary, this text is concerned with the peculiarities of sampling and inference commonly encountered in business, the social sciences, and natural resource management. Specifically, we will consider methods for actually selecting the sample from an existing population and ways of circumventing various difficulties that arise. Methods for designing surveys that capitalize on characteristics of the population will be presented along with associated estimators to reduce the cost for acquiring an estimate of specified accuracy.

Chapter 2 reviews some of the basic concepts encountered in introductory statistics, including the fundamental role that probability plays in making inferences. Chapter 3 presents some of the basic terminology of sampling, as well as a discussion of problems arising in sample survey design. Simple random sampling, familiar to the beginning student, is carefully presented in chapter 4; it includes physical procedures for actually selecting the sample. Following chapters cover economical methods for selecting a sample and associated methods for estimating population parameters.

In reading this text, keep in mind that the ultimate objective of each chapter is *inference*. Identify the sampling procedure associated with each chapter, the population parameters of interest, their estimators and associated bounds on the errors of estimation. Develop an intuitive understanding and appreciation for the benefits to be derived from specialized sampling procedures. Focus on the broad concepts and do not become hypnotized by the formulas for estimators and variances that sometimes are unavoidably complicated. In short, one should focus on the forest rather than the trees. Work some exercises and the details will fall into place.

REFERENCES

"Careers in Statistics." *American Statistical Association* and the *Institute of Mathematical Statistics*, 1973.

Mendenhall, W. *Introduction to Probability and Statistics.* 4th ed. N. Scituate, Mass.: Duxbury Press, 1975.

Tanur, J. M.; Mosteller, F.; Kruskal, W. H.; Pieters, R. S.; and Rising, G. R., eds. *Statistics: A Guide to the Unknown.* San Francisco: Holden-Day, 1972.

2.
A Review of Some Basic Concepts

2.1 INTRODUCTION

Knowledge of the basic concepts of statistics is a prerequisite for a study of sample survey design. Thus in this chapter we will review some of these basic concepts.

The ultimate objective of statistics is to make inferences about a population based on information contained in a sample. The target of our inference, the population, is a set of measurements, finite or infinite, existing or conceptual. Hence the first step in statistics is to find a way to phrase an inference about a population or, equivalently, to describe a set of measurements. Thus frequency distributions and numerical descriptive measures are the first topics of our review.

The second step in statistics is to consider how inferences can be made about the population based on information contained in a sample. To do this we must consider probability distributions of sample quantities and the related concept of expectation. Knowledge of probability distributions associated with the sample allows us to choose proper inference-making procedures and to attach measures of goodness to such inferences.

The method of inference primarily employed in business and the social sciences is estimation. We may wish to estimate the total assets of a corporation, the fraction of voters favoring candidate Jones, or the number of campers using a state park during a given period of time. Hence we must understand the basic concepts underlying the selection of an estimator of a population parameter, the method for evaluating its goodness, and the concepts involved in interval estimation. Because the bias and variance of estimators determine their goodness, we need to review the basic ideas concerned with the expectation of a random variable and the notions of variance and covariance.

The subsequent sections follow the outline given above. We begin with a review of the primary problem, namely, how to describe a set of measurements. We then rapidly review the probabilistic model for the repetition of an experiment. We explain how the model can be used to infer the characteristics of a population and discuss random variables, probability distributions, and expectations. Finally, we present the basic concepts associated with point and interval estimation.

2.2 DESCRIBING A SET OF MEASUREMENTS

It is often useful to summarize a set of measurements (population or sample) by constructing a relative frequency histogram (see Mendenhall, 1975, chapter 3). This graph gives a useful display of the data, but it is not of much use for inferential purposes. Thus we need to consider numerical descriptive measures, particularly the mean, variance, and standard deviation.

The populations we consider in this text generally contain a finite number N of elements. Let $\mathcal{U} = \{u_1, u_2, \ldots, u_N\}$ denote such a population, where u_i is the measurement of interest on the ith element, and let $\{y_1, \ldots, y_n\}$ denote a sample selected from $\mathcal{U}$. The population mean, μ, is the average of the elements of $\mathcal{U}$, that is,

$$\mu = \frac{1}{N} \sum_{i=1}^{N} u_i$$

and the population variance, σ^2, is the average of the square of the deviations about μ, or

$$\sigma^2 = \frac{1}{N} \sum_{i=1}^{N} (u_i - \mu)^2$$

The mean μ measures the "center" of the population and σ^2 measures the spread of the observations about the mean. The sample mean and variance are given, respectively, by

$$\bar{y} = \frac{1}{n} \sum_{i=1}^{n} y_i$$

and

$$s^2 = \frac{\sum_{i=1}^{n} (y_i - \bar{y})^2}{n - 1}$$

2.3 Probability

[Note that the sample variance has a divisor of $(n - 1)$.] The standard deviation is the square root of the variance, σ for the population and s for the sample.

One result that connects the concepts of mean, standard deviation, and relative frequency is Tchebysheff's Theorem, which states that, for any $k \geq 1$, *at least* $(1 - 1/k^2)$ of a set of measurements will lie within k standard deviations of their mean. For example, letting $k = 2$, at least 3/4 of a set of measurements must lie within 2 standard deviations of their mean. Usually this fraction is much greater than 3/4. Looking at this another way, the range of a set of measurements is likely to equal approximately four standard deviations.

2.3 PROBABILITY

Although a formal definition of probability will not be given here, the basic notions of probability, and the related concept of random variable, must be briefly mentioned so that you will understand why so much emphasis is placed on methods of drawing samples in later chapters. Suppose from the population $\mathcal{U} = \{u_1, \ldots, u_N\}$ we sample one element. Let y denote the value that the sampled element will take on. Before actually carrying out the sampling, y can range over all the values $u_1, u_2, \ldots, u_N$. Thus before the sampling is actually completed, we can talk about the *probability*, or chance, that y will take on a specific value, say u_i. The subscript i can denote any of the values $1, 2, \ldots, N$. Notationally, we are interested in $P[y = u_i]$, the probability that y takes on the value u_i. The quantity y is called a *random variable* since the actual value it takes on for a specific sample varies from u_1 to u_N and there is a certain chance, or probability, associated with each possible value.

What is the probability that $y = u_i$? This question *cannot* be answered until we know specifically how the one element is to be selected from the population. Suppose that the measurements $\{u_1, \ldots, u_N\}$ are thoroughly mixed in a box and one is drawn "at random." Then it seems reasonable to suppose that all values $u_1, \ldots, u_N$ are equally likely to occur, or $P[y = u_i] = 1/N$. The possible values for y $(u_1, \ldots, u_N)$ along with the respective probabilities $(1/N, \ldots, 1/N$ in this case) form the *probability distribution* for the random variable y.

It is not always true that y will have equal probabilities for all possible values. Suppose you have a dime and a half-dollar in your pocket. If you reach into your pocket and choose the first coin you touch, will the coins each have probability 1/2 of being selected? Certainly not. You are more likely to select the half-dollar simply because of its larger relative size.

The inferential procedures outlined in the following chapters are tied very strictly to specific probability distributions for the sample. The methods will not work well unless the sampling rules with which they are associated are carefully obeyed. It is of the utmost importance to realize that *no* scientific inferential method can be used with samples that do not have a discernible probability distribution attached to them.

We will frequently be interested in the probabilistic behavior of functions of sample observations, such as the sample mean. To gain more insight into the behavior of probability distributions, consider the following specific numerical example. Let $\mathcal{U} = \{1, 2, 3, 4\}$ and suppose a sample of size $n = 2$ is to be selected, with elements selected without replacement. The possible samples are then $\{1, 2\}$, $\{1, 3\}$, $\{1, 4\}$, $\{2, 3\}$, $\{2, 4\}$, and $\{3, 4\}$. The respective possible values for $\bar{y} = 1/2(y_1 + y_2)$ are 1.5, 2, 2.5, 2.5, 3, and 3.5. If the six samples are equally likely (a method of constructing samples like this is given in chapter 4), then $P[\bar{y} = 1.5] = 1/6$. Note, however, that $P[\bar{y} = 2.5] = 1/3$ since two samples result in this same value.

We see that the possible values of $\bar{y}$ do not encompass the range of population values (1 to 4 in this case). Also, the probabilities associated with values of $\bar{y}$ tend to become larger for the values near the center. We will see more of the phenomenon later.

Looking back at the preceding numerical example, we see that the outcome on the first draw greatly influences the outcome on the second. For example, if the first draw is a 3, then the second draw must be a 1, 2, or 4. Thus we say that the second outcome is *dependent* upon the first. Now, there are occasions in sampling (chapter 5 will furnish one example) in which outcomes for one variable do not depend on what has happened to another. As an illustration, suppose that the four integers in $\mathcal{U}$ are divided before sampling so that we have, in effect, two populations, $\mathcal{U}_1 = \{1, 2\}$ and $\mathcal{U}_2 = \{3, 4\}$. If the first sampled element is randomly drawn from $\mathcal{U}_1$ and the second from $\mathcal{U}_2$, then the outcome of the second draw cannot be affected by what happened on the first draw. Letting y_1 represent the outcome on the first draw and y_2 the outcome on the second, we say that the random variables y_1 and y_2 are *independent*.

The rules for calculating probability distributions for various functions and sampling plans get quite complicated, and it is not our intention to investigate this problem in detail. However, keep in mind that each sampling scheme discussed in future chapters will allow the calculation of probabilities for possible sample values, and it is this fact that allows us to attribute certain properties to the various inference procedures.

2.4 EXPECTATIONS

It is sometimes difficult or inconvenient to work with the entire probability distribution for a random variable, and so we narrow our study

2.5 Covariance and Correlation

to some numerical descriptive measures of the distribution, usually obtained as expectations. If $g(y)$ denotes a function of y and $p(y)$ denotes the probability that the random variable takes on the value y, then the *expected value* or *mean value* of $g(y)$ is given by

$$E[g(y)] = \sum_y g(y)p(y)$$

where the summation is over all values of y for which $p(y) > 0$.

Suppose, for example, that y denotes an observation selected at random from $\mathcal{U} = \{u_1, \ldots, u_N\}$. Then $p(y) = 1/N$ for y equal to any of the values $u_1, \ldots, u_N$ and

$$E(y) = \sum_y yp(y) = \sum_{i=1}^{N} u_i\left(\frac{1}{N}\right) = \mu$$

where μ is the population mean. If one observation is drawn from $\mathcal{U}$ and recorded, and if this process is repeated over and over again, each time drawing from the same $\mathcal{U}$, then after many trials, the average value of these sample measurements will be close to μ. Thus μ provides a theoretical average value (or expected value) for y.

The variance of y, denoted by $V(y)$, is defined to be $E(y - \mu)^2$ and hence

$$V(y) = E(y - \mu)^2 = \sum_{i=1}^{N} (u_i - \mu)^2 \left(\frac{1}{N}\right) = \sigma^2$$

where σ^2 is as defined in section 2.2.

Consider the numerical example for $\bar{y}$ given in section 2.3. There $\bar{y}$ can take on the values 1.5, 2, 2.5, 2.5, 3, and 3.5 with equal probabilities, and thus it follows that

$$E(\bar{y}) = \sum_{\bar{y}} \bar{y}p(\bar{y}) = \tfrac{1}{6}(1.5 + 2 + 2.5 + 2.5 + 3 + 3.5) = 2.5$$

Note that if y is a single observation chosen from $\mathcal{U} = \{1, 2, 3, 4\}$ at random, then $E(y) = \mu = 2.5$, also. The fact that $E(\bar{y}) = \mu$ will be pursued in more detail in chapter 4.

2.5 COVARIANCE AND CORRELATION

Often an experiment yields more than one random variable of interest. For example, the psychologist measures more than one characteristic per individual in a study of human behavior. Typical variables might be a measure of intelligence, y_1, a personality measure, y_2, and other variables representing test scores or measures of physical characteristics. Often we are interested in the simple dependence of pairs of variables, such as the relationship between personality and intelligence, or between college

2. A Review of Some Basic Concepts

achievement and college board scores. Particularly, we ask whether data representing paired observations of y_1 and y_2 on a number of people imply a dependence between the two variables. If so, how strong is the dependence?

Intuitively, we think of dependence of two random variables, y_1 and y_2, as implying that one, say y_1, either increases or decreases as y_2 changes. We will confine our attention to two measures of dependence, the *covariance* and the *simple coefficient of linear correlation*, and will utilize figures 2.1(a) and (b) to justify choosing them as measures of dependence. These figures represent plotted points for two (random) samples of $n = 10$ experimental units drawn from a population. Measurements of y_1 and y_2 were made on each experimental unit. If all of the points lie on a straight line, as indicated in figure 2.1(a), y_1 and y_2 are obviously dependent. In contrast, figure 2.1(b) indicates little or no dependence between y_1 and y_2.

Suppose we actually know μ_1 and μ_2, the means of y_1 and y_2, respectively, and locate this point on the graphs, figure 2.1. Now locate a plotted point on figure 2.1(a) and measure the deviations, $(y_1 - \mu_1)$ and $(y_2 - \mu_2)$. Note that both deviations assume the same algebraic sign for a particular point; hence, their product, $(y_1 - \mu_1)(y_2 - \mu_2)$, is positive. This will be true for all plotted points on figure 2.1(a). Points to the right of (μ_1, μ_2) will yield pairs of positive deviations, points to the left will produce pairs of negative deviations, and the average of the product of the deviations $(y_1 - \mu_1)(y_2 - \mu_2)$ will be "large" and positive. If the linear relation indicated in figure 2.1(a) had sloped downward to the right, all corresponding pairs of deviations would be of the opposite sign, and the average value of $(y_1 - \mu_1)(y_2 - \mu_2)$ would be a large negative number.

The situation described above will not occur for figure 2.1(b), where little or no dependence exists between y_1 and y_2. Corresponding

Figure 2.1/*Plotted points of two samples*

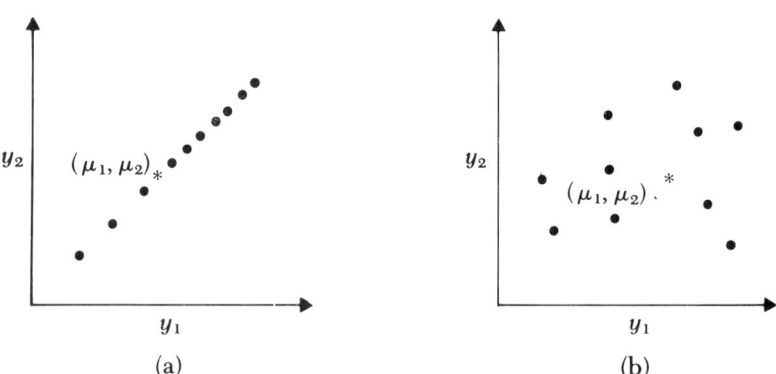

2.6 Expectations of Linear Functions of Random Variables

deviations, $(y_1 - \mu_1)$ and $(y_2 - \mu_2)$, will assume the same algebraic sign for some points and opposite signs for others. Thus the product $(y_1 - \mu_1)(y_2 - \mu_2)$ will be positive for some points, negative for others, and will average to some value near zero.

Clearly, then, the expected (average) value of $(y_1 - \mu_1)(y_2 - \mu_2)$ provides a measure of the linear dependence of y_1 and y_2. This quantity, defined over the two corresponding populations associated with y_1 and y_2, is called the *covariance* of y_1 and y_2. We denote the covariance between y_1 and y_2 thus:

$$\text{Cov}(y_1, y_2) = E[(y_1 - \mu_1)(y_2 - \mu_2)]$$

The larger the absolute value of the covariance of y_1 and y_2, the greater will be the linear dependence between y_1 and y_2. Positive values indicate that y_1 increases as y_2 increases; negative values indicate that y_1 decreases as y_2 increases. A zero value of the covariance indicates no linear dependence between y_1 and y_2.

Unfortunately, it is difficult to use the covariance as an absolute measure of dependence, because its value depends upon the scale of measurement. Consequently, it is difficult to determine whether a particular covariance is "large" at first glance. We can eliminate this difficulty by standardizing its value, using the simple coefficient of linear correlation. Thus the population linear coefficient of correlation,

$$\rho = \frac{\text{Cov}(y_1, y_2)}{\sigma_1 \sigma_2}$$

(where σ_1 and σ_2 are the standard deviations of y_1 and y_2, respectively) is related to the covariance and can assume values in the interval $-1 \leq \rho \leq 1$. The sample coefficient of correlation is used as an estimator of ρ and is discussed in most introductory courses. Further information on this subject can be found in Mendenhall (1975, chapter 10).

2.6 EXPECTATIONS OF LINEAR FUNCTIONS OF RANDOM VARIABLES

We are very often interested in functions of sample observations that can be expressed as linear functions. That is, if $y_1, \ldots, y_n$ denotes a sample of size n, then a linear function L is of the form

$$L = \sum_{i=1}^{n} a_i y_i$$

for known constants $a_1, a_2, \ldots, a_n$. The sample mean

$$\bar{y} = \frac{1}{n} \sum_{i=1}^{n} y_i$$

2. A Review of Some Basic Concepts

is such a function, with $a_i = 1/n$ for $i = 1, \ldots, n$. It will be necessary on many occasions to investigate the mean and variance of functions of the form of L, and to this end the following results are of fundamental importance:

$$E(L) = \sum_{i=1}^{n} a_i E(y_i)$$

and

$$V(L) = \sum_{i=1}^{n} a_i^2 V(y_i) + 2 \sum\sum_{i<j} a_i a_j \operatorname{Cov}(y_i, y_j)$$

The double sum is taken over all pairs (y_i, y_j) with $i < j$. We will defer the discussion of examples until chapter 4 and the appendix.

For *independent* random variables, y_i and y_j, it can be shown that $\operatorname{Cov}(y_i, y_j) = 0$. Thus the formula for $V(L)$ simplifies in the case of independence and becomes

$$V(L) = \sum_{i=1}^{n} a_i^2 V(y_i)$$

2.7 ESTIMATION

The objective of any sample survey is to make inferences about a population of interest based on information obtained in a sample from that population. Inferences in sample surveys are usually aimed at the *estimation* of certain numerical characteristics of the population, such as the mean, total, or variance. These numerical descriptive measures of the population are called *parameters*.

An *estimator* is a function of observable random variables, and perhaps other known constants, used to estimate a parameter. For example, the sample mean $\bar{y}$ can be used as an estimator of the population mean μ. $\bar{y}$ is an estimator since it is a function of sample observations. Note that $\bar{y}$ is, however, a random variable and has a probability distribution that depends on the sampling mechanism, as pointed out in section 2.3. Some of the possible values that $\bar{y}$ can take on will be close to μ and others might be quite far from μ on either the positive or negative side. If we are to take a sample and calculate a specific value as our best estimate of μ, it would be nice to know that, on the average, $\bar{y}$ generates values that center about μ and are in general quite close to μ. Thus we would want to select a sampling plan that ensures us that $E(\bar{y}) = \mu$ and $V(\bar{y})$ is "small."

In general, suppose that $\hat{\theta}$ is an estimator of the parameter θ. Two properties that we would like $\hat{\theta}$ to possess are

1. $E(\hat{\theta}) = \theta$.
2. $V(\hat{\theta}) = \sigma_{\hat{\theta}}^2$ is small.

An estimator possessing property 1 is said to be *unbiased*. As for property 2, we will not discuss minimum-variance unbiased estimators in this text,

2.7 Estimation

but we will compare unbiased estimators on the basis of their variances. If two unbiased estimators are available for θ, we will generally give preference to the one with the smaller variance.

To summarize, this text will investigate a number of combinations of sampling plans and estimators which give rise to unbiased estimators with small variance.

Although the probability distribution of $\bar{y}$, a common estimator, will depend on the sampling mechanism and the sizes of the sample and population, in many instances the sample mean tends to have a bell-shaped symmetric distribution known as the *normal distribution*. This is especially true if n is large, say $n \geq 30$. We see a normal curve sketched through the histogram of figure 2.2.

To get some further idea of the shape of probability distributions for sample means consider the following two examples.

Example 2.1
A population of size $N = 100$ measurements was generated by computer and found to have a mean μ of 52.575 and a variance σ^2 of 886.847. The actual population values are given in table 4 of the appendix. A sample of size $n = 20$ was drawn from this population in such a manner that every possible sample of that size had an equal chance of being selected (see chapter 4). This process was repeated until 50 such samples were generated. The frequency histogram of the sample means turned out as displayed in figure 2.2. (The relative frequency histogram would assume this same shape.) Note the tendency of the histogram to be bell-shaped and symmetric, although any histogram involving only 50 samples is not likely to be perfectly symmetric.

Figure 2.2/*Distribution of sample means for $N = 100$ and $n = 20$*

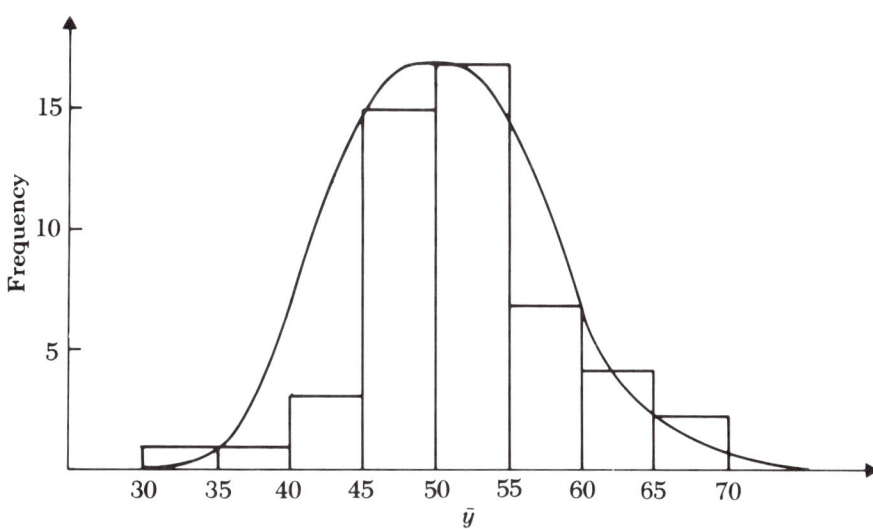

2. A Review of Some Basic Concepts

Example 2.2
This example is like example 2.1 in all respects except that $N = 20$ and $n = 15$. The actual population values are given in table 5 of the appendix and show $\mu = 9.035$ and $\sigma^2 = 52.019$. Again, 50 samples were selected and the frequency distribution of sample means is given in figure 2.3. Note once again a tendency toward a bell-shaped symmetric distribution. However, this distribution differs considerably from that of example 2.1 in spread. Here the sample means are grouped tightly about the population mean, as should be expected since the sample size of 15 is nearly equal to the population size of 20. One might suggest that this distribution does not resemble the normal distribution nearly so much as does the one of example 2.1. Of course, if $n = N$, then $\bar{y} = \mu$ and there will be no variation among sample means.

Once we know which estimator, $\hat{\theta}$, we are using in a given situation and something about its probability distribution, we can assess the magnitude of the error of estimation. We define the *error of estimation* to be $|\hat{\theta} - \theta|$. How good will a single estimate be? We cannot state that an observed estimate will be within a specified distance of θ, but we can, at least approximately, find a bound B such that

$$P(|\hat{\theta} - \theta| \leq B) = 1 - \alpha$$

for any desired probability $1 - \alpha$, where $0 < \alpha < 1$. If $\hat{\theta}$ has a normal distribution, then $B = z_{\alpha/2}\sigma_{\hat{\theta}}$ where $z_{\alpha/2}$ is the value cutting off an area of

Figure 2.3/*Distribution of sample means for $N = 20$ and $n = 15$*

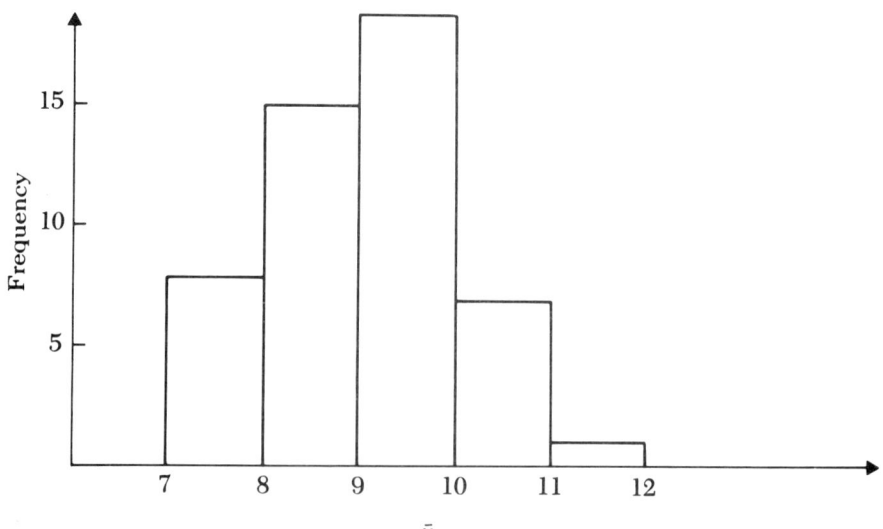

($\alpha/2$) in the right-hand tail of the standard normal distribution. The table values of $z_{\alpha/2}$ are given in table 1 of the appendix. If $1 - \alpha = .95$, then $z_{.025} = 1.96$, or approximately 2. Since many estimators we use throughout the text will not be precisely normally distributed for many values of n and N, and since Tchebysheff's Theorem states that at least 75% of the observations for *any* probability distribution will be within two standard deviations of their mean, we will use $2\sigma_{\hat{\theta}}$ as a bound on the error of estimation. This gives $P(|\hat{\theta} - \theta| \leq B) \doteq .95$ for the approximately normal cases and $P(|\hat{\theta} - \theta| \leq B) \geq .75$ in any case. Note that, in the case of normally distributed $\hat{\theta}$, a bound to satisfy any desired probability $(1 - \alpha)$ can be found through use of table 1.

If $P(|\hat{\theta} - \theta| \leq B) = 1 - \alpha$, then $P(\hat{\theta} - B \leq \theta \leq \hat{\theta} + B) = 1 - \alpha$. In this form, $(\hat{\theta} - B, \hat{\theta} + B)$ is called a *confidence interval* for θ with *confidence coefficient* $(1 - \alpha)$. The quantity $\hat{\theta} - B$ is called the lower confidence limit (LCL), and $\hat{\theta} + B$ is called the upper confidence limit (UCL).

2.8 SUMMARY

Chapter 2 presents a capsule review of the basic concepts of statistics. Making an inference about a population requires a method for describing a set of measurements and, consequently, requires a discussion of frequency histograms and numerical descriptive measures. Two very useful numerical descriptive measures are the mean and standard deviation. Although the mean is an easily understood measure of central tendency, the standard deviation acquires meaning as a measure of variation only when interpreted using Tchebysheff's Theorem or some specific distribution such as the normal.

Another important concept is the role that probability plays in making inferences about a population. The probabilist reasons from a known population to a sample. In contrast, the statistician uses probability as the vehicle to make inferences about a population based on information contained in a sample. Although a good background in probability is desirable, knowledge of the basic concepts of probability and the use of probability in inference making provides a sufficient background for understanding this text.

Random variables and their probability distributions are presented to provide a background for describing the properties of estimators of population parameters. The notions of expectations, covariance, and correlation assist in evaluating the properties of estimators.

The estimation of population parameters is the primary method of inference making used in sample survey methods. The concept of a point estimator with its corresponding measure of goodness (bound on the

2. A Review of Some Basic Concepts

error of estimation) is presented and is used as the method of inference in all subsequent chapters.

REFERENCE

Mendenhall, W. *Introduction to Probability and Statistics.* 4th ed. N. Scituate, Mass.: Duxbury Press, 1975.

EXERCISES

2.1 What is the objective of statistics?

2.2 How does a course on sample survey design differ from the standard introductory course on statistics?

2.3 Why is it essential to know how to describe a set of measurements?

2.4 How can you describe a set of measurements?

2.5 What is a parameter?

2.6 State Tchebysheff's Theorem.

2.7 Show that the sample variance s^2, given in section 2.2, is equivalent to

$$s^2 = \frac{1}{n-1}\left[\sum_{i=1}^{n} y_i^2 - n\bar{y}^2\right]$$

The latter form is usually easier for numerical calculation.

2.8 Given $n = 20$ sample measurements: 1, 2, 0, 2, 2, 4, 0, 3, 1, 2, 3, 2, 0, 1, 2, 2, 4, 2, 1, 3.
  (a) Calculate the sample mean $\bar{y}$.
  (b) Calculate s^2.
  (c) What fraction of the measurements lie within one standard deviation of the mean? Two? Three? How do these fractions agree with those given by Tchebysheff's Theorem? (This example illustrates the effectiveness of the standard deviation as a measure of the variability of a set of measurements.)

2.9 Given $n = 10$ sample measurements: 5, 2, 4, 4, 3, 4, 1, 3, 5, 4.
  (a) Calculate the sample mean.
  (b) Calculate the sample variance.
  (c) Find the fraction of measurements lying within one standard deviation of the mean. Compare these with the corresponding figures given by Tchebysheff's Theorem and the normal distribution.

2.10 What is the objective when calculating a sample mean and variance?

2.11 What do we mean when we say that two random variables are positively correlated? Negatively correlated?

2.12 What is an estimator?

2.13 How does one evaluate the goodness of an estimator?

Exercises

2.14 Describe two desirable properties for an estimator.

2.15 What is an unbiased estimator?

2.16 What is the "error of estimation"?

2.17 What is a reasonable bound on the error of estimation?

2.18 Of what value is Tchebysheff's Theorem in making statements about the error of estimation?

2.19 Refer to section 2.3 and consider the six equally likely samples of size $n = 2$ that can be generated (sampling without replacement) from $\mathcal{U} = \{1, 2, 3, 4\}$. Show numerically that $E(y_1 - y_2) = 0$ and $E(2y_1 + y_2) = 7.5$. Also, derive these results by using section 2.6.

3.
Elements of the Sampling Problem

3.1 INTRODUCTION

You will recall that the objective of statistics is to make inferences about a population based on information contained in a sample. This same objective motivates our discussion of the sampling problem. We will consider the particular problem of sampling from a finite collection of measurements (population). We will refer occasionally to populations composed of an infinite number of measurements. In most cases the inference will be in the form of an estimate of a population parameter, such as a mean, total, or proportion, with a bound on the error of estimation. For those more interested in methodology than theory, intuitive arguments will be given whenever possible to justify the use of estimators.

The first part of our discussion of the sampling problem introduces certain technical terms common to sample surveys. Next we discuss how to select a sample from the population of interest.

Each observation, or item, taken from the population contains a certain amount of information about the population parameter or parameters of interest. Since information costs money, the experimenter must determine how much information he or she should buy. Too little information prevents the experimenter from making good estimates, while too much information results in a waste of money. The quantity of information obtained in the sample depends upon the number of items sampled and upon the amount of variation in the data. This latter factor

3. Elements of the Sampling Problem

can be controlled by the method of selecting the sample, called the *design of the sample survey*; it, along with the sample size, determines the quantity of information in the sample pertinent to a population parameter. Several sample survey designs are introduced in section 3.3.

The design of the sample survey does not determine how the data are to be obtained once an item has been chosen for the sample. Thus we need to discuss methods of data collection. This is done in section 3.4, with special emphasis on the advantages and limitations of each method.

3.2 TECHNICAL TERMS

Technical terminology is kept to a minimum in this text; however, certain common terms must be defined. Let us introduce these terms by way of an example. In a certain community an opinion poll was conducted to determine public sentiment toward a bond issue in an upcoming election. The objective of the survey was to estimate the proportion of voters in the community who favored the bond issue.

Definition 3.1 An *element* is an object on which a measurement is taken.

In our example an element is a registered voter in the community. The measurement taken on an element is the voter's preference on the bond issue. Since measurements are usually considered to be numbers, the experimenter could obtain numerical data by recording a one for a voter in favor of the bond issue and a zero for a voter not in favor.

Definition 3.2 A *population* is a collection of elements about which we wish to make an inference.

The population of interest should be clearly specified by the investigator. The characteristic (numerical measurement) of interest for each member of this population is his or her preference on the bond issue, but the same population could have different numerical characteristics attached in other problems.

Definition 3.3 *Sampling units* are nonoverlapping collections of elements from the population.

A registered voter in the community is an element in the bond issue example. However, it might be more convenient and less costly to sample households (groups of elements) rather than individual voters to obtain voter preferences. In that case the units to be sampled (sampling

3.3 How to Select the Sample: The Design of the Sample Survey

units) would be households within the community. Note that each sampling unit consists of either none, one, or more than one element from the population, depending on the number of eligible voters within a given household.

If each sampling unit contains one and only one element of the population, then a sampling unit and an element from the population are identical. This situation arises if we sample individual voters rather than households within the community.

Definition 3.4   A *frame* is a list of sampling units.

If we specify the individual voter as the sampling unit, a list of all registered voters could serve as a frame for a public opinion poll. Note that this frame would not include all the elements in the population, because it would be impossible to update the list daily. If we take the household as the sampling unit, then a telephone directory, a city directory, or a list of household heads obtained from census data could serve as a frame.

All these frames would have some inadequacies. The lists would not be up to date. They would contain many names of unregistered household heads, and hence a sample drawn from the lists would contain many units that are not in the population of interest. Also, some registered voters might not appear on any of these lists. It is hoped, however, that the gap between the frame and the population is small enough to permit inferences to be made about the population based on a sample drawn from the frame.

Definition 3.5   A *sample* is a collection of sampling units
drawn from a frame.

Data are obtained from the elements of the sample and used in describing the population of interest. Let the individual voter be our sampling unit and the list of registered voters be our frame. In the public opinion poll, a number of voters (the sample) would be contacted to determine their preference for the upcoming bond issue. We then could use the information obtained from these voters to make an inference about the voter preference throughout the community.

3.3   HOW TO SELECT THE SAMPLE: THE DESIGN OF THE SAMPLE SURVEY

The objective of sampling is to estimate population parameters, such as the mean or total, from information contained in a sample. As stated previously, the experimenter controls the quantity of information contained in the sample by the number of sampling units he or she includes in the sample and by the method used to select the sample data. How do we determine which procedure to use and the number of observations (sampling units) to include in the sample? The answer depends upon how much information we want to buy. If θ is the parameter of interest and $\hat{\theta}$ is an estimator of θ, we should specify a bound on our error of estimation; that is, we should specify that θ and $\hat{\theta}$ differ in absolute value by less than some value B. Stated symbolically,

$$\text{error of estimation} = |\theta - \hat{\theta}| < B$$

We also must state a probability, $(1 - \alpha)$, which specifies the fraction of times in repeated sampling we require the error of estimation to be less than B. This can be stated as

$$P[\text{error of estimation} < B] = 1 - \alpha$$

We will usually select $B = 2\sigma_{\hat{\theta}}$, and hence $(1 - \alpha)$ will be approximately .95 for bell-shaped distributions. Most estimators used in this book will exhibit bell-shaped distributions for reasonably large sample sizes, even when the parent population is skewed.

After we obtain a specified bound with its associated probability, $(1 - \alpha)$, we can compare different designs (methods of selecting the sample) to determine which procedure yields the desired precision at minimum cost. The problem of selecting the sample size to achieve a certain bound on error is discussed in Mendenhall (1975, chapter 8).

The basic design (*simple random sampling*) consists of selecting a group of n sampling units in such a way that each sample of size n has the same chance of being selected. Thus we could obtain a random sample of n eligible voters in the bond issue poll by drawing names from the list of registered voters in such a way that each sample of size n has the same probability of selection. The details of simple random sampling are discussed in chapter 4. At this point, we merely state that a simple random sample would contain as much information on the community preference as any other sample survey design, provided all voters in the community have similar socioeconomic backgrounds.

Suppose, however, that the community consists of people in two distinct income brackets, high and low. Voters in the high bracket may have opinions on the bond issue which are quite different from those in the low bracket. Therefore, to obtain accurate information about the population, we want to sample voters from each bracket. We could divide the population elements into two groups, or strata, according to income and select a simple random sample from each group. The resulting sample is called a *stratified random sample*.

Note that stratification is accomplished by using knowledge of an auxiliary variable, namely, personal income. By stratifying on high and low values of income, we increase the accuracy of our estimator. *Ratio estimation* is a second method for using the information contained in an auxiliary variable. Ratio estimators not only use measurements on the response of interest but also incorporate measurements on an auxiliary variable. Ratio estimation can also be used with stratified random sampling.

Although individual preferences are desired in the survey, it may be much more economical, especially in urban areas, to sample specific families, apartment buildings, or city blocks rather than individual voters. Individual preferences could then be obtained from each eligible voter within the unit sampled. This technique is called *cluster sampling*. Although we divide the population into groups for both cluster sampling and stratified random sampling, the techniques differ. In stratified random sampling we take a simple random sample within each group, while in cluster sampling we take a simple random sample of groups and then sample all items within the selected groups (clusters).

Sometimes the names of persons in the population of interest are available in a list, such as a registration list, or on file cards stored in a drawer. It is sometimes economical to draw the sample by selecting one name near the beginning of the list and then selecting every tenth or fifteenth name thereafter. If the sampling is conducted in this manner, we obtain a *systematic sample*. As you might expect, systematic sampling offers a convenient means of obtaining sample information; unfortunately, we do not necessarily obtain the most information for a specified amount of money.

We know that observations cost money. Note that the cost of an observation may vary from design to design, and even within a design, depending on the method of data collection. The experimenter should choose the design that gives the desired bound on error with the smallest number of observations (assuming the same cost per observation). However, if the cost per observation varies from design to design, the experimenter should choose the design that gives the desired bound on the error of estimation at a minimum cost.

3.4 METHODS OF DATA COLLECTION

There are many different methods of collecting the sample data once the sampling design has been chosen. All sampling techniques and estimation procedures are based on the assumption that the sample data are drawn from the population of interest. Hence drawing the sample is of prime importance. There are several problems to recognize. First, a nonresponse to a question put to an individual selected to be included in the sample can introduce a bias into the sample data. Those in the sample who do respond may not represent the population about which we wish to make inferences. For example, in a survey to determine employee

3. Elements of the Sampling Problem

acceptance of a monthly parking fee, it is quite likely only those people violently opposed to the fee would respond to a mailed questionnaire. If we were to consider the percentage of respondents favoring the fee, we would probably obtain a distorted estimate of the true percentages for the entire population.

An interviewer should be supplied with a carefully drawn-up set of instructions to minimize nonresponse. A fixed number of callbacks should be required for each sampled unit and all these should be on different days and different hours of the day. For example, one call could be made on a weekday evening, another on a weekday morning, and a third on a weekend. A specific method for determining the number of callbacks will be considered in chapter 11. The important point is that some effort must be made to obtain responses from the group that does not respond initially.

The second problem is that respondents or measuring equipment frequently give false information. For example, if a person is asked in an interview whether he cheated on his income tax, for fear of discovery, he would probably respond negatively whether he had or had not. The same person, however, might give a truthful statement to the same question posed on a mailed questionnaire. As another example, forest areas measured on aerial photographs may always read either high or low because of an improperly calibrated planimeter. The important point is that we have both nonresponse and response errors that may creep into our sample data, and either can lead to results that are not representative of the population of interest.

The third problem concerns arbitrary changes in the sampled elements. Data must be obtained from the exact sampling units that were selected in accordance with a sampling design. An interviewer must not substitute a next-door neighbor for a person whose name was sampled. Theoretically, samples selected according to a design have known probabilities associated with them. These known probabilities allow us to calculate the expected values and variances of estimators, such as the sample mean, and thus to determine the goodness of these estimators. If haphazard substitutions are made in the sample, this probability structure is altered and the goodness of the estimator is uncertain.

Practically speaking, haphazard substitutions may bias the results. For example, suppose next-door neighbors are substituted for families not at home. This may lead to a sample that contains an unduly high proportion of families with children, because these families will more frequently be found at home. If the response of interest is dependent on the number of children in the family, the resulting estimate will be biased.

A classical example of errors in surveys is the *Literary Digest* poll taken before the 1936 presidential election. In that poll some 10 million sample ballots were mailed to subscribers of the *Digest* and to selected

3.4 Methods of Data Collection

persons having telephones. The results of the poll showed Landon to be the winner over Roosevelt. The gross error was probably due in part to the restricted frame and in part to the high nonresponse rate. Only 2.3 million ballots were returned. See the article by Maurice C. Bryson listed in the references for an interesting account of this poll and its aftermath.

Various methods of data collection are described in the following paragraphs.

1. *Personal interviews.* Data are frequently obtained by *personal interviews.* For example, we could use personal interviews with eligible voters to obtain a sample of the public sentiments toward a community bond issue. The procedure usually requires the interviewer to ask prepared questions and to record the respondent's answers. The primary advantage of these interviews is that people will usually respond when confronted in person. In addition, the interviewer can note specific reactions and eliminate misunderstandings about the questions being asked. The major limitations of the personal interview (aside from the cost involved) concern the interviewers. If they are not thoroughly trained, they may deviate from the required protocol, thus introducing a bias into the sample data. Any movement, facial expression, or statement by the interviewer could affect the response obtained. For example, a leading question such as, "Are you also in favor of the bond issue?" might tend to elicit a positive response. Finally, errors in recording the responses could also lead to erroneous results.

2. *Telephone interviews.* Information can also be obtained from persons in the sample through *telephone interviews.* With the advent of wide area telephone service lines (WATS lines), an interviewer can place any number of calls to specified areas of the country for a fixed monthly rate. Surveys conducted through telephone interviews are frequently less expensive than personal interviews due to the elimination of travel expenses. The investigator can also monitor the interviews to be certain the specified interview procedure is being followed.

We recommend that interviews conducted over the telephone be kept short and impersonal to maintain the interest of the respondent. The most important limitation on these interviews is that we restrict ourselves to persons who can be reached by telephone. This could lead to the selection of a sample that would not be from the population of interest.

3. *Self-administered questionnaires.* Another useful method of data collection we will discuss is the *self-administered questionnaire,* to be completed by the respondent. These questionnaires usually are mailed to the individuals included in the sample, although other distribution methods could be used. To encourage participation by the respondents, a questionnaire must be carefully constructed.

The self-administered questionnaire does not require interviewers, and thus its use results in a savings in the cost of the survey. This savings in cost is usually bought at the expense of a lower response rate.

Nonresponse can be a problem in any form of data collection, but since we have the least contact with respondents in a mailed questionnaire, we frequently have the lowest rate of response. The low response rate can introduce a bias into the sample because the people who answer questionnaires may not be representative of the population of interest. To eliminate some of this bias, we frequently contact the nonrespondents through follow-up letters, telephone interviews, or personal interviews.

4. *Direct observation.* The fourth method for collecting data is *direct observation*. For example, if we were interested in estimating the number of trucks that use a particular road during the 4–6 P.M. rush hours, we could assign a person to count the number of trucks passing a specified point during this period. Possibly electronic counting equipment could also be used. The disadvantage in using an observer is the possibility of errors in observation.

A closely related notion is that of getting data from objective sources that are not affected by the respondents themselves. Health information can sometimes be obtained from hospital records, income information from employer's records (especially for state and federal government workers). This approach may take more time but may yield large rewards in important surveys.

3.5 DESIGNING A QUESTIONNAIRE

We previously mentioned that a questionnaire should be constructed to encourage participation by the respondents. The most frequently used questionnaires are the dichotomous, multiple-choice, and open-end types.

The *dichotomous* type is the simplest form and requires that the respondent choose between one of two responses. For example, we could conduct a mail questionnaire on the bond issue by asking the following question:

> Are you in favor of the bond issue that is to be presented
> to the people in the upcoming election?
> ( ) YES   ( ) NO

Although the dichotomous questionnaire is easy to construct, it sometimes oversimplifies an issue and does not provide room for compromise. The *multiple-choice* type is more appropriate in certain situations. In our public opinion poll, we could ask the following question:

> How would you indicate your opinion on the bond issue
> to be presented to the people in the upcoming election?
> ( ) Strongly in favor
> ( ) In favor

3.5 Designing a Questionnaire

( ) Undecided
( ) Not in favor
( ) Strongly not in favor

The type of questionnaire that allows a person the most freedom of response is the *open-end* questionnaire. For example, we could ask the following question:

What is your opinion on the bond issue to be presented to the people in the upcoming election?
Response_____

As you might expect, the disadvantage of such a questionnaire is the difficulty the experimenter has in classifying the results obtained.

Several general comments can be made regardless of the type of questionnaire being used. Questions must be simple and phrased to imply the same meaning to all persons. The question, "How many children are in your family?" may lead to confusion over what is meant by "children" and "in your family." The following question would be less ambiguous:

How many persons under the age of 21 live in your household and receive more than one-half their financial support from you?

The experimenter should avoid leading questions such as

Don't you think the courts are too lenient with criminals?

These questions suggest the answer the interviewer wants to hear, and the respondent may agree with the interviewer simply because that is the easiest response.

Questions involving a numerical response must be carefully phrased, with the nature of the desired response clearly indicated. A question such as

How much water do you drink?

is unnecessarily vague. It is generally better to say something like

Here is an eight-ounce glass. (Hold one up.) How many eight-ounce glasses of water do you drink per day?

If total water intake is of interest, remind the person of coffee, iced tea, and other drinks that are mostly water. Do not expect respondents to think deeply and thoroughly on questions presented to them. Lead them along as simply and directly as possible.

Questions must offer an adequate choice of answers to avoid forcing an unrepresentative response. It is particularly important to allow for no response, even on simple questions. For example, some people do not

3. Elements of the Sampling Problem

know their own age, and many have no opinion on the government of the state.

The questionnaire should be kept as short as possible and should contain only questions pertinent to the objectives of the survey. People quickly become bored when answering a long list of questions, and this boredom leads to incorrect answers.

Questionnaires should be pretested on a small group of people before the actual survey is performed. This gives the experimenter an opportunity to observe errors and shortcomings.

We could spend many more pages on the practical problems of designing a survey and controlling the field work. But instead of doing that, let us get on with describing the various designs. If you would like to know more about the practical problems, consult another text, such as the excellent book by Des Raj (1968).

3.6 SUMMARY

The objective of a sample survey is to make inferences about the population of interest based on information contained in a sample. The population consists of the body of data about which we wish to make an inference and is composed of elements or bits of information. Nonoverlapping collections of elements from the population are called sampling units. The frame is a list of sampling units that we use to represent the population of interest. The sample is a collection of sampling units drawn from the frame. Using the sample data, we will estimate certain population parameters and place bounds on our error of estimation.

The quantity of information obtained from the sample can be controlled by the number of sampling units drawn and the sample design or method of data collection used. Some of the designs introduced are simple random sampling, stratified random sampling, cluster sampling, and systematic sampling. Each is discussed in detail in a later chapter. The best design for a given problem is the one that provides the necessary precision in terms of a bound on the error of estimation for a minimum cost.

After the design has been selected, there are various methods of collecting the sample data. Personal interviews, telephone interviews, direct observations, and questionnaires were discussed and assessed as means of collecting the sample data. Each method has its advantages and limitations.

In section 3.5 we discussed the actual construction of questionnaires with reference to dichotomous, multiple-choice, and open-end types of questionnaires. Again we emphasize the importance of obtaining information in the sample that is representative of the population of

3.6 Summary

interest. This problem is of prime significance when we consider methods of data collection.

REFERENCES

Bryson, M. C. "The Literary Digest Poll: Making of a Statistical Myth." *American Statistician*, vol. 30, no. 4 (1976).
Cochran, W. G. *Sampling Techniques.* 3d ed. New York: Wiley, 1977.
Deming, W. E. *Sample Design in Business Research.* New York: Wiley, 1960.
Kish, L. *Survey Sampling.* New York: Wiley, 1965.
Mendenhall, W. *Introduction to Probability and Statistics.* 4th ed. N. Scituate, Mass.: Duxbury Press, 1975.
Raj, Des. *Sampling Theory.* New York: McGraw-Hill, 1968.

EXERCISES

3.1 An experimenter wants to estimate the average water consumption per family in a city. Discuss the relative merits of choosing individual families, dwelling units (single family houses, apartment buildings, etc.), and city blocks as sampling units. What would you use as a frame in each case?

3.2 A forester wants to estimate the total number of trees on a tree farm that possess diameters exceeding 12 inches. A map of the farm is available. Discuss the problem of choosing appropriate sampling units and an appropriate frame.

3.3 A safety expert is interested in estimating the proportion of automobile tires with unsafe tread. Should he use individual cars or collections of cars, such as those in parking lots, as sampling units? What could he use as a frame?

3.4 An industry is composed of many small plants located throughout the United States. An executive wants to survey the opinions of the employees on the vacation policy of the industry. What would you suggest she use as sampling units? What could she use as a frame?

3.5 A state department of agriculture desires to estimate the number of acres planted in corn within the state. Suggest possible sampling units and frames.

3.6 A political scientist wants to estimate the proportion of adult residents of a state who favor a unicameral legislature. Discuss possible units and frames. Also, discuss the relative merits of personal interviews, telephone interviews, and mailed questionnaires as methods of data collection.

3.7 Discuss the relative merits of using personal interviews, telephone interviews, and mailed questionnaires as methods of data collection for each of the following situations:
(a) A television executive wants to estimate the proportion of viewers in the country who are watching the network at a certain hour.

3. Elements of the Sampling Problem

(b) A newspaper editor wants to survey the attitudes of the public toward the type of news coverage offered by his paper.
(c) A city commissioner is interested in determining how homeowners feel about a proposed zoning change.
(d) A county health department wants to estimate the proportion of dogs that have had rabies shots within the last year.

4.
Simple Random Sampling

4.1 INTRODUCTION

The objective of a sample survey is to make an inference about the population of interest based on information contained in a sample. Two factors affect the quantity of information contained in the sample and hence affect the precision of our inference-making procedure. The first is the size of the sample selected from the population. The second is the amount of variation in the data; this can frequently be controlled by the method of selecting the sample. The procedure for selecting the sample is called the *sample survey design.* For a fixed sample size n, we will consider various designs or *sampling* procedures for obtaining the n observations in the sample. Since observations cost money, a design that provides a precise estimator of the parameter of interest for a fixed sample size yields a savings in cost to the experimenter. The basic design or sampling technique, simple random sampling, is discussed in this chapter.

Definition 4.1 If a sample of size n is drawn from a population of size N in such a way that every possible sample of size n has the same chance of being selected, the sampling procedure is called *simple random sampling.* The sample thus obtained is called a *simple random sample.*

4. Simple Random Sampling

We will use simple random sampling to obtain estimators for population means, totals, and proportions.

Consider the following problem. A federal auditor is to examine the accounts for a city hospital. The hospital records obtained from a computer show a particular accounts receivable total, and the auditor must verify this total. If there are 28,000 open accounts in the hospital, the auditor cannot afford the time to examine every patient record to obtain a total accounts receivable figure. Hence it becomes necessary to choose some sampling scheme for obtaining a representative sample of patient records. After examining the patient accounts in the sample, the auditor can then estimate the accounts receivable total for the entire hospital. If the computer figure lies within a specified distance of the auditor's estimate, the computer figure is accepted as valid. Otherwise more hospital records must be examined for possible discrepancies between the computer figure and the sample data.

Suppose that all $N = 28,000$ patient records are recorded on IBM cards and a sample size $n = 100$ is to be drawn. The sample is called a simple random sample if every possible sample of $n = 100$ records has the same chance of being selected.

Two problems now face the experimenter: (1) how does he or she draw the simple random sample, and (2) how can he or she estimate the various population parameters of interest? These topics are discussed in the following sections.

4.2 HOW TO DRAW A SIMPLE RANDOM SAMPLE

To draw a simple random sample from the population of interest is not as trivial as it may first appear. How can we draw a sample from a population in such a way that every possible sample of size n has the same chance of being selected? We might use our own judgment to "randomly" select the sample. This technique is frequently called haphazard sampling. A second technique, representative sampling, involves choosing a sample that we consider to be typical or representative of the population. Both haphazard and representative sampling are subject to investigator bias and, more importantly, they lead to estimators whose properties cannot be evaluated. Thus neither of these techniques leads to a simple random sample.

Simple random samples can be selected using tables of random numbers. A table of random numbers is shown in table 3 of the appendix.

A random number table is set of integers generated so that, in the long run, the table will contain all ten integers $(0, 1, \ldots, 9)$ in approximately equal proportions, with no trends in the pattern in which the digits were generated. Thus if one number is selected from a random point in the table, it is equally likely to be any of the digits 0 through 9.

4.2 How to Draw a Simple Random Sample

Choosing numbers from the table is analogous to drawing numbers out of a hat containing those numbers on thoroughly mixed pieces of paper. Suppose we want a simple random sample of three persons to be selected from seven. We could number the people from 1 to 7, put slips of paper containing these numbers (one number to a slip) into a hat, mix them, and draw out three, without replacing drawn numbers. Analogously, we could drop a pencil point on a random starting point in table 3 of the appendix. Suppose the point falls on the 15th line of column 9 and we decide to use the right-most digit (a 5, in this case). This is like drawing a 5 from the hat. We may now proceed in any direction to obtain the remaining numbers in the sample. Suppose we decide before starting to proceed down the page. The number immediately below the 5 is a 2, so our second sampled person would be number 2. Proceeding, we next come to an 8, but there are only seven people in our population; hence the 8 must be ignored. Two more 5s then appear, but both must be ignored since person 5 has already been selected. (The 5 has been removed from the hat.) Finally, we come to a 1, and our sample of three is completed with persons numbered 5, 2, and 1.

Note that any starting point can be used and one can move in any predetermined direction. If more than one sample is to be used in any problem, each should have its own unique starting point.

A more realistic illustration is given in example 4.1.

Example 4.1
For simplicity, assume there are $N = 1000$ patient records from which a simple random sample of $n = 20$ is to be drawn. We know that a simple random sample will be obtained if every possible example of $n = 20$ records has the same chance of being selected. The digits in table 3 of the appendix, and in any other table of random numbers, are generated to satisfy the conditions of simple random sampling. Determine which records are to be included in a sample of size $n = 20$.

Solution
We can think of the accounts as being numbers 001, 002, ..., 999, 000. That is, we have 1000 three-digit numbers, where 001 represents the first record, 999 the 999th patient record, and 000 the 1000th.

Refer to table 3 of the appendix and use the first column; if we drop the last two digits of each number, we see that the first three-digit number formed is 104, the second is 223, the third is 241, and so on. Taking a random sample of 20 digits, we obtain the numbers shown in table 4.1.

If the records are actually numbered, we merely choose the records with the corresponding numbers, and these represent a simple random sample of $n = 20$ from $N = 1000$. If the patient accounts are not numbered, we can refer to a list of the accounts

4. Simple Random Sampling

Table 4.1 / Patient records to be included in the sample

104	963	071
223	895	510
241	854	023
421	289	010
375	635	521
779	094	070
995	103	

and count from the first to the 10th, 23rd, 70th, and so on until the desired numbers are reached. If a random number occurs twice, the second occurrence is omitted and another number is selected as its replacement.

4.3 ESTIMATION OF A POPULATION MEAN AND TOTAL

We stated previously that the objective of survey sampling is to draw inferences about a population based on information contained in a sample. One way to make inferences is to estimate certain population parameters by utilizing the sample information. The objective of a sample survey is often to estimate a population mean, denoted by μ, or a population total, denoted by τ. Thus the auditor of example 4.1 might be interested in the mean dollar value for the accounts receivable or the total dollar amount in these accounts. Hence we consider estimation of the two population parameters, μ and τ, in this section.

Suppose that a simple random sample of n accounts is drawn, and we are to estimate the mean value per account for the total population of hospital records. Intuitively, we would employ the same average,

$$\bar{y} = \frac{\sum\limits_{i=1}^{n} y_i}{n}$$

to estimate μ.

Of course, a single value of $\bar{y}$ tells us very little about the population mean μ, unless we are able to evaluate the goodness of our estimator. Hence, in addition to estimating μ, we would like to place a bound on the error of estimation. It can be shown that $\bar{y}$ possesses many desirable properties for estimating μ.

We saw in section 2.4 that $E(\bar{y}) = \mu$ for a particular numerical example involving simple random sampling. The fact that this result is

4.3 Estimation of a Population Mean and Total

true in general for simple random sampling will now be shown. Let $y_1, \ldots, y_n$ denote a simple random sample from a population containing N elements. Then, as seen in section 2.4,

$$E(y_i) = \frac{1}{N} \sum_{i=1}^{N} u_i = \mu \qquad (4.1)$$

and this is true for any $i = 1, \ldots, n$. Thus from a result given in section 2.6,

$$E(\bar{y}) = E\left(\frac{1}{n} \sum_{i=1}^{n} y_i\right) = \frac{1}{n} \sum_{i=1}^{n} E(y_i)$$

$$= \frac{1}{n} \sum_{i=1}^{n} \mu = \mu$$

So $\bar{y}$ is an unbiased estimator of μ.

Using the other results of section 2.6, it is shown in the appendix that

$$V(\bar{y}) = \frac{\sigma^2}{n}\left(\frac{N-n}{N-1}\right)$$

[Notice that $V(\bar{y})$ approaches zero as n tends to N.]

Similar techniques can be used to show that

$$E(s^2) = \frac{N}{N-1} \sigma^2$$

so that $V(\bar{y})$ can be unbiasedly estimated from the sample by

$$\hat{V}(\bar{y}) = \frac{s^2}{n}\left(\frac{N-n}{N}\right)$$

where

$$s^2 = \frac{1}{n-1} \sum_{i=1}^{n} (y_i - \bar{y})^2$$

The variance of the estimator $\bar{y}$ is the same as that given in an introductory course except that it is multiplied by a correction factor to adjust for sampling from a finite population. The correction factor takes into account the fact that an estimate based on a sample $n = 10$ from a population of $N = 20$ items contains more information about the population than a sample of $n = 10$ from a population of $N = 20{,}000$.

4. Simple Random Sampling

Estimator of the population mean μ:

$$\hat{\mu} = \bar{y} = \frac{\sum_{i=1}^{n} y_i}{n} \qquad (4.2)$$

Estimated variance of $\bar{y}$:

$$\hat{V}(\bar{y}) = \frac{s^2}{n}\left(\frac{N-n}{N}\right) \qquad (4.3)$$

where

$$s^2 = \frac{\sum_{i=1}^{n}(y_i - \bar{y})^2}{n-1} = \frac{\sum_{i=1}^{n} y_i^2 - n\bar{y}^2}{n-1}$$

Bound on the error of estimation:

$$2\sqrt{\hat{V}(\bar{y})} = 2\sqrt{\frac{s^2}{n}\left(\frac{N-n}{N}\right)} \qquad (4.4)$$

The quantity $(N - n)/N$ is called the finite population correction (*fpc*). Note that this correction factor differs slightly from the one encountered in the true variance of $\bar{y}$. When n remains small relative to the population size N, the *fpc* is close to unity. Practically speaking, the *fpc* can be ignored if $(N - n)/N \geq .95$, or, equivalently, $n \leq (1/20)N$. In that case the estimated variance of $\bar{y}$ is the more familiar quantity, s^2/n.

To show the behavior of confidence intervals for the mean, 50 random samples of size $n = 20$ were selected from the population of $N = 100$ elements given in table 4 of the appendix. An approximate 95% confidence interval was constructed for each sample, with the results shown in table 4.2. Note that four (or 8%) of the observed intervals fail to cover the true population mean. This is quite close to the nominal value of 5%.

Table 4.3 shows the results of a similar experiment drawn from table 5 of the appendix. Here only two (4%) of the intervals fail to cover the true mean.

Example 4.2
Refer to the hospital audit of example 4.1 and suppose that a random sample of $n = 200$ accounts is selected from the total of $N = 1000$. The sample mean of the accounts is found to be $\bar{y} = \$94.22$, and the sample variance is $s^2 = 445.21$. Estimate μ, the average due for all 1000 hospital accounts, and place a bound on the error of estimation.

4.3 Estimation of a Population Mean and Total

Table 4.2 / Confidence intervals for $N = 100$ and $n = 20$

$\bar{y}$	s^2	LCL	UCL
56.020	1047.629	43.332	68.708
53.650	973.679	41.418	65.882
60.052	1044.769	47.381	72.722
49.350	606.324	39.697	59.002
49.082	994.433	36.721	61.444
49.038	1058.878	36.282	61.794
42.857	937.009	30.858	54.856
46.682	901.619	34.911	58.453
42.694	677.978	32.487	52.901
52.922	1086.781	39.999	65.844
47.778	926.727	35.845	59.712
48.950	705.443	38.539	59.362
52.200	1227.258	38.467	65.933
50.395	714.205	39.919	60.871
54.384	845.914	42.982	65.785
49.296	968.221	37.099	61.494
50.167	957.080	38.040	62.295
50.082	948.243	38.010	62.153
58.146	840.061	46.785	69.508
51.010	1144.449	37.749	64.271
54.947	1021.469	42.418	67.476
51.596	907.564	39.787	63.405
60.053	612.693	50.350	69.756
61.360	730.304	50.767	71.954
37.612	642.730	27.674	47.550
45.641	788.646	34.632	56.640
47.266	678.076	37.059	57.474
51.645	815.394	40.452	62.839
48.601	760.584	37.790	59.412
49.368	1003.110	36.953	61.784
52.723	874.174	41.133	64.313
43.005	622.081	33.228	52.782
33.760	586.996	24.262	43.257
57.683	656.446	47.639	67.726
68.100	750.229	57.363	78.837
59.298	695.199	48.962	69.634
47.474	1021.986	34.942	60.006
47.749	962.295	35.588	59.909
50.098	785.590	39.111	61.085
51.697	893.741	39.978	63.416
45.989	731.062	35.390	56.588
54.382	735.614	42.392	66.373
56.294	898.002	44.547	68.041
52.548	1333.015	38.236	66.860
53.236	1147.398	39.958	66.514
57.694	766.730	46.840	68.548
63.771	860.750	52.270	75.271
48.835	875.848	37.234	60.437
66.375	645.377	56.416	76.333
56.731	1070.385	43.906	69.556

$\mu = 52.575$

4. Simple Random Sampling

Table 4.3/*Confidence intervals for N = 20 and n = 15*

$\bar{y}$	s^2	LCL	UCL	$\mu = 9.035$
10.172	62.698	8.168	12.175	
10.312	53.296	8.465	12.160	
10.435	58.390	8.501	12.368	
8.198	15.953	6.340	10.057	
7.410	46.677	5.681	9.139	
10.455	49.063	8.682	12.227	
9.133	64.951	7.094	11.172	
9.255	51.192	7.445	11.066	
9.392	54.933	7.516	11.267	
10.386	59.018	8.442	12.330	
8.700	62.707	6.696	10.703	
8.126	46.516	6.401	9.852	
8.869	53.483	7.018	10.719	
9.074	58.610	7.137	11.012	
7.719	52.275	5.889	9.548	
7.815	49.723	6.031	9.600	
8.794	54.153	6.932	10.656	
8.778	53.764	6.923	10.634	
11.350	50.345	9.554	13.145	
8.205	55.182	6.326	10.085	
8.371	56.787	6.464	10.278	
9.556	57.116	7.644	11.468	
9.442	58.971	7.499	11.385	
7.865	53.681	6.011	9.719	
9.323	67.261	7.248	11.398	
9.300	48.507	7.538	11.062	
9.400	47.895	7.667	11.133	
9.738	56.042	7.844	11.632	
10.100	50.812	8.297	11.904	
9.540	58.265	7.608	11.471	
9.204	55.947	7.311	11.096	
9.057	55.205	7.177	10.937	
9.514	48.569	7.750	11.277	
10.533	50.279	8.738	12.327	
9.076	51.918	7.252	10.899	
8.159	52.775	6.321	9.997	
7.453	55.096	5.575	9.331	
8.323	58.580	6.386	10.260	
8.704	57.380	6.787	10.620	
9.146	57.078	7.234	11.057	
9.301	53.757	7.446	11.156	
8.908	59.789	6.951	10.864	
7.418	55.680	5.530	9.306	
7.335	49.494	5.555	9.115	
9.601	58.002	7.674	11.528	
8.175	55.629	6.288	10.063	
8.634	52.570	6.799	10.468	
9.200	55.837	7.310	11.091	
7.136	41.977	5.496	8.775	
8.032	50.013	6.243	9.822	

4.3 Estimation of a Population Mean and Total

Solution
We use $\bar{y} = \$94.22$ to estimate μ. A bound on the error of estimation can be found by using equation (4.4).

$$2\sqrt{\hat{V}(\bar{y})} = 2\sqrt{\frac{s^2}{n}\left(\frac{N-n}{N}\right)} = 2\sqrt{\frac{445.21}{200}\left(\frac{1000-200}{1000}\right)}$$
$$= 2\sqrt{1.7808} = \$2.67$$

Thus we estimate the mean value per account, μ, to be $\bar{y} = \$94.22$. Since n is large, the sample mean should possess approximately a normal distribution, so that $\$94.22 \pm \$2.67$ is approximately a 95% confidence interval for the population mean.

Example 4.3
A simple random sample of $n = 9$ hospital records is drawn to estimate the average amount of money due on $N = 484$ open accounts. The sample values for these nine records are listed in table 4.4. Estimate μ, the average amount outstanding, and place a bound on your error of estimation.

Table 4.4/Amount of money owed

y_1	33.50
y_2	32.00
y_3	52.00
y_4	43.00
y_5	40.00
y_6	41.00
y_7	45.00
y_8	42.50
y_9	39.00

Solution
It is convenient to display the sample data and computations as indicated in table 4.5.
Summing the entries in the y column, we get

$$\sum_{i=1}^{9} y_i = 368.00$$

Using the y^2 column we have

$$\sum_{i=1}^{9} y_i^2 = 15{,}332.50$$

4. Simple Random Sampling

Table 4.5 / Data and computations for example 4.3

y	y^2
33.50	1,122.25
32.00	1,024.00
52.00	2,704.00
43.00	1,849.00
40.00	1,600.00
41.00	1,681.00
45.00	2,025.00
42.50	1,806.25
39.00	1,521.00
$\sum y_i = 368.00$	$\sum y_i^2 = 15{,}332.50$

We need both of these quantities to calculate $\bar{y}$ and s^2. Our estimate of μ is

$$\bar{y} = \frac{\sum_{i=1}^{9} y_i}{9} = \frac{368.00}{9} = \$40.89$$

To find a bound on the error of estimation we must compute

$$s^2 = \frac{\sum_{i=1}^{n}(y_i - \bar{y})^2}{n-1} = \frac{\sum_{i=1}^{9} y_i^2 - \left(\sum_{i=1}^{9} y_i\right)^2/9}{8}$$

$$= \frac{1}{8}\left[15{,}332.50 - \frac{(368)^2}{9}\right] = \frac{1}{8}[15{,}332.50 - 15{,}047.11]$$

$$= 35.67$$

Utilizing equation (4.4), we obtain the bound on the error of estimation,

$$2\sqrt{\hat{V}(\bar{y})} = 2\sqrt{\frac{s^2}{n}\left(\frac{N-n}{N}\right)} = 2\sqrt{\frac{35.67}{9}\left(\frac{484-9}{484}\right)}$$

$$= 2\sqrt{3.890} = 3.944 = \$3.94$$

To summarize, the estimate of the mean amount of money owed per account, μ, is $\bar{y} = \$40.89$. Although we cannot be certain how close $\bar{y}$ is to μ, we are reasonably confident that the error of estimation is less than $3.94.

Many sample surveys are conducted to obtain information about a population total. The federal auditor of example 4.1 would probably be interested in verifying the computer figure for the total accounts receivable (in dollars) for the $N = 1000$ open accounts.

4.3 Estimation of a Population Mean and Total

You recall that the mean for a population of size N is the sum of all observations in the population divided by N. The population total, that is, the sum of all observations in the population, is denoted by the symbol τ. Hence

$$N\mu = \tau$$

Intuitively, we expect the estimator of τ to be N times the estimator of μ. In fact this is the case.

Estimator of the population total τ:

$$\hat{\tau} = N\bar{y} = \frac{N \sum_{i=1}^{n} y_i}{n} \qquad (4.5)$$

Estimated variance of $\hat{\tau}$:

$$\hat{V}(\hat{\tau}) = \hat{V}(N\bar{y}) = N^2 \left(\frac{s^2}{n}\right)\left(\frac{N-n}{N}\right) \qquad (4.6)$$

where

$$s^2 = \frac{\sum_{i=1}^{n}(y_i - \bar{y})^2}{n-1}$$

Bound on the error of estimation:

$$2\sqrt{\hat{V}(N\bar{y})} = 2\sqrt{N^2\left(\frac{s^2}{n}\right)\left(\frac{N-n}{N}\right)} \qquad (4.7)$$

Note that the estimated variance of $\hat{\tau} = N\bar{y}$ in equation (4.6) is N^2 times the estimated variance of $\bar{y}$ given in equation (4.3).

Example 4.4
An industrial firm is concerned about the time per week spent by scientists on certain trivial tasks. The time log sheets of a simple random sample of $n = 50$ employees show the average amount of time spent on these tasks is 10.31 hours with a sample variance $s^2 = 2.25$. If the company employs $N = 750$ scientists, estimate the total number of man-hours lost per week on trivial tasks, and place a bound on the error of estimation.

4. Simple Random Sampling

Solution
We know the population consists of $N = 750$ employees from which a random sample of $n = 50$ time log sheets was obtained. The average amount of time lost for the fifty employees was $\bar{y} = 10.31$ hours per week. Therefore, the estimate of τ is

$$\hat{\tau} = N\bar{y} = 750(10.31) = 7{,}732.5 \text{ hours}$$

To place a bound on the error of estimation, we apply equation (4.7) to obtain

$$2\sqrt{\hat{V}(\hat{\tau})} = 2\sqrt{(750)^2\left(\frac{2.25}{50}\right)\left(\frac{750-50}{750}\right)}$$

$$= 2\sqrt{23{,}625} = 307.4 \text{ hours}$$

Thus the estimate of total time lost is $\hat{\tau} = 7{,}732.5$ hours. We are reasonably confident that the error of estimation is less than 307.4 hours.

4.4 SELECTING THE SAMPLE SIZE FOR ESTIMATING POPULATION MEANS AND TOTALS

At some point in the design of the survey, someone must make a decision about the size of the sample to be selected from the population. So far, we have discussed a sampling procedure (simple random sampling) but have said nothing about the number of observations to be included in the sample. The implications of such a decision are obvious. Observations cost money. Hence if the sample is too large, time and talent are wasted. Conversely, if the number of observations included in the sample is too small, we have bought inadequate information for the time and effort expended and have again been wasteful.

The number of observations needed to estimate a population mean μ with a bound on the error of estimation of magnitude B is found by setting two standard deviations of the estimator, $\bar{y}$, equal to B and solving this expression for n. That is, we must solve

$$2\sqrt{V(\bar{y})} = B \qquad (4.8)$$

for n.

You will recall that the estimated variance of $\bar{y}$, $\hat{V}(\bar{y})$, is given by

$$\hat{V}(\bar{y}) = \frac{s^2}{n}\left(\frac{N-n}{N}\right) \qquad (4.9)$$

Also,

$$V(\bar{y}) = \frac{\sigma^2}{n}\left(\frac{N-n}{N-1}\right) \qquad (4.10)$$

4.4 Selecting the Sample Size for Estimating Population Means and Totals

You will recognize equation (4.10) from an introductory course as the familiar variance of $\bar{y}$, that is, σ^2/n, multiplied by the factor $(N - n)/(N - 1)$.

The required sample size can now be found by solving the following equation for n:

$$2\sqrt{V(\bar{y})} = 2\sqrt{\frac{\sigma^2}{n}\left(\frac{N-n}{N-1}\right)} = B \qquad (4.11)$$

The solution is given in equation (4.12).

Sample size required to estimate μ with a bound on the error of estimation B:

$$n = \frac{N\sigma^2}{(N-1)D + \sigma^2} \qquad (4.12)$$

where

$$D = \frac{B^2}{4}$$

Solving for n in a practical situation presents a problem because the population variance σ^2 is unknown. Since a sample variance s^2 is frequently available from prior experimentation, we can obtain an approximate sample size by replacing σ^2 with s^2 in equation (4.12). We will illustrate a method for guessing a value of σ^2 when very little prior information is available. If N is large, as it usually is, the $(N - 1)$ can be replaced by N in the denominator of equation (4.12).

Example 4.5
It is necessary to estimate the average amount of money μ for a hospital's accounts receivable. Although no prior data is available to estimate the population variance σ^2, it is known that most accounts lie within a $100 range. If there are $N = 1000$ open accounts, find the sample size needed to estimate μ with a bound on the error of estimation $B = \$3$.

Solution
We need an estimate of σ^2, the population variance. Since the range is often approximately equal to 4 standard deviations (4σ), one-fourth of the range will provide an approximate value of σ.

4. Simple Random Sampling

Hence

$$\sigma \approx \frac{\text{range}}{4} = \frac{100}{4} = 25$$

and

$$\sigma^2 \approx (25)^2 = 625$$

Using equation (4.12), we obtain

$$n = \frac{N\sigma^2}{(N-1)D + \sigma^2}$$

where

$$D = \frac{B^2}{4} = \frac{(3)^2}{4} = 2.25$$

So

$$n = \frac{1000(625)}{999(2.25) + 625} = 217.56$$

That is, we need approximately 218 observations to estimate μ, the mean accounts receivable, with a bound on the error of estimation of $3.00.

In like manner, we can determine the number of observations needed to estimate a population total τ, with a bound on the error of estimation of magnitude B. The required sample size is found by setting two standard deviations of the estimator equal to B and solving this expression for n. That is, we must solve

$$2\sqrt{V(N\bar{y})} = B$$

or, equivalently,

$$2N\sqrt{V(\bar{y})} = B \qquad (4.13)$$

[The reason for this equivalence is given directly after equation (4.7).]

Sample size required to estimate τ with a bound on error B:

$$n = \frac{N\sigma^2}{(N-1)D + \sigma^2} \qquad (4.14)$$

where

$$D = \frac{B^2}{4N^2}$$

Example 4.6
An investigator is interested in estimating the total weight gain in 0 to 4 weeks for N = 1000 chicks fed on a new ration. Obviously it would be time-consuming and tedious to weigh each bird. Therefore, determine the number of chicks to be sampled in this study in order to estimate τ with a bound on the error of estimation equal to 1000 grams. Many similar studies on chick nutrition have been run in the past. Using data from these studies, the investigator found that σ^2, the population variance, was approximately equal to 36.00 grams. Determine the required sample size.

Solution
We can obtain an approximate sample size using equation (4.14) with σ^2 equal to 36.00 and

$$D = \frac{B^2}{4N^2} = \frac{(1000)^2}{4(1000)^2} = .25$$

That is,

$$n = \frac{N\sigma^2}{(N-1)D + \sigma^2} = \frac{1000(36.00)}{999(0.25) + 36.00} = 125.98$$

The investigator, therefore, needs to weigh n = 126 chicks to estimate τ, the total weight gain for N = 1000 chickens in 0 to 4 weeks, with a bound on the error of estimation equal to 1000 grams.

4.5 ESTIMATION OF A POPULATION PROPORTION

The investigator conducting a sample survey is frequently interested in estimating the proportion of the population that possesses a specified characteristic. For example, a congressional leader investigating the merits of an 18-year-old voting age might want to estimate the proportion of the potential voters in the district between the ages of 18 and 21. A marketing research group might be interested in the proportion of the total sales market in diet preparations that is attributable to a particular product. That is, what percentage of sales is accounted for by a particular product? A forest manager might be interested in the proportion of trees with a diameter of 12 inches or more. Television ratings are often determined by estimating the proportion of the viewing public that watches a particular program.

You will recognize that all these examples exhibit a characteristic of the binomial experiment, that is, an observation either does belong or does not belong to the category of interest. For example, one could estimate the proportion of eligible voters in a particular district by examining population census data for several of the precincts within the district. An estimate of the proportion of voters between 18 and 21 years of age for the entire district would be the fraction of potential voters from the precincts sampled that fell into this age range.

In subsequent discussion we denote the population proportion and its estimator by the symbols p and $\hat{p}$, respectively. The properties of $\hat{p}$ for simple random sampling parallel those of the sample mean $\bar{y}$ if the response measurements are defined as follows: let $y_i = 0$ if the ith element sampled does not possess the specified characteristic and $y_i = 1$ if it does. Then the total number of elements in a sample of size n possessing a specified characteristic is

$$\sum_{i=1}^{n} y_i$$

If we draw a simple random sample of size n, the sample proportion $\hat{p}$ would be the fraction of the elements in the sample that possess the characteristic of interest. For example, the estimate $\hat{p}$ of the proportion of eligible voters between the ages of 18 and 21 in a certain district would be

$$\hat{p} = \frac{\text{number of voters sampled between the ages of 18 and 21}}{\text{number of voters sampled}}$$

or

$$\hat{p} = \frac{\sum_{i=1}^{n} y_i}{n} = \bar{y}$$

In other words, $\hat{p}$ is the average of the 0 and 1 values from the sample. Similarly, we can think of the population proportion as the average of the 0 and 1 values for the entire population (i.e., $p = \mu$).

Estimator of the population proportion p:

$$\hat{p} = \bar{y} = \frac{\sum_{i=1}^{n} y_i}{n} \tag{4.15}$$

Estimated variance of $\hat{p}$:

$$\hat{V}(\hat{p}) = \frac{\hat{p}\hat{q}}{n-1}\left(\frac{N-n}{N}\right) \tag{4.16}$$

where

$$\hat{q} = 1 - \hat{p}$$

Bound on the error of estimation:

$$2\sqrt{\hat{V}(\hat{p})} = 2\sqrt{\frac{\hat{p}\hat{q}}{n-1}\left(\frac{N-n}{N}\right)} \tag{4.17}$$

4.5 Estimation of a Population Proportion

Example 4.7
A simple random sample of $n = 100$ college seniors was selected to estimate (1) the fraction of $N = 300$ seniors going on to graduate school and (2) the fraction of students that have held part-time jobs during college. Let y_i and x_i ($i = 1, 2, \ldots, 100$) denote the responses of the ith student sampled. We will set $y_i = 0$ if the ith student does not plan to attend graduate school and $y_i = 1$ if he does. Similarly, let $x_i = 0$ if he has not held a part-time job sometime during college and $x_i = 1$ if he has. Using the sample data presented in the accompanying table, estimate p_1, the proportion of seniors planning to attend graduate school, and p_2, the proportion of seniors who have had a part-time job sometime during their college careers (summers included).

Student	y	x
1	1	0
2	0	1
3	0	1
4	1	1
5	0	0
6	0	0
7	0	1
⋮	⋮	⋮
96	0	1
97	1	0
98	0	1
99	0	1
100	1	1
	$\sum_{i=1}^{100} y_i = 15$	$\sum_{i=1}^{100} x_i = 65$

Solution
The sample proportions from equation (4.15) are given by

$$\hat{p}_1 = \frac{\sum_{i=1}^{n} y_i}{n} = \frac{15}{100} = .15$$

and

$$\hat{p}_2 = \frac{\sum_{i=1}^{n} x_i}{n} = \frac{65}{100} = .65$$

4. Simple Random Sampling

The bounds on the errors of estimation of p_1 and p_2 are, respectively,

$$2\sqrt{\hat{V}(\hat{p}_1)} = 2\sqrt{\frac{\hat{p}_1\hat{q}_1}{n-1}\left(\frac{N-n}{N}\right)}$$

$$= 2\sqrt{\frac{(.15)(.85)}{99}\left(\frac{300-100}{300}\right)} = 2(.0293) = .059$$

and

$$2\sqrt{\hat{V}(\hat{p}_2)} = 2\sqrt{\frac{\hat{p}_2\hat{q}_2}{n-1}\left(\frac{N-n}{N}\right)}$$

$$= 2\sqrt{\frac{(.65)(.35)}{99}\left(\frac{300-100}{300}\right)} = 2(.0391) = .078$$

Thus we estimate that .15 (15%) of the seniors plan to attend graduate school, with a bound on the error of estimation equal to .059 (5.9%). Similarly, we estimate that .65 (65%) of the seniors have held a part-time job during college, with a bound on the error of estimation equal to .078 (7.8%).

We have shown that the population proportion, p, can be regarded as the average (μ) of the zero and one values for the entire population. Hence the problem of determining the sample size required to estimate p to within B units should be analogous to determining a sample size for estimating μ with a bound on the error of estimation, B. You will recall that the required sample size for estimating μ is given by

$$n = \frac{N\sigma^2}{(N-1)D + \sigma^2} \tag{4.18}$$

where $D = B^2/4$ [see equation (4.12)]. The corresponding sample size needed to estimate p can be found by replacing σ^2 in equation (4.18) with the quantity pq.

Sample size required to estimate p with a bound on the error of estimation, B:

$$n = \frac{Npq}{(N-1)D + pq} \tag{4.19}$$

where

$$q = 1 - p \quad \text{and} \quad D = \frac{B^2}{4}$$

4.5 Estimation of a Population Proportion

In a practical situation, we do not know p. An approximate sample size can be found by replacing p with an estimated value. Frequently such an estimate can be obtained from similar past surveys. However, if no such prior information is available, we can substitute $p = .5$ into equation (4.19) to obtain a conservative sample size (one that is likely to be larger than required).

Example 4.8
Student government leaders at a college want to conduct a survey to determine the proportion of students that favors a proposed honor code. Since it is almost impossible to interview $N = 2000$ students in a reasonable length of time, determine the sample size (number of students to be interviewed) needed to estimate p with a bound on the error of estimation of magnitude $B = .05$. Assume that no prior information is available to estimate p.

Solution
We can approximate the required sample sizes when no prior information is available by setting $p = .5$ in equation (4.19). We have

$$D = \frac{B^2}{4} = \frac{(.05)^2}{4} = .000625$$

Hence

$$n = \frac{Npq}{(N-1)D + pq}$$
$$= \frac{(2000)(.5)(.5)}{(1999)(.000625) + (.5)(.5)} = \frac{500}{1.499}$$
$$= 333.56$$

That is, 334 students must be interviewed to estimate the proportion of students that favors the proposed honor code with a bound on the error of estimation of $B = .05$.

Example 4.9
Referring to example 4.8, suppose that in addition to estimating the proportion of students that favors the proposed honor code, student government leaders also want to estimate the number of students who feel the student union building adequately serves their needs. Determine the combined sample size required for a survey to estimate p_1, the proportion that favors the proposed honor code, and p_2, the proportion that believes the student union adequately serves its needs, with bounds on the errors of estimation of magnitude $B_1 = .05$ and $B_2 = .07$. Although no

4. Simple Random Sampling

prior information is available to estimate p_2, approximately 60% of the students believed the union adequately met their needs in a similar survey run the previous year.

Solution

In this example we must determine a sample size n that will allow us to estimate p_1 with a bound $B_1 = .05$ and p_2 with a bound $B_2 = .07$. First, we determine the sample sizes that satisfy each objective separately. The larger of the two will then be the combined sample size for a survey to meet both objectives. From example 4.8, the sample size required to estimate p_1 with a bound on the error of estimation of $B_1 = .05$ was $n = 334$ students. We can use data from the survey of the previous year to determine the sample size needed to estimate p_2. We have

$$D = \frac{B^2}{4} = \frac{(.07)^2}{4} = .001225$$

and hence, using $p_2 = .60$,

$$n = \frac{Npq}{(N-1)D + pq}$$

$$= \frac{(2000)(.6)(.4)}{(1999)(.001225) + (.6)(.4)} = \frac{480}{2.68877}$$

$$= 178.52$$

That is, 179 students must be interviewed to estimate p_2, the proportion of the $N = 2000$ students that believes the student union meets its needs, with a bound on the error of estimation equal to .07.

The sample size required to achieve both objectives in one survey is 334, the larger of the two sample sizes.

4.6 SUMMARY

The objective of statistics is to make inferences about a population based on information contained in a sample. Two factors affect the quantity of information in a given investigation. The first is the sample size. The larger the sample size, the more information we expect to obtain about the population. The second factor that affects the quantity of information is the amount of variation in the data. This can be controlled by the design of the sample survey, that is, the method by which observations are obtained.

In this chapter we discussed the simplest type of sample survey design, namely, simple random sampling. This design does not attempt to reduce the effect of data variation on the error of estimation. A simple

4.6 Summary

random sample of size n occurs if each sample of n elements from the population has the same chance of being selected. Random number tables are quite useful in determining the elements that are to be included in a simple random sample.

In estimating a population mean μ and total τ, we use the sample mean $\bar{y}$ and sample total $N\bar{y}$, respectively. Both estimators are unbiased; that is, $E(\bar{y}) = \mu$ and $E(N\bar{y}) = \tau$. The estimated variance and bound on the error of estimation are given for both estimators.

Sometime during the design of an actual survey, the experimenter must decide how much information is desired, that is, how large a bound on the error of estimation can be tolerated. Sample-size requirements were presented for estimating μ and τ with a specified bound on the error of estimation.

The third parameter estimated was the population proportion, p. The properties of $\hat{p}$ were presented and related to the properties of $\bar{y}$, the estimator of the population mean μ. Selecting the sample size to estimate p with a specified bound on the error of estimation was based on the same principle employed in selecting a sample size for estimating μ and τ.

REFERENCES

Barr, A. J.; Goodnight, J. H.; Sall, J. P.; and Helwig, J. T. *A User's Guide to SAS.* Raleigh, N.C.: SAS Institute, Inc., 1976.

Cochran, W. G. *Sampling Techniques.* 3d ed. New York: Wiley, 1977.

Dixon, W. J., ed. *BMDP, Biomedical Computer Programs.* Berkeley: University of California Press, 1975.

Hansen, M. H.; Hurwitz, W. N.; and Madow, W. G. *Sample Survey Methods and Theory*, vol. I. New York: Wiley, 1953.

Kish, L. *Survey Sampling.* New York: Wiley, 1965.

Nie, N. H.; Hull, C. H.; Jenkins, J. G.; Steinbrenner, K.; and Bent, D. H. *Statistical Package for the Social Sciences.* 2d ed. New York: McGraw-Hill, 1975.

Ryan, T. A.; Joiner, B. L.; and Ryan, B. F. *Minitab Student Handbook.* N. Scituate, Mass.: Duxbury Press, 1976.

EXERCISES

4.1 List all possible simple random samples of size $n = 2$ that can be selected from the population $\mathcal{U} = \{1, 2, 3, 4\}$. Calculate σ^2 for the population and $V(\bar{y})$ for the sample mean $\bar{y}$. (Six equally likely values of $\bar{y}$ will appear.) Thus show by direct calculation that

$$V(\bar{y}) = \frac{N-n}{N-1}\left(\frac{\sigma^2}{n}\right)$$

4. Simple Random Sampling

4.2 For the simple random samples generated in exercise 4.1, calculate s^2 for each sample. Show numerically that

$$E(s^2) = \frac{N}{N-1}\sigma^2$$

4.3 Suppose you were to estimate the number of weed clusters of a certain type in a field. What is the population and what would you use for sampling units? How would you construct a frame? How would you select a simple random sample? If a sampling unit is an area, such as a square yard, does the size chosen for a sampling unit affect the accuracy of the results? What considerations would go into your choice of size of sampling unit?

4.4 Using the random number table in the appendix, select a simple random sample of $n = 10$ observations from the population given in either table 4 or table 5 of the appendix. Construct an approximate 95% confidence interval for μ. Does the interval include the true μ given in the table? Is your value of s^2 close to $[N/(N-1)]\sigma^2$?

4.5 State park officials were interested in the proportion of campers who consider the campsite spacing adequate in a particular campground. They decided to take a simple random sample of $n = 30$ from the first $N = 300$ camping parties that visit the campground. Let $y_i = 0$ if the head of the ith party sampled does not think the spacing is adequate and $y_i = 1$ if he does ($i = 1, 2, \ldots, 30$). Use the data in the accompanying table to estimate p, the proportion of campers who consider the campsite spacing adequate. Place a bound on the error of estimation.

Camper Sampled	Response, y_i
1	1
2	0
3	1
⋮	⋮
29	1
30	1
	$\sum_{i=1}^{30} y_i = 25$

4.6 Use the data in exercise 4.5 to determine the sample size required to estimate p with a bound on the error of estimation of magnitude $B = .05$.

4.7 A simple random sample of 100 water meters within a community is monitored to estimate the average daily water consumption per household over a specified dry spell. The sample mean and same variance are found to be $\bar{y} = 12.5$ and $s^2 = 1{,}252$. If we assume that there are $N = 10{,}000$ households within the community, estimate μ, the true average daily consumption, and place a bound on the error of estimation.

Exercises

4.8 Using exercise 4.7, estimate the total number of gallons of water, τ, used daily during the dry spell. Place a bound on the error of estimation.

4.9 Resource managers of forest game lands are concerned about the size of the deer and rabbit populations during the winter months in a particular forest. As an estimate of population size, they propose using the average number of pellet groups for rabbits and deer per 30-foot-square plots. Using an aerial photograph, the forest was divided into $N = 10,000$ thirty-foot-square grids. A simple random sample of $n = 500$ plots was taken, and the number of pellet groups was observed for rabbits and for deer. The results of this study are summarized in the accompanying table.

Deer	Rabbits
sample mean = 2.30	sample mean = 4.52
sample variance = .65	sample variance = .97

Estimate μ_1 and μ_2, the average number of pellet groups for deer and rabbits, respectively, per 30-square-foot plots. Place bounds on the errors of estimation.

4.10 A simple random sample of $n = 40$ college students was interviewed to determine the proportion of students in favor of converting from the semester to the quarter system. If 25 of the students answered affirmatively, estimate the proportion of students on campus in favor of the change. (Assume $N = 2000$.) Place a bound on the error of estimation.

4.11 A dentist was interested in the effectiveness of a new toothpaste. A group of $N = 1000$ school children participated in a study. Prestudy records showed there was an average of 2.2 cavities every six months for the group. After three months on the study, the dentist sampled $n = 10$ children to determine how they were progressing on the new toothpaste. Using the data in the table, estimate the mean number of cavities for the entire group and place a bound on the error of estimation.

Child	Number of Cavities in the Three-Month Period
1	0
2	4
3	2
4	3
5	2
6	0
7	3
8	4
9	1
10	1

4. Simple Random Sampling

4.12 The Fish and Game Department of a particular state was concerned about the direction of its future hunting programs. To provide for a greater potential for future hunting, the department wanted to determine the proportion of hunters seeking any type of game bird. A simple random sample of $n = 1,000$ of the $N = 99,000$ licensed hunters was obtained. If 430 indicated they hunted game birds, estimate p, the proportion of licensed hunters seeking game birds. Place a bound on the error of estimation.

4.13 Using the data in exercise 4.12, determine the sample size the department must obtain to estimate the proportion of game bird hunters, given a bound on the error of estimation of magnitude $B = .02$.

4.14 A company auditor was interested in estimating the total number of travel vouchers that were incorrectly filed. In a simple random sample of $n = 50$ vouchers taken from a group of $N = 250$, 20 were filed incorrectly. Estimate the total number of vouchers from the $N = 250$ that have been filed incorrectly, and place a bound on the error of estimation. [Hint: If p is the population proportion of incorrect vouchers, then Np is the total number of incorrect vouchers. An estimator of Np is $N\hat{p}$, which has an estimated variance given by $N^2 \hat{V}(\hat{p})$.]

4.15 A psychologist wishes to estimate the average reaction time to a stimulus among 200 patients in a hospital specializing in nervous disorders. A simple random sample of $n = 20$ patients was selected and their reaction times were measured with the following results:

$$\bar{y} = 2.1 \text{ seconds} \qquad s = .4 \text{ seconds}$$

Estimate the population mean μ, and place a bound on the error of estimation.

4.16 In exercise 4.15, how large a sample should be taken in order to estimate μ with a bound of 1 second on the error of estimation? Use 1.0 second as an approximation of the population standard deviation.

4.17 The manager of a machine shop wishes to estimate the average time that it takes for an operator to complete a simple task. The shop has 98 operators. Eight operators are selected at random and timed. The observed results are shown in the accompanying table. Estimate the average time for completion of the task among all operators, and place a bound on the error of estimation.

Time (in minutes)	
4.2	5.3
5.1	4.6
7.9	5.1
3.8	4.1

4.18 A sociological study conducted in a small town calls for the estimation of the proportion of households that contain at least one member over 65 years of age. The city has 621 households according to the most recent city

Exercises

directory. A simple random sample of $n = 60$ households was selected from the directory. At the completion of the field work, out of the 60 households sampled, 11 contained at least one member over 65 years of age. Estimate the true population proportion p, and place a bound on the error of estimation.

4.19 In exercise 4.18, how large a sample should be taken in order to estimate p with a bound of .08 on the error of estimation? Assume the true proportion p is approximately .2.

4.20 An investigator is interested in estimating the total number of "count trees" (trees larger than a specified size) on a plantation of $N = 1500$ acres. This information is used to determine the total volume of lumber for trees on the plantation. A simple random sample of $n = 100$ one-acre plots was selected, and each plot was examined for the number of count trees. If the sample average for the $n = 100$ one-acre plots was $\bar{y} = 25.2$ with a sample variance of $s^2 = 136$, estimate the total number of count trees on the plantation. Place a bound on the error of estimation.

4.21 Using the results of the survey conducted in exercise 4.20, determine the sample size required to estimate τ, the total number of trees on the plantation, with a bound on the error of estimation of magnitude $B = 1500$.

4.22 A large construction firm has 120 houses in various stages of completion. To estimate the total dollar amount to be listed as inventory of construction in progress, a simple random sample of 12 of these houses is selected and accumulated costs determined on each. Assume the following costs were obtained for the 12 sample houses:

15,500	10,200	8,900
16,400	9,800	14,100
12,600	6,400	18,000
18,200	12,200	7,500

Estimate the total accumulated costs for the 120 houses and place a bound on the error of estimation.

EXPERIENCES WITH REAL DATA

1. Table 4.6 lists state appropriations for higher education for 1976–1977. Treating these figures as a population of 50 elements, select a random sample of n states and estimate the total appropriations amount, placing a bound on the error of estimation. Without making use of the actual appropriations figures (these would be unknown in a real problem), choose as best you can a sample size that should guarantee a bound of $100 million or less.

2. Identify a problem in your own area of interest for which you can actually draw a simple random sample to estimate a population mean, total, or proportion. Clearly define the population and the sampling units, and construct a frame. Select a simple random sample from the frame by using

4. Simple Random Sampling

Table 4.6/*State appropriations for higher education, 1976–1977*

	1976–1977 Appropriations Amount (add 000)	Rank	Appropriations Per Capita Amount	Rank	Approp. Per $1,000 of Personal Income Amount	Rank
Alabama	$ 268,919	16	$ 74.41	21	$16.03	7
Alaska	64,829	40	184.17	1	19.50	1
Arizona	184,786	27	83.09	8	15.52	8
Arkansas	114,936	34	54.32	39	11.76	26
California	1,825,400	1	86.38	5	13.10	19
Colorado	206,226	24	81.38	10	13.60	15
Connecticut	145,888	32	47.14	44	6.76	47
Delaware	44,928	44	77.60	13	11.50	29
Florida	434,857	8	52.10	41	9.24	41
Georgia	265,562	17	53.91	40	10.60	35
Hawaii	97,884	37	114.89	2	17.25	3
Idaho	70,158	39	85.45	6	16.57	4
Illinois	680,971	4	61.10	32	9.00	43
Indiana	322,224	12	60.67	33	10.73	33
Iowa	222,671	21	77.59	14	12.77	22
Kansas	173,777	29	76.66	17	12.73	23
Kentucky	200,503	26	59.04	34	12.12	24
Louisiana	214,998	22	56.71	35	11.56	28
Maine	42,260	46	39.91	49	8.33	45
Maryland	256,777	18	62.66	31	9.68	39
Massachusetts	240,034	19	41.26	48	6.75	48
Michigan	593,930	6	64.86	27	10.51	37
Minnesota	323,554	11	82.43	9	14.20	12
Mississippi	154,036	30	65.66	26	16.21	5
Missouri	236,782	20	49.71	42	9.02	42
Montana	47,099	43	62.97	30	11.62	27
Nebraska	121,980	33	79.11	11	13.00	20
Nevada	42,357	45	71.55	22	10.76	32
New Hampshire	22,859	49	27.94	50	5.26	50
New Jersey	315,338	14	43.10	46	6.41	49
New Mexico	82,047	38	71.53	23	14.98	10
New York	1,251,096	2	69.04	25	10.52	36
North Carolina	407,977	9	74.84	19	15.11	9
North Dakota	48,865	42	76.71	16	13.38	17
Ohio	502,225	7	46.68	45	8.03	46
Oklahoma	152,263	31	56.14	37	10.69	34
Oregon	176,653	28	77.21	15	13.38	16
Pennsylvania	659,781	5	55.78	38	9.39	40
Rhode Island	64,771	41	69.87	24	11.97	25
South Carolina	210,239	23	74.61	20	16.15	6

Table 4.6/*Continued*

	1976–1977 Appropriations Amount (add 000)	Rank	Appropriations Per Capita Amount	Rank	Approp. Per $1,000 of Personal Income Amount	Rank
South Dakota	$ 38,382	47	$56.20	36	$11.41	30
Tennessee	200,889	25	47.97	43	9.80	38
Texas	918,589	3	75.07	18	13.33	18
Utah	102,937	36	85.35	7	17.34	2
Vermont	20,138	50	42.76	47	8.62	44
Virginia	316,042	13	63.63	28	11.00	31
Washington	310,131	15	87.43	4	14.00	13
West Virginia	114,460	35	63.48	29	12.91	21
Wisconsin	364,056	10	79.04	12	13.94	14
Wyoming	33,821	48	90.43	3	14.74	11
Total U.S.	$13,911,885		$65.21		$11.05	

Source: Appeared originally in *The Chronicle of Higher Education*, October 25, 1976, Pg. 1. Reprinted with permission. Copyright 1978 by Editorial Projects for Education, Inc.

the random number tables in the appendix. Then collect the data and make the necessary calculations.

Some suggested projects are as follows.

Business: Estimate the average gross income for firms of a certain type in your area, or the average amount spent for entertainment among college males.

Social sciences: Estimate the proportion of registered voters favoring some current political proposal, or estimate the average number of persons per household for a certain section of your city.

Physical sciences: Consider a laboratory experiment such as measuring the tensile strength of wire or the diameter of a machined rod. Take n independent observations on such an experiment and treat them as a simple random sample. Construct an interval estimate of the "population" mean. Here the population is merely conceptual (one could take many measurements of the phenomenon in question) and its mean represents the average strength of wire of this type or the average diameter of the rod.

Biological sciences: Estimate the average weight of animals fed on a certain diet for a specified time period, or the average height of trees in a certain plot. As an example of working with totals instead of means, estimate the total number of insect colonies (of a certain type) infesting a plot. Be careful here on selecting the sampling units and constructing the frame.

If your real example involves a large data set, you may want to use a computer for calculation purposes. Most computing centers have standard

4. Simple Random Sampling

programs that will compute sample means and variances. Four widely used packages of such programs are SPSS, SAS, BIOMED, and MINITAB (see the references for this chapter).

5.
Stratified Random Sampling

5.1 INTRODUCTION

The purpose of sample survey design is to maximize the amount of information for a given cost. Simple random sampling, the basic sampling design, often provides good estimates of population quantities at low cost. In this chapter we define a second sampling procedure, stratified random sampling, which in many instances increases the quantity of information for a given cost.

Definition 5.1 A *stratified random sample* is one obtained by separating the population elements into nonoverlapping groups, called *strata*, and then selecting a simple random sample from each stratum.

A public opinion poll is to be conducted over a state that contains two large cities and a rural area. The elements in the population of interest are all the men and women over 21 years of age in the state. A stratified random sample from this state could be obtained by selecting a simple random sample of adults from each city and another simple random sample from the rural area. That is, the two cities and the rural area represent three separate strata from which we obtain simple random samples.

5. Stratified Random Sampling

There are three reasons stratified random sampling often results in increased information for a given cost:

1. The data should be more homogeneous within each stratum than in the population as a whole.
2. The cost of conducting the actual sampling tends to be less for stratified random sampling than for simple random sampling because of administrative convenience.
3. When stratified sampling is used, separate estimates of population parameters can be obtained for each stratum without additional sampling.

Reduced variability within each stratum produces stratified sampling estimators that have smaller variances than do the corresponding simple random sampling estimators from the same sample size.

Each stratum has fewer people and covers a smaller geographic area than does the whole population. Therefore, it is more convenient to choose the samples and to collect the data in the smaller strata. Also, separate teams of investigators can work in each stratum and hence the survey can be completed more quickly.

In the preceding example, each of the cities in the public opinion poll could be surveyed by using the simple random sample from that stratum and by following methods set forth in chapter 4.

It should be noted that stratification can be used with other types of sampling within strata. We will see some examples of this in later chapters.

5.2 HOW TO DRAW A STRATIFIED RANDOM SAMPLE

The first step in the selection of a stratified random sample is to clearly specify the strata; then we place each sampling unit of the population into its appropriate stratum. This may be more difficult than it sounds. For example, suppose that you plan to stratify the sampling units, say households, into rural and urban units. What should be done with households in a town of 1000 inhabitants? Are these households rural or urban? They may be rural if the town is isolated in the country, or they may be urban if the town is adjacent to a large city. Hence it is essential to specify what is meant by urban and rural so that each sampling unit clearly falls into only one stratum.

After the sampling units are divided into strata, we select a simple random sample from each stratum by using the techniques given in chapter 4. We discuss the problem of choosing appropriate sample sizes for the strata later in this chapter. We must be certain that the samples selected from the strata are independent. That is, different random sam-

5.2 How to Draw a Stratified Random Sample

pling schemes should be used within each stratum so that the observations chosen in one stratum do not depend upon those chosen in another.

The following example illustrates the problem of estimating a population mean from a stratified random sample.

Example 5.1
An advertising firm is interested in determining how much to emphasize television advertising in a given county. The firm decides to conduct a sample survey to estimate the average number of hours per week that households in the county watch television (that is, the average number of hours per week the television set is actually turned on). Suggest a survey design for this problem.

Solution
The county contains two towns. Therefore, the households in this county are grouped into three distinct segments, town A, town B, and the surrounding rural area. Town A is built around a factory, and most of the households contain factory workers with school-age children. Town B is an exclusive suburb of a city in a neighboring county and contains older people with few children at home. A stratified random sample with three strata appears to be an appropriate sample survey design because of administrative conveniences and similarities in behavior patterns within each group. We would expect small variability within each stratum.

Let L denote the number of strata, N_i the number of sampling units in stratum i, and N the number of sampling units in the population. Then $N = N_1 + N_2 + \cdots + N_L$. For example 5.1, $N_1 = 155$ households in town A, $N_2 = 62$ in town B, and $N_3 = 93$ rural households; therefore, $N = 310$ households in the population.

The advertising firm has enough time and money to interview only $n = 40$ households, and it decides to select random samples of size $n_1 = 20$ from town A, $n_2 = 8$ from town B, and $n_3 = 12$ from the rural area. (We will give the reason for choosing unequal sample sizes later.) The simple random samples are selected and the interviews conducted. The results of the survey are shown in table 5.1.

Table 5.1 / *Television viewing time, in hours per week*

Stratum 1, Town A	Stratum 2, Town B	Stratum 3, Rural Area
35 28 26 41	27 4 49 10	8 15 21 7
43 29 32 37	15 41 25 30	14 30 20 11
36 25 29 31		12 32 34 24
39 38 40 45		
28 27 35 34		

5. Stratified Random Sampling

Table 5.2/*Calculations for table 5.1*

Stratum 1	Stratum 2	Stratum 3
$n_1 = 20$	$n_2 = 8$	$n_3 = 12$
$\bar{y}_1 = 33.900$	$\bar{y}_2 = 25.125$	$\bar{y}_3 = 19.000$
$s_1^2 = 35.358$	$s_2^2 = 232.411$	$s_3^2 = 87.636$
$N_1 = 155$	$N_2 = 62$	$N_3 = 93$

The terms s_1^2, s_2^2, and s_3^2 in table 5.2 are the sample variances for strata 1, 2, and 3, respectively; they are given by the formula

$$s_i^2 = \frac{\sum_{j=1}^{n_i}(y_{ij} - \bar{y}_i)^2}{n_i - 1} = \frac{\sum_{j=1}^{n_i} y_{ij}^2 - n_i \bar{y}_i^2}{n_i - 1}$$

$i = 1, 2, 3$, where y_{ij} is the jth observation in stratum i. These variances estimate the corresponding true stratum variances σ_1^2, σ_2^2, and σ_3^2.

5.3 ESTIMATION OF A POPULATION MEAN AND TOTAL

How can we use the data of table 5.1 to estimate the population mean? Let $\bar{y}_i$ denote the sample mean for the simple random sample selected from stratum i, μ_i the population mean for stratum i, and τ_i the population total for stratum i. Then the population total, τ, is equal to $\tau_1 + \tau_2 + \cdots + \tau_L$. We have a simple random sample within each stratum. Therefore, we know from chapter 4 that $\bar{y}_i$ is an unbiased estimator of μ_i and $N_i\bar{y}_i$ is an unbiased estimator of the stratum total $\tau_i = N_i\mu_i$. It seems reasonable to form an estimator of τ, which is the sum of the τ_i's, by summing the estimators of the τ_i's. Similarly, since the population mean μ equals the population total τ divided by N, an unbiased estimator of μ is obtained by summing the estimators of the τ_i's over all strata and then dividing by N. We denote this estimator by $\bar{y}_{st}$, where the subscript st indicates that stratified random sampling is used.

Estimator of the population mean μ:

$$\bar{y}_{st} = \frac{1}{N}[N_1\bar{y}_1 + N_2\bar{y}_2 + \cdots + N_L\bar{y}_L] = \frac{1}{N}\sum_{i=1}^{L} N_i\bar{y}_i \quad (5.1)$$

Estimated variance of $\bar{y}_{st}$:

$$\hat{V}(\bar{y}_{st}) = \frac{1}{N^2}[N_1^2\hat{V}(\bar{y}_1) + N_2^2\hat{V}(\bar{y}_2) + \cdots + N_L^2\hat{V}(\bar{y}_L)]$$

5.3 Estimation of a Population Mean and Total

$$= \frac{1}{N^2}\left[N_1^2\left(\frac{N_1 - n_1}{N_1}\right)\left(\frac{s_1^2}{n_1}\right) + \cdots + N_L^2\left(\frac{N_L - n_L}{N_L}\right)\left(\frac{s_L^2}{n_L}\right)\right]$$

$$= \frac{1}{N^2}\sum_{i=1}^{L} N_i^2\left(\frac{N_i - n_i}{N_i}\right)\left(\frac{s_i^2}{n_i}\right) \tag{5.2}$$

Bound on the error of estimation:

$$2\sqrt{\hat{V}(\bar{y}_{st})} = 2\sqrt{\frac{1}{N^2}\sum_{i=1}^{L} N_i^2\left(\frac{N_i - n_i}{N_i}\right)\left(\frac{s_i^2}{n_i}\right)} \tag{5.3}$$

Example 5.2
Using the data in table 5.1, estimate the average television viewing time (in hours per week) for the following:
(a) all households in the county
(b) all households in town B
In both cases place a bound on the error of estimation.

Solution
(a) From table 5.1 and equation (5.1),

$$\bar{y}_{st} = \frac{1}{N}[N_1\bar{y}_1 + N_2\bar{y}_2 + N_3\bar{y}_3]$$

$$= \frac{1}{310}[(155)(33.900) + (62)(25.125) + (93)(19.000)]$$

$$= 27.675$$

is the best estimate of the average number of hours per week spent watching television by all households in the county. Also,

$$\hat{V}(\bar{y}_{st}) = \frac{1}{N^2}\sum_{i=1}^{3} N_i^2\left(\frac{N_i - n_i}{N_i}\right)\left(\frac{s_i^2}{n_i}\right)$$

$$= \frac{1}{(310)^2}\left[\frac{(155)^2(.871)(35.358)}{20} + \frac{(62)^2(.871)(232.411)}{8} + \frac{(93)^2(.871)(87.636)}{12}\right]$$

$$= 1.97$$

The estimate of the population mean with an approximate two-standard-deviation bound on the error of estimation is given by

$$\bar{y}_{st} \pm 2\sqrt{\hat{V}(\bar{y}_{st})}, \quad 27.675 \pm 2\sqrt{1.97}, \quad 27.675 \pm (2.807)$$

5. Stratified Random Sampling

Thus we estimate the average number of hours per week that households in the county view television to be 27.675 hours. The error of estimation should be less than 2.807 hours with probability approximately equal to .95.

(b) The $n_2 = 8$ observations from stratum 2 constitute a simple random sample; hence we can apply formulas from chapter 4. The estimate of the average viewing time for town B with an approximate two-standard-deviation bound on the error of estimation is given by

$$\bar{y}_2 \pm 2 \sqrt{\left(\frac{N_2 - n_2}{N_2}\right)\left(\frac{s_2^2}{n_2}\right)} \quad \text{or} \quad 25.125 \pm 2 \sqrt{\left(\frac{62 - 8}{62}\right)\left(\frac{232.411}{8}\right)}$$

or

$$25.125 \pm 10.06$$

This estimate has a large bound on the error of estimation because s_2^2 is large and the sample size, n_2, is small. Thus the estimate $\bar{y}_{st}$ of the population mean is quite good but the estimate $\bar{y}_2$ of the mean of stratum 2 is poor. If an estimate is desired for a particular stratum, the sample from that stratum must be large enough to provide a reasonable bound on the error of estimation.

Procedures for the estimation of a population total, τ, follow directly from the procedures presented for estimating μ. Since τ is equal to $N\mu$, an unbiased estimator of τ is given by $N\bar{y}_{st}$.

Estimator of the population total τ:

$$N\bar{y}_{st} = N_1\bar{y}_1 + N_2\bar{y}_2 + \cdots + N_L\bar{y}_L = \sum_{i=1}^{L} N_i\bar{y}_i \quad (5.4)$$

Estimated variance of $N\bar{y}_{st}$:

$$\hat{V}(N\bar{y}_{st}) = N^2 \hat{V}(\bar{y}_{st}) = \sum_{i=1}^{L} N_i^2 \left(\frac{N_i - n_i}{N_i}\right)\left(\frac{s_i^2}{n_i}\right) \quad (5.5)$$

Bound on the error of estimation:

$$2\sqrt{\hat{V}(N\bar{y}_{st})} = 2\sqrt{\sum_{i=1}^{L} N_i^2 \left(\frac{N_i - n_i}{N_i}\right)\left(\frac{s_i^2}{n_i}\right)} \quad (5.6)$$

Example 5.3
Refer to example 5.1 and estimate the total number of hours per week that households in the county view television. Place a bound on the error of estimation.

5.4 Selecting the Sample Size for Estimating Population Means and Totals

Solution
For the data in table 5.1,
$$N\bar{y}_{st} = 310(27.675) = 8{,}579.250 \text{ hours}$$
The estimated variance of $N\bar{y}_{st}$ is given by
$$\hat{V}(N\bar{y}_{st}) = N^2\hat{V}(\bar{y}_{st}) = (310)^2(1.97) = 189{,}278.560$$
The estimate of the population total with a bound on the error of estimation is given by
$$N\bar{y}_{st} \pm 2\sqrt{\hat{V}(N\bar{y}_{st})}, \qquad 8{,}579.25 \pm 2\sqrt{189{,}278.560}$$
or
$$8{,}579.25 \pm 2(435.06) \quad \text{or} \quad 8{,}579.25 \pm 870.12$$

Thus we estimate the total weekly viewing time for households in the county to be 8,579.25 hours. The error of estimation should be less than 870.12 hours.

5.4 SELECTING THE SAMPLE SIZE FOR ESTIMATING POPULATION MEANS AND TOTALS

The amount of information in a sample depends on the sample size n, since $V(\bar{y}_{st})$ decreases as n increases. Let us examine a method of choosing the sample size to obtain a fixed amount of information for estimating a population parameter. Suppose we specify that the estimate $\bar{y}_{st}$ should lie within B units of the population mean, with probability approximately equal to .95. Symbolically, we want
$$2\sqrt{V(\bar{y}_{st})} = B$$
or
$$V(\bar{y}_{st}) = \frac{B^2}{4}$$

The equation above contains the actual population variance of $\bar{y}_{st}$ rather than the estimated variance. The actual variance, $V(\bar{y}_{st})$, looks very similar to equation (5.2), with $s_1^2, s_2^2, \ldots, s_L^2$ replaced by $\sigma_1^2, \sigma_2^2, \ldots, \sigma_L^2$.

Although we set $V(\bar{y}_{st})$ equal to $B^2/4$, we cannot solve for n unless we know something about the relationships among $n_1, n_2, \ldots, n_L$ and n. There are many ways of allocating a sample of size n among the various strata. In each case, however, the number of observations n_i allocated to the ith stratum is some fraction of the total sample size n. We denote this fraction by w_i. Hence we can write

$$n_i = nw_i \qquad i = 1, \ldots, L \tag{5.7}$$

5. Stratified Random Sampling

Using equation (5.7), we can then set $V(\bar{y}_{st})$ equal to $B^2/4$ and solve for n.

Similarly, estimation of the population total τ with a bound of B units on the error of estimation leads to the equation

$$2\sqrt{V(N\bar{y}_{st})} = B$$

or, using equation (5.5),

$$V(\bar{y}_{st}) = \frac{B^2}{4N^2}$$

The approximate sample size required to estimate μ or τ with a bound B on the error of estimation:

$$n = \frac{\sum_{i=1}^{L} \frac{N_i^2 \sigma_i^2}{w_i}}{N^2 D + \sum_{i=1}^{L} N_i \sigma_i^2} \tag{5.8}$$

where w_i is the fraction of observations allocated to stratum i and σ_i^2 the population variance for stratum i.

$$D = \frac{B^2}{4} \quad \text{when estimating } \mu$$

$$D = \frac{B^2}{4N^2} \quad \text{when estimating } \tau$$

We must obtain approximations of the population variances $\sigma_1^2, \sigma_2^2, \ldots, \sigma_L^2$ before we can use formula (5.8). One method of obtaining these approximations is to use the sample variances $s_1^2, s_2^2, \ldots, s_L^2$ from a previous experiment to estimate $\sigma_1^2, \sigma_2^2, \ldots, \sigma_L^2$. A second method requires knowledge of the range of the observations within each stratum. From Tchebysheff's Theorem and the normal distribution it follows that the range should be roughly four to six standard deviations.

Methods of choosing the fractions $w_1, w_2, \ldots, w_L$ are given in section 5.5.

Example 5.4
A prior survey suggests that the stratum variances in example 5.1 are approximately $\sigma_1^2 \approx 25$, $\sigma_2^2 \approx 225$, and $\sigma_3^2 \approx 100$. We wish to estimate the population mean by using $\bar{y}_{st}$. Choose the sample size to obtain a bound on the error of estimation equal to 2 hours if the allocation fractions are given by $w_1 = 1/3$, $w_2 = 1/3$, and $w_3 = 1/3$. In other words, you are to take an equal number of observations from each stratum.

5.4 Selecting the Sample Size for Estimating Population Means and Totals

Solution
A bound on the error of 2 hours means that

$$2\sqrt{V(\bar{y}_{st})} = 2 \quad \text{or} \quad V(\bar{y}_{st}) = 1$$

Therefore, $D = 1$.
In example 5.1, $N_1 = 155$, $N_2 = 62$, and $N_3 = 93$. Therefore,

$$\sum_{i=1}^{3} \frac{N_i^2 \sigma_i^2}{w_i} = \frac{N_1^2 \sigma_1^2}{w_1} + \frac{N_2^2 \sigma_2^2}{w_2} + \frac{N_3^2 \sigma_3^2}{w_3}$$

$$= \frac{(155)^2(25)}{(1/3)} = \frac{(62)^2(225)}{(1/3)} + \frac{(93)^2(100)}{(1/3)}$$

$$= (24{,}025)(75) + (3{,}844)(675) + (8{,}649)(300)$$

$$= 6{,}991{,}275$$

$$\sum_{i=1}^{3} N_i \sigma_i^2 = N_1 \sigma_1^2 + N_2 \sigma_2^2 + N_3 \sigma_3^2$$

$$= (155)(25) + (62)(225) + (93)(100) = 27{,}125$$

$$N^2 D = (310)^2(1) = 96{,}100$$

From equation (5.8) we then have

$$n = \frac{\sum_{i=1}^{3} \dfrac{N_i^2 \sigma_i^2}{w_i}}{N^2 D + \sum_{i=1}^{3} N_i \sigma_i^2} = \frac{6{,}991{,}275}{96{,}100 + 27{,}125} = \frac{6{,}991{,}275}{123{,}225} = 56.7$$

Thus the experimenter should take $n = 57$ observations with

$$n_1 = n(w_1) = 57(1/3) = 19$$
$$n_2 = 19$$
$$n_3 = 19$$

Example 5.5
As in example 5.4, suppose the variances of example 5.1 are approximated by $\sigma_1^2 \approx 25$, $\sigma_2^2 \approx 225$, and $\sigma_3^2 \approx 100$. We wish to estimate the population total τ with a bound of 400 hours on the error of estimation. Choose the appropriate sample size if an equal number of observations is to be taken from each stratum.

Solution
The bound on the error of estimation is to be 400 hours and, therefore,

$$D = \frac{B^2}{4N^2} = \frac{(400)^2}{4N^2} = \frac{40{,}000}{N^2}$$

5. Stratified Random Sampling

To calculate n from equation (5.8), we need the following quantities:

$$\sum_{i=1}^{3} \frac{N_i^2 \sigma_i^2}{w_i} = 6{,}991{,}275 \quad \text{(from example 5.4)}$$

$$\sum_{i=1}^{3} N_i \sigma_i^2 = 27{,}125 \quad \text{(from example 5.4)}$$

$$N^2 D = N^2 \left(\frac{40{,}000}{N^2}\right) = 40{,}000$$

Using equation (5.8),

$$n = \frac{\sum_{i=1}^{3} \frac{N_i^2 \sigma_i^2}{w_i}}{N^2 D + \sum_{i=1}^{3} N_i \sigma_i^2} = \frac{6{,}991{,}275}{40{,}000 + 27{,}125} = 104.2, \text{ or } 105$$

Then $n_1 = n_2 = n_3 = 35$.

5.5 ALLOCATION OF THE SAMPLE

You recall that the objective of a sample survey design is to provide estimators with small variances at the lowest possible cost. After the sample size n is chosen, there are many ways to divide n into the individual stratum sample sizes, $n_1, n_2, \ldots, n_L$. Each division may result in a different variance for the sample mean. Hence our objective is to use an allocation that gives a specified amount of information at minimum cost.

In terms of our objective, the best allocation scheme is affected by three factors. They are

1. the total number of elements in each stratum
2. the variability of observations within each stratum
3. the cost of obtaining an observation from each stratum

The number of elements in each stratum affects the quantity of information in the sample. A sample of size 20 from a population of 200 elements should contain more information than a sample of 20 from 20,000 elements. Thus large sample sizes should be assigned to strata containing large numbers of elements.

Variability must be considered because a larger sample is needed to obtain a good estimate of a population parameter when the observations are less homogeneous.

If the cost of obtaining an observation varies from stratum to stratum, we will take small samples from strata with high costs. We will do so because our objective is to keep the cost of sampling at a minimum.

5.5 Allocation of the Sample

> The approximate allocation that minimizes cost for a fixed value of $V(\bar{y}_{st})$ or minimizes $V(\bar{y}_{st})$ for a fixed cost:
>
> $$n_i = n \frac{N_i \sigma_i / \sqrt{c_i}}{N_1 \sigma_1 / \sqrt{c_1} + N_2 \sigma_2 / \sqrt{c_2} + \cdots + N_L \sigma_L / \sqrt{c_L}} \quad (5.9)$$
>
> $$= n \frac{N_i \sigma_i / \sqrt{c_i}}{\sum_{k=1}^{L} N_k \sigma_k / \sqrt{c_k}}$$
>
> where N_i denotes the size of the ith stratum, σ_i^2 denotes the population variance for the ith stratum, and c_i denotes the cost of obtaining a single observation from the ith stratum.

It is necessary to approximate the variance of each stratum before sampling in order to use the allocation formula (5.9). The approximations can be obtained from earlier surveys or from knowledge of the range of the measurements within each stratum.

Substituting the n_i/n given by formula (5.9) for w_i in equation (5.8) gives

$$n = \frac{\left[\sum_{k=1}^{L} N_k \sigma_k / \sqrt{c_k}\right]\left[\sum_{i=1}^{L} N_i \sigma_i \sqrt{c_i}\right]}{N^2 D + \sum_{i=1}^{L} N_i \sigma_i^2}$$

for optimal allocation with the variance of $\bar{y}_{st}$ fixed at D.

Example 5.6
The advertising firm in example 5.1 finds that it costs more to obtain an observation from a rural household than to obtain a response in town A or B. The increase is due to costs of traveling from one rural household to another. The cost per observation in each town is estimated to be $9.00 (that is, $c_1 = c_2 = 9$), and the costs per observation in the rural area to be $16.00 (that is, $c_3 = 16$). The stratum standard deviations (approximated by the strata sample variances from a prior survey) are $\sigma_1 \approx 5$, $\sigma_2 \approx 15$, and $\sigma_3 \approx 10$. Find the overall sample size n and the stratum sample sizes, n_1, n_2, and n_3, that allow the firm to estimate, at minimum cost, the average television viewing time with a bound on the error of estimation equal to 2 hours.

5. Stratified Random Sampling

Solution
We have

$$\sum_{k=1}^{3} \frac{N_k \sigma_k}{\sqrt{c_k}} = \frac{N_1 \sigma_1}{\sqrt{c_1}} + \frac{N_2 \sigma_2}{\sqrt{c_2}} + \frac{N_3 \sigma_3}{\sqrt{c_3}}$$

$$= \frac{155(5)}{\sqrt{9}} + \frac{62(15)}{\sqrt{9}} + \frac{93(10)}{\sqrt{16}} = 800.83$$

and

$$\sum_{i=1}^{3} N_i \sigma_i \sqrt{c_i} = N_1 \sigma_1 \sqrt{c_1} + N_2 \sigma_2 \sqrt{c_2} + N_3 \sigma_3 \sqrt{c_3}$$

$$= 155(5)\sqrt{9} + 62(15)\sqrt{9} + 93(10)\sqrt{16}$$

$$= 8835$$

Thus

$$n = \frac{\left[\sum_{k=1}^{3} N_k \sigma_k / \sqrt{c_k}\right]\left[\sum_{i=1}^{3} N_i \sigma_i \sqrt{c_i}\right]}{N^2 D + \sum_{i=1}^{3} N_i \sigma_i^2}$$

$$= \frac{(800.83)(8835)}{(310)^2(1) + 27{,}125} = 57.42 \text{ or } 58$$

Then

$$n_1 = n\left[\frac{N_1 \sigma_1 / \sqrt{c_1}}{\sum_{k=1}^{3} N_k \sigma_k / \sqrt{c_k}}\right] = n\left(\frac{155(5)/3}{800.83}\right) = .32n = 18.5 \text{ or } 18$$

Similarly,

$$n_2 = n\left(\frac{62(15)/3}{800.83}\right) = .39n = 22.6 \text{ or } 23$$

$$n_3 = n\left(\frac{93(10)/4}{800.83}\right) = .29n = 16.8 \text{ or } 17$$

Hence the experimenter should select 18 households at random from town A, 23 from town B, and 17 from the rural area. He can then estimate the average number of hours spent watching television at minimum cost with a bound of 2 hours on the error of estimation.

In some stratified sampling problems, the cost of obtaining an observation is the same for all strata. If the costs are unknown, we may be willing to assume that the costs per observation are equal. In this case the allocation formula (5.9) can still be used by letting $c_1 = c_2 = \cdots = c_L =$

5.5 Allocation of the Sample

1. When $c_1 = c_2 = \cdots = c_L$ and $w_1, w_2, \ldots, w_L$ are obtained by formula (5.9), the method of selecting the proportion of the sample size n to be assigned to each stratum is called *Neyman* allocation.

Example 5.7

The advertising firm of example 5.1 decides to use telephone interviews rather than personal interviews because all households in the county have telephones, and this method reduces costs. The cost of obtaining an observation is then the same in all three strata. The stratum standard deviations are again approximated by $\sigma_1 \approx 5$, $\sigma_2 \approx 15$, and $\sigma_3 \approx 10$. The firm desires to estimate the population mean μ with a bound on the error of estimation equal to 2 hours. Find the appropriate sample size n and stratum sample sizes, n_1, n_2, and n_3.

Solution

We will now use the original formulas, (5.8) and (5.9). The costs are the same in all strata. Therefore, to find the allocation fractions, w_1, w_2, and w_3, we replace the costs by 1 in formula (5.9). Then

$$\sum_{i=1}^{3} N_i \sigma_i = N_1 \sigma_1 + N_2 \sigma_2 + N_3 \sigma_3$$
$$= (155)(5) + (62)(15) + (93)(10) = 2635$$

and from equation (5.9)

$$n_1 = n\left[\frac{N_1 \sigma_1}{\sum_{i=1}^{3} N_i \sigma_i}\right] = n\left[\frac{(155)(5)}{2635}\right] = n(.30)$$

Similarly,

$$n_2 = n\left[\frac{(62)(15)}{2635}\right] = n(.35)$$

$$n_3 = n\left[\frac{(93)(10)}{2635}\right] = n(.35)$$

Thus $w_1 = .30$, $w_2 = .35$, and $w_3 = .35$.

Now let us use equation (5.8) to find n. A bound of 2 hours on the error of estimation means that

$$2\sqrt{V(\bar{y}_{st})} = 2 \quad \text{or} \quad V(\bar{y}_{st}) = 1$$

Therefore,

$$D = \frac{B^2}{4} = 1 \quad \text{and} \quad N^2 D = (310)^2(1) = 96{,}100$$

Also,

$$\sum_{i=1}^{3} \frac{N_i^2 \sigma_i^2}{w_i} = \frac{N_1^2 \sigma_1^2}{w_1} + \frac{N_2^2 \sigma_2^2}{w_2} + \frac{N_3^2 \sigma_3^2}{w_3}$$

$$= \frac{(155)^2(5)^2}{.30} + \frac{(62)^2(15)^2}{.35} + \frac{(93)^2(10)^2}{.35} = 6{,}944{,}369$$

$$\sum_{i=1}^{3} N_i \sigma_i^2 = 27{,}125$$

from example 5.5, and, from equation (5.8),

$$n = \frac{\sum_{i=1}^{3} \frac{N_i^2 \sigma_i^2}{w_i}}{N^2 D + \sum_{i=1}^{3} N_i \sigma_i^2} = \frac{6{,}944{,}369}{96{,}100 + 27{,}125} = 56.35 \text{ or } 57$$

Then

$$n_1 = nw_1 = (57)(.30) = 17$$
$$n_2 = nw_2 = (57)(.35) = 20$$
$$n_3 = nw_3 = (57)(.35) = 20$$

The sample size n in this last example is nearly the same as in example 5.6, but the allocation has changed. More observations are taken from the rural area because these observations no longer have a higher cost.

Example 5.8
An experimenter wanted to estimate the average weight of 90 rats (50 male and 40 female) being fed a certain diet. The rats were separated by sex; hence it seemed appropriate to use stratified random sampling with two strata. To approximate the variability within each stratum, the experimenter selected the smallest and largest rats in each stratum and weighed them. She found that the range was 10 grams for the males and 8 grams for the females. How large a sample should have been taken in order to estimate the population average with a bound of 1 gram on the error of estimation? Assume cost of sampling was the same for both strata.

Solution
Let us denote males as stratum 1 and females as stratum 2. To use equation (5.9) we must first approximate σ_1 and σ_2. The standard deviation should be about one-fourth of the range, assuming that the weights have a bell-shaped distribution. Thus

$$\sigma_1 \approx \frac{10}{4} = 2.5 \quad \text{and} \quad \sigma_2 \approx \frac{8}{4} = 2.0$$

5.5 Allocation of the Sample

From formula (5.9), with $c_1 = c_2 = 1$,

$$n_i = n\left[\frac{N_i\sigma_i}{\sum_{k=1}^{2} N_k\sigma_k}\right]$$

where

$$\sum_{k=1}^{2} N_k\sigma_k = (50)(2.5) + (40)(2.0) = 125 + 80 = 205$$

Then

$$n_1 = n\left[\frac{N_1\sigma_1}{\sum_{k=1}^{2} N_k\sigma_k}\right] = n\left(\frac{125}{205}\right) = .61n$$

and

$$n_2 = n\left(\frac{80}{205}\right) = .39n$$

Thus $w_1 = .61$ and $w_2 = .39$.

We must calculate the following quantities in order to find n:

$$\sum_{i=1}^{2} \frac{N_i^2\sigma_i^2}{w_i} = \frac{(50)^2(2.5)^2}{.61} + \frac{(40)^2(2.0)^2}{.39} = 42{,}025.01$$

$$\sum_{i=1}^{2} N_i\sigma_i^2 = (50)(2.5)^2 + (40)(2.0)^2 = 472.50$$

$$D = \frac{B^2}{4} = \frac{(1)^2}{4} = .25$$

Using equation (5.8)

$$n = \frac{\sum_{i=1}^{2} \frac{N_i^2\sigma_i^2}{w_i}}{N^2 D + \sum_{i=1}^{2} N_i\sigma_i^2} = \frac{42{,}025.01}{(90)^2(.25) + 472.50} = 16.83$$

The sample size n should have been 17 with

$$n_1 = nw_1 = (17)(.61) = 10$$
$$n_2 = nw_2 = (17)(.39) = 7$$

Just as we sometimes encounter equal costs per observation in all strata, we sometimes encounter approximately equal variances, σ_1^2, $\sigma_2^2, \ldots, \sigma_L^2$. If the variances are equal in all strata, then each of the variances $\sigma_1^2, \sigma_2^2, \ldots, \sigma_L^2$ can be replaced by 1 in formula (5.9) to simplify the calculation of the allocation fractions.

5. Stratified Random Sampling

If costs $c_1, c_2, \ldots, c_L$ are also equal for all strata, both the costs and the variances can be replaced by 1 in formula (5.9), and

$$n_i = n\frac{N_i}{N} \qquad i = 1, \ldots, L \tag{5.10}$$

This method of assigning sample sizes to the strata is called *proportional* allocation because sample sizes $n_1, n_2, \ldots, n_L$ are proportional to stratum sizes $N_1, N_2, \ldots, N_L$. Of course, proportional allocation can be, and often is, used when stratum variances and costs are not equal. One advantage to using this allocation is the fact that the estimator $\bar{y}_{st}$ becomes simply the sample mean for the entire sample. This can be an important time-saving feature in some surveys.

Under proportional allocation, formula (5.8) for the value of n, which yields $V(\bar{y}_{st}) = D$, becomes

$$n = \frac{\sum_{i=1}^{L} N_i \sigma_i^2}{ND + \dfrac{1}{N}\sum_{i=1}^{L} N_i \sigma_i^2}$$

Example 5.9
The advertising firm in example 5.1 thinks that the approximate variances used in previous examples are in error and that the stratum variances are approximately equal. The common value of σ_i was approximated by 10 in a preliminary study. Telephone interviews are to be used and hence costs will be equal in all strata. It is desired to estimate the average number of hours per week that households in the county watch television with a bound on the error of estimation equal to 2 hours. Find the sample size and stratum sample sizes necessary to achieve this accuracy.

Solution
We have

$$\sum_{i=1}^{3} N_i \sigma_i^2 = N_1 \sigma_1^2 + N_2 \sigma_2^2 + N_3 \sigma_3^2$$

$$= (155)(100) + (62)(100) + (93)(100)$$

$$= 310(100) = 31{,}000$$

Thus, since $D = 1$,

$$n = \frac{31{,}000}{310(1) + (1/310)(31{,}000)} = 75.6 \text{ or } 76$$

5.5 Allocation of the Sample

It follows that

$$n_1 = n \frac{N_1}{\sum_{i=1}^{3} N_i} = n \frac{N_1}{N} = n\left(\frac{155}{310}\right) = n(.5) = 38$$

$$n_2 = n \frac{N_2}{N} = n\left(\frac{62}{310}\right) = n(.2) = 15$$

$$n_3 = n \frac{N_3}{N} = n\left(\frac{93}{310}\right) = n(.3) = 23$$

These results differ from those of example 5.7 because here the variances are assumed to be equal in all strata and are approximated by a common value.

The amount of money to be spent on sampling is sometimes fixed before the experiment is started. Then the experimenter must find a sample size and allocation scheme that minimizes the variance of the estimator for a fixed expenditure.

Example 5.10
In the television-viewing example, suppose the costs are as specified in example 5.6. That is, $c_1 = c_2 = 9$ and $c_3 = 16$. Let the stratum variances be approximated by $\sigma_1 \approx 5$, $\sigma_2 \approx 15$, and $\sigma_3 \approx 10$. Given that the advertising firm has only \$500 to spend on sampling, choose the sample size and allocation that minimize $V(\bar{y}_{st})$.

Solution
The allocation scheme is still given by formula (5.9). In example 5.6 we found $w_1 = .32$, $w_2 = .39$, and $w_3 = .29$.
Since the total cost must equal \$500, we have

$$c_1 n_1 + c_2 n_2 + c_3 n_3 = 500$$

or

$$9n_1 + 9n_2 + 16n_3 = 500$$

Since $n_i = nw_i$, we can substitute as follows:

$$9nw_1 + 9nw_2 + 16nw_3 = 500$$

or

$$9n(.32) + 9n(.39) + 16n(.29) = 500$$

5. Stratified Random Sampling

Solving for n we obtain

$$11.03n = 500$$

$$n = \frac{500}{11.03} = 45.33$$

Therefore, we must take $n = 45$ to insure that the cost remains below \$500. The corresponding allocation is given by

$$n_1 = nw_1 = (45)(.32) = 14$$
$$n_2 = nw_2 = (45)(.39) = 18$$
$$n_3 = nw_3 = (45)(.29) = 13$$

We can make the following summary statement on stratified random sampling. In general, stratified random sampling with proportional allocation will produce an estimator with smaller variance than that produced by simple random sampling (with the same sample size) if there is considerable variability among the stratum means. If sampling costs are nearly equal from stratum to stratum, stratified random sampling with optimal allocation [formula (5.8)] will yield estimators with smaller variance than will proportional allocation when there is variability among the stratum variances.

5.6 ESTIMATION OF A POPULATION PROPORTION

In our numerical examples we have been interested in estimating the average or the total number of hours per week spent watching television. In contrast, suppose that the advertising firm wants to estimate the proportion (fraction) of households that watches a particular show. The population is divided into strata, just as before, and a simple random sample is taken from each stratum. Interviews are then conducted to determine the proportion $\hat{p}_i$ of households in stratum i that view the show. This $\hat{p}_i$ is an unbiased estimator of p_i, the population proportion in stratum i (as described in chapter 4). Reasoning as we did in section 5.3, we conclude that $N_i \hat{p}_i$ is an unbiased estimator of the total number of households in stratum i that view this particular show. Hence $N_1 \hat{p}_1 + N_2 \hat{p}_2 + \cdots + N_L \hat{p}_L$ is a good estimator of the total number of viewing households in the population. Dividing this quantity by N, we obtain an unbiased estimator of the population proportion p of households viewing the show.

5.6 Estimation of a Population Proportion

Estimator of the population proportion p:

$$\hat{p}_{st} = \frac{1}{N}[N_1\hat{p}_1 + N_2\hat{p}_2 + \cdots + N_L\hat{p}_L] = \frac{1}{N}\sum_{i=1}^{L} N_i\hat{p}_i \quad (5.11)$$

Estimated variance of $\hat{p}_{st}$:

$$\hat{V}(\hat{p}_{st}) = \frac{1}{N^2}[N_1^2\hat{V}(\hat{p}_1) + N_2^2\hat{V}(\hat{p}_2) + \cdots + N_L^2\hat{V}(\hat{p}_L)]$$

$$= \frac{1}{N^2}\sum_{i=1}^{L} N_i^2\hat{V}(\hat{p}_i)$$

$$= \frac{1}{N^2}\sum_{i=1}^{L} N_i^2\left(\frac{N_i - n_i}{N_i}\right)\left(\frac{\hat{p}_i\hat{q}_i}{n_i - 1}\right) \quad (5.12)$$

Bound on the error of estimation:

$$2\sqrt{\hat{V}(\hat{p}_{st})} = 2\sqrt{\frac{1}{N^2}\sum_{i=1}^{L} N_i^2\left(\frac{N_i - n_i}{N_i}\right)\left(\frac{\hat{p}_i\hat{q}_i}{n_i - 1}\right)} \quad (5.13)$$

Example 5.11
The advertising firm wanted to estimate the proportion of households in the county of example 5.1 that view show X. The county is divided into three strata, town A, town B, and the rural area. The strata contain $N_1 = 155$, $N_2 = 62$, and $N_3 = 93$ households, respectively. A stratified random sample of $n = 40$ households is chosen with proportional allocation. In other words, a simple random sample is taken from each stratum; the sizes of the samples are $n_1 = 20$, $n_2 = 8$, and $n_3 = 12$. Interviews are conducted in the 40 sampled households; results are shown in table 5.3. Estimate the proportion of households viewing show X and place a bound on the error of estimation.

Table 5.3/Data for example 5.11

Stratum	Sample Size	Number of Households Viewing Show, X	$\hat{p}_i$
1	$n_1 = 20$	16	.80
2	$n_2 = 8$	2	.25
3	$n_3 = 12$	6	.50

5. Stratified Random Sampling

Solution
The estimate of the proportion of households viewing show X is given by $\hat{p}_{st}$. Using equation (5.11), we calculate

$$\hat{p}_{st} = \frac{1}{310}[(155)(.80) + 62(.25) + 93(.50)] = .60$$

The variance of $\hat{p}_{st}$ can be estimated by using equation (5.12). First, let us calculate the $\hat{V}(\hat{p}_i)$ terms. We have

$$\hat{V}(\hat{p}_1) = \left(\frac{N_1 - n_1}{N_1}\right)\left(\frac{\hat{p}_1\hat{q}_1}{n_1 - 1}\right) = \left(\frac{155 - 20}{155}\right)\left[\frac{(.8)(.2)}{19}\right]$$

$$= (.871)(.008) = .007$$

$$\hat{V}(\hat{p}_2) = \left(\frac{N_2 - n_2}{N_2}\right)\left(\frac{\hat{p}_2\hat{q}_2}{n_2 - 1}\right) = \left(\frac{62 - 8}{62}\right)\left[\frac{(.25)(.75)}{7}\right]$$

$$= (.871)(.027) = .024$$

$$\hat{V}(\hat{p}_3) = \left(\frac{N_3 - n_3}{N_3}\right)\left(\frac{\hat{p}_3\hat{q}_3}{n_3 - 1}\right) = \left(\frac{93 - 12}{93}\right)\left[\frac{(.5)(.5)}{11}\right]$$

$$= (.871)(.023) = .020$$

From equation (5.12),

$$\hat{V}(\hat{p}_{st}) = \frac{1}{N^2} \sum_{i=1}^{3} N_i^2 \hat{V}(\hat{p}_i)$$

$$= \frac{1}{(310)^2}[(155)^2(.007) + (62)^2(.024) + (93)^2(.020)]$$

$$= .0045$$

Then the estimate of proportion of households in the county that view show X with a bound on the error of estimation is given by

$$\hat{p}_{st} \pm 2\sqrt{\hat{V}(\hat{p}_{st})}, \quad .60 \pm 2\sqrt{.0045}$$

$$.60 \pm 2(.0671), \quad .60 \pm .1342$$

The bound on the error in example 5.11 is quite large. We could reduce this bound and make the estimator more precise by increasing the sample size. The problem of choosing a sample size is considered in the next section.

5.7 SELECTING THE SAMPLE SIZE AND ALLOCATING THE SAMPLE TO ESTIMATE PROPORTIONS

To estimate a population proportion, we first indicate how much information we desire by specifying the size of the bound; the sample size is chosen accordingly.

5.7 Selecting Sample Size and Allocating the Sample to Estimate Proportions

The formula for the sample size n (for a given bound B on the error of estimation) is the same as equation (5.8) except that σ_i^2 becomes $p_i q_i$.

The approximation sample size required to estimate p with a bound B on the error of estimation:

$$n = \frac{\sum_{i=1}^{L} \frac{N_i^2 p_i q_i}{w_i}}{N^2 D + \sum_{i=1}^{L} N_i p_i q_i} \qquad (5.14)$$

where w_i is the fraction of observations allocated to stratum i, p_i is the population proportion for stratum i, and

$$D = \frac{B^2}{4}$$

The allocation formula that gives the variance of $\hat{p}_{st}$ equal to some fixed constant at minimum cost is the same as formula (5.9) with σ_i replaced by $\sqrt{p_i q_i}$.

The approximate allocation that minimizes cost for a fixed value of $V(\hat{p}_{st})$ or minimizes $V(\hat{p}_{st})$ for a fixed cost:

$$n_i = n \frac{N_i \sqrt{p_i q_i / c_i}}{N_1 \sqrt{p_1 q_1 / c_1} + N_2 \sqrt{p_2 q_2 / c_2} + \cdots + N_L \sqrt{p_L q_L / c_L}}$$

$$= n \frac{N_i \sqrt{p_i q_i / c_i}}{\sum_{k=1}^{L} N_k \sqrt{p_k q_k / c_k}} \qquad (5.15)$$

where N_i denotes the size of the ith stratum, p_i denotes the population proportion for the ith stratum, and c_i denotes the cost of obtaining a single observation from the ith stratum.

Example 5.12
The data of table 5.2 were obtained from a sample conducted last year. The advertising firm now wants to conduct a new survey in the same county to estimate the proportion of households viewing show X. Although the fractions p_1, p_2, and p_3 that appear in equations (5.14) and (5.15) are unknown, they can be approximated by the estimates from the earlier study, that is,

5. Stratified Random Sampling

$\hat{p}_1 = .80$, $\hat{p}_2 = .25$, and $\hat{p}_3 = .50$. The cost of obtaining an observation is \$9 for either town and \$16 for the rural area, that is, $c_1 = c_2 = 9$ and $c_3 = 16$. The number of households within the strata are $N_1 = 155$, $N_2 = 62$, and $N_3 = 93$. The firm wants to estimate the population proportion p with a bound on the error of estimation equal to .1. Find the sample size n and the strata sample sizes, n_1, n_2, and n_3, that will give the desired bound at minimum cost.

Solution

We first use equation (5.15) to find the allocation fractions, w_i. Using $\hat{p}_i$ to approximate p_i,

$$\sum_{i=1}^{3} N_i \sqrt{\hat{p}_i \hat{q}_i / c_i} = N_1 \sqrt{\hat{p}_1 \hat{q}_1 / c_1} + N_2 \sqrt{\hat{p}_2 \hat{q}_2 / c_2} + N_3 \sqrt{\hat{p}_3 \hat{q}_3 / c_3}$$

$$= 155\sqrt{(.8)(.2)/9} + 62\sqrt{(.25)(.75)/9} + 93\sqrt{(.5)(.5)/16}$$

$$= \frac{62.000}{3} + \frac{26.846}{3} + \frac{46.500}{4}$$

$$= 20.667 + 8.949 + 11.625 = 41.241$$

and

$$n_1 = n \frac{N_1 \sqrt{\hat{p}_1 \hat{q}_1 / c_1}}{\sum_{i=1}^{3} N_i \sqrt{\hat{p}_i \hat{q}_i / c_i}} = n\left(\frac{20.667}{41.241}\right) = n(.50)$$

Similarly,

$$n_2 = n\left(\frac{8.949}{41.241}\right) = n(.22)$$

$$n_3 = n\left(\frac{11.625}{41.241}\right) = n(.28)$$

Thus $w_1 = .50$, $w_2 = .22$, and $w_3 = .28$.

The next step is to use equation (5.14) to find n. First, the following quantities must be calculated:

$$\sum_{i=1}^{3} \frac{N_i^2 \hat{p}_i \hat{q}_i}{w_i} = \frac{N_1^2 \hat{p}_1 \hat{q}_1}{w_1} + \frac{N_2^2 \hat{p}_2 \hat{q}_2}{w_2} + \frac{N_3^2 \hat{p}_3 \hat{q}_3}{w_3}$$

$$= \frac{(155)^2(.8)(.2)}{.50} + \frac{(62)^2(.25)(.75)}{.22} + \frac{(93)^2(.5)(.5)}{.28}$$

$$= 18{,}686.46$$

5.7 Selecting Sample Size and Allocating the Sample to Estimate Proportions

$$\sum_{i=1}^{3} N_i \hat{p}_i \hat{q}_i = N_1 \hat{p}_1 \hat{q}_1 + N_2 \hat{p}_2 \hat{q}_2 + N_3 \hat{p}_3 \hat{q}_3$$

$$= (155)(.8)(.2) + (62)(.25)(.75) + (93)(.5)(.5)$$

$$= 59.675$$

To find D we let $2\sqrt{V(\hat{p}_{st})} = .1$ (the bound on the error of estimation). Then

$$V(\hat{p}_{st}) = \frac{(.1)^2}{4} = .0025 = D$$

and

$$N^2 D = (310)^2 (.0025) = 240.25$$

Finally, from equation (5.14), n is given approximately by

$$n = \frac{\sum_{i=1}^{3} \frac{N_i^2 \hat{p}_i \hat{q}_i}{w_i}}{N^2 D + \sum_{i=1}^{3} N_i \hat{p}_i \hat{q}_i} = \frac{18,686.46}{240.25 + 59.675} = 62.3 \text{ or } 63$$

Hence

$$n_1 = n w_1 = (63)(.50) = 31$$
$$n_2 = n w_2 = (63)(.22) = 14$$
$$n_3 = n w_3 = (63)(.28) = 18$$

If the cost of sampling does not vary from stratum to stratum, then the cost factors, c_i, can be replaced by 1 in formula (5.15).

Example 5.13
Suppose that in example 5.12 telephone interviews are to be conducted, and, hence the cost of sampling is the same in all strata. The fraction p_i will be approximated by $\hat{p}_i$, $i = 1, 2, 3$. We desire to estimate the population proportion p with a bound of .1 on the error of estimation. Find the appropriate sample size to achieve this bound at minimum cost.

Solution
Equation (5.15) is used to find the fractions w_1, w_2, and w_3, but now all c_i terms can be replaced by 1. Hence

$$\sum_{i=1}^{3} N_i \sqrt{\hat{p}_i \hat{q}_i} = 155\sqrt{(.8)(.2)} + 62\sqrt{(.25)(.75)} + 93\sqrt{(.5)(.5)}$$

$$= 62.000 + 26.846 + 46.500 = 135.346$$

5. Stratified Random Sampling

and

$$n_1 = n \frac{N_1\sqrt{\hat{p}_1 \hat{q}_1}}{\sum_{i=1}^{3} N_i\sqrt{\hat{p}_i \hat{q}_i}} = n\left(\frac{62.000}{135.346}\right) = n(.46)$$

Similarly,

$$n_2 = n\left(\frac{26.846}{135.346}\right) = n(.20)$$

$$n_3 = n\left(\frac{46.500}{135.346}\right) = n(.34)$$

Thus $w_1 = .46$, $w_2 = .20$, and $w_3 = .34$.

Equation (5.14) is now used to solve for n. We must first calculate

$$\sum_{i=1}^{3} \frac{N_i^2 \hat{p}_i \hat{q}_i}{w_i} = \frac{(155)^2(.8)(.2)}{.46} + \frac{(62)^2(.25)(.75)}{.20} + \frac{(93)^2(.5)(.5)}{.34}$$

$$= 18{,}319.83$$

$$\sum_{i=1}^{3} N_i \hat{p}_i \hat{q}_i = 59.675 \quad \text{(from example 5.12)}$$

$$N^2 D = 240.25 \quad \text{(from example 5.12)}$$

From equation (5.14) n is approximately

$$n = \frac{\sum_{i=1}^{3} \frac{N_i^2 \hat{p}_i \hat{q}_i}{w_i}}{N^2 D + \sum_{i=1}^{3} N_i \hat{p}_i \hat{q}_i} = \frac{18{,}319.83}{240.25 + 59.675} = 61.08 \text{ or } 62$$

Hence we take a sample of 62 observations to estimate p with a bound on the error of magnitude $B = .1$. The corresponding allocation is given by

$$n_1 = nw_1 = 62(.46) = 29$$
$$n_2 = nw_2 = 62(.20) = 12$$
$$n_3 = nw_3 = 62(.34) = 21$$

These answers are close to those of example 5.12. The changes in allocation are due to the fact that costs do not vary in this example.

Recall that the allocation formula (5.9) assumes a very simple form when the variances, as well as costs, are equal for all strata. Equation (5.15) simplifies in the same way, provided all stratum proportions p_i are

5.7 Selecting Sample Size and Allocating the Sample to Estimate Proportions

equal and all costs c_i are equal. Then equation (5.15) becomes

$$n_i = n\frac{N_i}{N} \quad i = 1, \ldots, L$$

As previously noted, this method for assignment of sample sizes to the strata is called *proportional* allocation.

Example 5.14
In the television survey of example 5.12, the advertising firm plans to use telephone interviews; therefore, the cost of sampling will not vary from stratum to stratum. The stratum sizes are $N_1 = 155$, $N_2 = 62$, and $N_3 = 93$. The results of last year's survey (see table 5.3) do not appear to hold for this year. The firm believes that the proportion of households viewing show X is close to .4 in each of the three strata. It is desired to estimate the population proportion p with a bound of .1 on the error of estimation. Find the sample size n and the allocation that gives this bound at minimum cost.

Solution
The allocation fractions are found by using equation (5.15) with $p_1, \ldots, p_L$ and $c_1, \ldots, c_L$ replaced by 1. Thus

$$n_1 = n\frac{N_1}{\sum\limits_{i=1}^{3} N_i} = n\frac{N_1}{N} = n\left(\frac{155}{310}\right) = n(.5)$$

$$n_2 = n\frac{N_2}{N} = n\left(\frac{62}{310}\right) = n(.2)$$

$$n_3 = n\frac{N_3}{N} = n\left(\frac{93}{310}\right) = n(.3)$$

or

$$w_1 = .5, \quad w_2 = .2, \quad \text{and} \quad w_3 = .3$$

The sample size n is found from equation (5.14), using .4 as an approximation to p_1, p_2, and p_3. It follows that

$$\sum_{i=1}^{3} \frac{N_i^2 p_i q_i}{w_i} = \frac{(155)^2(.4)(.6)}{.5} + \frac{(62)^2(.4)(.6)}{.2} + \frac{(93)^2(.4)(.6)}{.3}$$

$$= 23{,}064$$

and

$$\sum_{i=1}^{3} N_i p_i q_i = (155)(.4)(.6) + (62)(.4)(.6) + (93)(.4)(.6)$$

$$= (.4)(.6)(155 + 62 + 93) = (.4)(.6)(310)$$

$$= 74.4$$

5. Stratified Random Sampling

A bound of .1 on the error of estimation gives

$$2\sqrt{V(\hat{p}_{st})} = .1$$
$$V(\hat{p}_{st}) = (.05)^2 = .0025$$

Hence $D = .0025$ and

$$N^2 D = (310)^2 (.0025) = 240.25$$

From equation (5.14)

$$n = \frac{\sum_{i=1}^{3} \frac{N_i^2 p_i q_i}{w_i}}{N^2 D + \sum_{i=1}^{3} N_i p_i q_i} = \frac{23{,}064}{240.25 + 74.4} = 73.3 \text{ or } 74$$

Then

$$n_1 = nw_1 = (74)(.5) = 37$$
$$n_2 = nw_2 = (74)(.2) = 15$$
$$n_3 = nw_3 = (74)(.3) = 22$$

5.8 ADDITIONAL COMMENTS ON STRATIFIED SAMPLING

Stratified random sampling does not always produce an estimator with a smaller variance than that of the corresponding estimator in simple random sampling. The following example illustrates this point.

Example 5.15
A wholesale food distributor in a large city wants to know if demand is great enough to justify adding a new product to his stock. To aid in making his decision, he plans to add this product to a sample of the stores he services in order to estimate average monthly sales. He only services four large chains in the city. Hence for administrative convenience, he decides to use stratified random sampling with each chain as a stratum. There are 24 stores in stratum 1, 36 in stratum 2, 30, in stratum 3, and 30 in stratum 4. Thus $N_1 = 24$, $N_2 = 36$, $N_3 = 30$, $N_4 = 30$, and $N = 120$. The distributor has enough time and money to obtain data on monthly sales in $n = 20$ stores. Because he has no prior information on the stratum variances, and because the cost of sampling is the same in each stratum, he decides to use proportional allocation, which gives

$$n_1 = n\left(\frac{N_1}{N}\right) = 20\left(\frac{24}{120}\right) = 4$$

5.8 Additional Comments on Stratified Sampling

Similarly,

$$n_2 = 20\left(\frac{36}{120}\right) = 6$$

$$n_3 = 20\left(\frac{30}{120}\right) = 5$$

$$n_4 = 5$$

The new product is introduced in four stores chosen at random from chain 1, six stores from chain 2, and five stores each from chains 3 and 4. The sales figures after a month show the results given in the accompanying table. Estimate the average sales for the month, and place a bound on the error of estimation.

		Stratum	
1	2	3	4
94	91	108	92
90	99	96	110
102	93	100	94
110	105	93	91
	111	93	113
	101		
$\bar{y}_1 = 99$	$\bar{y}_2 = 100$	$\bar{y}_3 = 98$	$\bar{y}_4 = 100$
$s_1^2 = 78.67$	$s_2^2 = 55.60$	$s_3^2 = 39.50$	$s_4^2 = 112.50$

Solution
From equation (5.1)

$$\bar{y}_{st} = \frac{1}{N} \sum_{i=1}^{4} N_i \bar{y}_i = 99.3$$

Note that the estimate $\bar{y}_{st}$ of the population mean is the average of all sample observations when proportional allocation is used.
The estimated variance of $\bar{y}_{st}$, from equation (5.2), is

$$\hat{V}(\bar{y}_{st}) = \frac{1}{N^2} \sum_{i=1}^{4} N_i^2 \left(\frac{N_i - n_i}{N_i}\right)\left(\frac{s_i^2}{n_i}\right)$$

where for this example

$$\left(\frac{N_i - n_i}{N_i}\right) = \frac{5}{6} \quad i = 1, 2, 3$$

5. Stratified Random Sampling

Then

$$\hat{V}(\bar{y}_{st}) = \frac{1}{(120)^2}\left(\frac{5}{6}\right)\left[(24)^2\left(\frac{78.67}{4}\right) + (36)^2\left(\frac{55.60}{6}\right)\right.$$
$$\left. + (30)^2\left(\frac{39.50}{5}\right) + (30)^2\left(\frac{112.50}{5}\right)\right]$$
$$= 2.9339$$

and the estimate of average monthly sales with a bound on the error of estimation is

$$\bar{y}_{st} \pm 2\sqrt{\hat{V}(\bar{y}_{st})}, \qquad 99.3 \pm 2\sqrt{2.9339}, \qquad 99.3 \pm 3.4257$$

Suppose the distributor had decided to take a simple random sample of $n = 20$ stores and the same 20 stores as above were selected. In other words, suppose the 20 stores constitute a simple random sample rather than a stratified random sample. Then the estimator of the population mean has the same value as that calculated above, that is,

$$\bar{y} = \bar{y}_{st} = 99.3$$

but the estimated variance becomes

$$\hat{V}(\bar{y}) = \left(\frac{N-n}{N}\right)\left(\frac{s^2}{n}\right) = \left(\frac{5}{6}\right)\left(\frac{59.8}{20}\right) = 2.492$$

We see that the estimated variance is *smaller* for simple random sampling. Thus we conclude simple random sampling may have been better than stratified random sampling for this problem. The experimenter did not consider the fact that sales vary greatly among stores within a chain when he stratified on chains. He could have obtained a smaller variance for his estimator by stratifying on amount of sales, that is, by putting stores with low monthly sales in one stratum, stores with high sales in another, and so forth.

In many sample survey problems, more than one measurement is taken on each sampling unit in order to estimate more than one population parameter. This situation causes complications in selecting the appropriate sample size and allocation, as is illustrated in the following example.

Example 5.16

A state forest service is conducting a study of the people who use state-operated camping facilities. The state has two camping areas, one located in the mountains and one located along the coast. The forest service wishes to estimate the average number of people per campsite and the proportion of campsites occupied by out-of-state campers during a particular weekend when all sites are expected to be used. The average number of people is to be estimated with a bound of 1 on the error of estimation, and

5.8 Additional Comments on Stratified Sampling

the proportion of out-of-state users is to be estimated with a bound of .1. The two camping areas conveniently form two strata, the mountain location forming stratum 1 and the coastal location stratum 2. It is known that $N_1 = 120$ campsites and $N_2 = 80$ campsites. Find the sample size and allocation necessary to achieve both of the bounds above.

Solution

Assuming that the costs of sampling are the same in each stratum, we could achieve the smallest sample size by using Neyman allocation. However, this allocation depends on the stratum variances and gives different allocations for the two different types of measurements involved in the problem. Instead, we use proportional allocation because it is usually close to optimum and it gives the same allocation for any desired measurement. It follows that

$$w_1 = \frac{N_1}{N} = \frac{120}{200} = .6$$

$$w_2 = \frac{N_2}{N} = \frac{80}{200} = .4$$

Now the sample size must be determined separately for each of the desired estimates. First consider estimating the average number of persons per campsite. It is necessary to have an approximation of the stratum variances in order to use equation (5.8) for the sample size. The forest service knows from experience that most sites contain from 1 to 9 persons. Therefore, we can use the approximation

$$\sigma_i \approx \frac{9-1}{4} = 2 \quad i = 1, 2$$

It follows that

$$\sum_{i=1}^{2} \frac{N_i^2 \sigma_i^2}{w_i} = \frac{(120)^2(4)}{.6} + \frac{(80)^2(4)}{.4} = 160{,}000$$

$$\sum_{i=1}^{2} N_i \sigma_i^2 = (120)(4) + (80)(4) = 800$$

$$N^2 D = N^2 \left(\frac{B^2}{4}\right) = (200)^2 \left(\frac{1}{4}\right) = 10{,}000$$

From equation (5.8)

$$n = \frac{\sum_{i=1}^{2} \frac{N_i^2 \sigma_i^2}{w_i}}{N^2 D + \sum_{i=1}^{2} N_i \sigma_i^2} = \frac{160{,}000}{10{,}000 + 800} = 14.8 \text{ or } 15$$

is the required sample size.

5. Stratified Random Sampling

Now let us consider estimating the proportion of out-of-state users. No prior estimates of the stratum proportions p_i are available, so we let $p_1 = p_2 = .5$ to obtain a maximum sample size. We use equation (5.14) to find n, and hence we must find

$$\sum_{i=1}^{2} \frac{N_i^2 p_i q_i}{w_i} = \frac{(120)^2(.5)(.5)}{.6} + \frac{(80)^2(.5)(.5)}{.4} = 10{,}000$$

$$N^2 D = N^2\left(\frac{B^2}{4}\right) = (200)^2\left(\frac{.01}{4}\right) = 100$$

$$\sum_{i=1}^{2} N_i p_i q_i = 120(.5)(.5) + 80(.5)(.5) = 50$$

From equation (5.14)

$$n = \frac{\sum_{i=1}^{2} \frac{N_i^2 p_i q_i}{w_i}}{N^2 D + \sum_{i=1}^{2} N_i p_i q_i} = \frac{10{,}000}{100 + 50} = 67$$

Thus

$$n_1 = n w_1 = (67)(.6) = 40$$
$$n_2 = n w_2 = (67)(.4) = 27$$

are the sample sizes required in order to achieve both bounds. Note that these sample sizes give an estimate of the average number of persons per campsite with a much smaller bound than required.

5.9 AN OPTIMAL RULE FOR CHOOSING STRATA

If our only objective of stratification is to produce estimators with small variance, then the best criterion by which to define strata is the set of values that the response of interest can take on. For example, suppose it is of interest to estimate the average income per household in a community. We could estimate this average quite accurately if we could put all low-income households in one stratum and all high-income households in another before actually sampling. Of course, this is often impossible because detailed knowledge of incomes before sampling might make the statistical problem unnecessary in the first place. However, we sometimes have some relating frequency data on broad categories of the variable of interest or on some highly correlated variable. In these cases the "cumulative square root of the frequency method" works well for delineating strata. Rather than attempt to explain this method in theory, we will simply show how it works in practice.

5.10 Summary

Example 5.17
It is desired to estimate the average yearly sales for 56 firms, using a sample of n = 15 firms. Frequency data on these firms is available in the form of classification by $50,000 increments and appears in the accompanying table. How can we best allocate the firms to L = 3 strata?

Income (thousands)	Frequency	$\sqrt{\text{Frequency}}$	Cumulative $\sqrt{\text{Frequency}}$
100–150	11	3.32	3.32
150–200	14	3.74	7.06
200–250	9	3.00	10.06
250–300	4	2.00	12.06
300–350	5	2.24	14.30
350–400	8	2.83	17.13
400–450	3	1.73	18.86
450–500	2	1.41	20.27
	56		

Solution
Note that we have added two columns to the frequency data for the population, namely, the square root of the frequencies and the cumulative square root. The approximately optimal method for stratification is to mark off equal intervals on the cumulative square root scale. (Note: On this scale, 7.06 is 3.32 + 3.74 etc.) Thus (20.27)/3 = 6.76 and our stratum boundaries should be as close as possible to 6.76 and 2(6.76) = 13.52. On the actual scale, 7.06 is closest to 6.76 and 14.30 is closest to 13.52. This results in three strata as follows:

stratum 1: firms with scales from 100,000 to 200,000
stratum 2: firms with scales from 200,001 to 350,000
stratum 3: firms with scales from 350,001 to 500,000

Assuming that firms in these strata can be identified before sampling, the sample of n = 15 can be allocated five to each stratum. (Equal stratum sample sizes are nearly optimal when employing this technique.)

5.10 SUMMARY

A stratified random sample is obtained by separating the population elements into groups, or strata, such that each element belongs to one and only one stratum, and then independently selecting a simple random sample from each stratum. This sample survey design has three major advantages over simple random sampling. First, the variance of the

5. Stratified Random Sampling

estimator of the population mean is usually reduced because the variance of observations within each stratum is usually smaller than the overall population variance. Second, the cost of collecting and analyzing the data is often reduced by the separation of a large population into smaller strata. Third, separate estimates can be obtained for individual strata without selecting another sample and, hence, without additional cost.

An unbiased estimator, $\bar{y}_{st}$, of the population mean is a weighted average of the sample means for the strata; it is given by equation (5.1). An unbiased estimator of the variance of $\bar{y}_{st}$ is given by equation (5.2); this estimator is used in placing bounds on the error of estimation. An unbiased estimator of the population total is also given, along with its estimated variance.

Before conducting a survey, experimenters should consider how large an error of estimation they will tolerate and then should select the sample size accordingly. The sample size n is given by equation (5.8) for a fixed bound B on the error of estimation. The sample must then be allocated among the various strata. The allocation that gives a fixed amount of information at minimum cost is given by equation (5.9); it is affected by the stratum sizes, the stratum variances, and the costs of obtaining observations.

The estimator $\hat{p}_{st}$ of a population proportion has the same form as $\bar{y}_{st}$ and is given by equation (5.11). An unbiased estimator of $V(\hat{p}_{st})$ is given by equation (5.12). The related allocation and sample size problems have the same solutions as above, except that σ^2 is replaced by $p_i q_i$.

REFERENCES

Cochran, W. G. *Sampling Techniques*. 3d ed. New York: Wiley, 1977.
Hansen, M. H.; Hurwitz, W. N.; and Madow, W. G. *Sample Survey Methods and Theory*, vol. 1. New York: Wiley, 1953.
Kish, L. *Survey Sampling*. New York: Wiley, 1965.

EXERCISES

5.1 A chain of department stores is interested in estimating the proportion of accounts receivable that are delinquent. The chain consists of four stores. To reduce the cost of sampling, stratified random sampling is used with each store as a stratum. Since no information on population proportions is available before sampling, proportional allocation is used. From the accompanying table estimate p, the proportion of delinquent accounts for the chain, and place a bound on the error of estimation.

Exercises

	Stratum			
	I	II	III	IV
Number of Accounts Receivable	$N_1 = 65$	$N_2 = 42$	$N_3 = 93$	$N_4 = 25$
Sample Size	$n_1 = 14$	$n_2 = 9$	$n_3 = 21$	$n_4 = 6$
Sample Proportion of Delinquent Accounts	$\hat{p}_1 = .3$	$\hat{p}_2 = .2$	$\hat{p}_3 = .4$	$\hat{p}_4 = .1$

5.2 A corporation desires to estimate the total number of man-hours lost, for a given month, because of accidents among all employees. Since laborers, technicians, and administrators have different accident rates, it is decided to use stratified random sampling with each group forming a separate stratum. Data from previous years suggest the variances shown in the table for the number of man-hours lost per employee in the three groups and current data give the stratum sizes. Determine the Neyman allocation for a sample of $n = 30$ employees.

I (Laborers)	II (Technicians)	III (Administrators)
$\sigma_1^2 = 36$	$\sigma_2^2 = 25$	$\sigma_3^2 = 9$
$N_1 = 132$	$N_2 = 92$	$N_3 = 27$

5.3 For exercise 5.2 estimate the total number of man-hours lost during the given month and place a bound on the error of estimation. Use the data in the table, obtained from sampling 18 laborers, 10 technicians, and 2 administrators.

I (Laborers)			II (Technicians)		III (Administrators)
8	24	0	4	5	1
0	16	32	0	24	8
6	0	16	8	12	
7	4	4	3	2	
9	5	8	1	8	
18	2	0			

5.4 A zoning commission is formed to estimate the average appraised value of houses in a residential suburb of a city. It is convenient to use the two voting districts in the suburb as strata because separate lists of dwellings are available for each district. From the data given in the table, estimate the average appraised value for all houses in the suburb and place a bound on the error of estimation (note that proportional allocation was used).

5. Stratified Random Sampling

Stratum I	Stratum II
$N_1 = 110$	$N_2 = 168$
$n_1 = 20$	$n_2 = 30$
$\sum_{i=1}^{n_1} y_i = 240{,}000$	$\sum_{i=1}^{n_2} y_i = 420{,}000$
$\sum_{i=1}^{n_1} y_i^2 = 2{,}980{,}000{,}000$	$\sum_{i=1}^{n_2} y_i^2 = 6{,}010{,}000{,}000$

5.5 A corporation wishes to obtain information on the effectiveness of a business machine. A number of division heads will be interviewed by telephone and asked to rate the equipment on a numerical scale. The divisions are located in North America, Europe, and Asia. Hence stratified sampling is used. The costs are larger for interviewing division heads located outside of North America. The accompanying table gives the costs per interview, approximate variances of the ratings, and N_i's that have been established. The corporation wants to estimate the average rating with $V(\bar{y}_{st}) = .1$. Choose the sample size n that achieves this bound and find the appropriate allocation.

	Stratum	
I (North America)	II (Europe)	III (Asia)
$c_1 = \$9$	$c_2 = \$25$	$c_3 = \$36$
$\sigma_1^2 = 2.25$	$\sigma_2^2 = 3.24$	$\sigma_3^2 = 3.24$
$N_1 = 112$	$N_2 = 68$	$N_3 = 39$

5.6 A school desires to estimate the average score that would be obtained on a reading comprehension exam for students in the sixth grade. The school has students divided into three tracks, with the fast learners in tract I and the slow learners in track III. It was decided to stratify on tracks since this method should reduce variability of test scores. The sixth grade contains

Track I		Track II		Track III	
80	92	85	82	42	32
68	85	48	75	36	31
72	87	53	73	65	29
85	91	65	78	43	19
90	81	49	69	53	14
62	79	72	81	61	31
61	83	53	59	42	30
		68	52	39	32
		71	61		
		59	42		

Exercises

55 students in track I, 80 in track II, and 65 in track III. A stratified random sample of 50 students is proportionally allocated and yields simple random samples of $n_1 = 14$, $n_2 = 20$, and $n_3 = 16$ from tracks I, II, and III. The test is administered to the sample of students with the results as shown in the table. Estimate the average score for the sixth grade, and place a bound on the error of estimation.

5.7 Suppose the average test score for the class in exercise 5.6 is to be estimated again at the end of the school year. The costs of sampling are equal in all strata, but the variances differ. Find the optimum (Neyman) allocation of a sample of size 50 using the data of exercise 5.6 to approximate the variances.

5.8 Using the data of exercise 5.6, find the sample size required to estimate the average score with a bound of 4 points on the error of estimation. Use proportional allocation.

5.9 Repeat exercise 5.8 using Neyman allocation. Compare the result with the answer to exercise 5.8.

5.10 A forester wants to estimate the total number of farm acres planted in trees for a state. Since the number of acres of trees varies considerably with the size of the farm, it is decided to stratify on farm sizes. The 240 farms in the state are placed in one of four categories according to size. A stratified random sample of 40 farms, selected using proportional allocation, yields the results shown in the table on number of acres planted in trees. Estimate the total number of acres of trees on farms in the state, and place a bound on the error of estimation.

Stratum I *0–200 Acres*		*Stratum II* *200–400 Acres*		*Stratum III* *400–600 Acres*		*Stratum IV* *Over 600 Acres*	
$N_1 = 86$		$N_2 = 72$		$N_3 = 52$		$N_4 = 30$	
$n_1 = 14$		$n_2 = 12$		$n_3 = 9$		$n_4 = 5$	
97	67	125	155	142	256	167	655
42	125	67	96	310	440	220	540
25	92	256	47	495	510	780	
105	86	310	236	320	396		
27	43	220	352	196			
45	59	142	190				
53	21						

5.11 The study of exercise 5.10 is to be made yearly, with the bound on the error of estimation of 500 acres. Find an approximate sample size to achieve this bound if Neyman allocation is to be used. Use the data in exercise 5.10.

5.12 A psychologist working with a group of mentally retarded adults desires to estimate their average reaction time to a certain stimulus. She feels that men and women probably will show a difference in reaction times so she wants to stratify on sex. The group of 96 people contains 43 men. In

5. Stratified Random Sampling

previous studies of this type it has been observed that the times range from 5 to 20 seconds for men and from 3 to 14 seconds for women. The costs of sampling are the same for both strata. Using optimum allocation find the approximate sample size necessary to estimate the average reaction time for the group to within 1 second.

5.13 A county government is interested in expanding the facilities of a day-care center for mentally retarded children. The expansion would increase the cost of enrolling a child in the center. A sample survey will be conducted to estimate the proportion of families with retarded children that would make use of the expanded facilities. The families are divided into those who use the existing facilities and those who do not. Some families live in the city in which the center is located and some live in the surrounding suburban and rural areas. Thus stratified random sampling is used, with users in the city, users in the surrounding county, nonusers in the city, and nonusers in the county forming strata 1, 2, 3, and 4, respectively. Approximately 90% of the present users and 50% of the present nonusers would use the expanded facilities. The costs of obtaining an observation from a user is $4.00 and from a nonuser is $8.00. The difference in cost is due to the fact that nonusers are difficult to locate.

Existing records give $N_1 = 97$, $N_2 = 43$, $N_3 = 145$, and $N_4 = 68$. Find the approximate sample size and allocation necessary to estimate the population proportion with a bound of .05 on the error of estimation.

5.14 The survey of exercise 5.13 was conducted and yields the following proportion of families who would use the new facilities:

$$\hat{p}_1 = .87, \quad \hat{p}_2 = .93, \quad \hat{p}_3 = .60, \quad \hat{p}_4 = .53$$

Estimate the population proportion p, and place a bound on the error of estimation. Was the desired bound achieved?

5.15 Suppose in exercise 5.13 the total cost of sampling is fixed at $400. Choose the sample size and allocation that minimizes the variance of the estimator $\hat{p}_{st}$ for this fixed cost.

5.16 Refer to the information on 56 business firms given in example 5.17.
(a) Suppose that the $n = 15$ observations are to comprise a stratified random sample with only two strata. Find the optimal dividing point between the strata. With $n_1 = 7$ and $n_2 = 8$, assume that the resulting sample measurements (in thousands of dollars) turn out to be 110, 142, 212, 227, 167, 130, 194 for stratum 1 and 387, 345, 465, 308, 280, 480, 355, 405 for stratum 2. Estimate μ by $\bar{y}_{st}$ and calculate the estimated variance of $\bar{y}_{st}$.
(b) Now suppose the dividing point between the two strata is shifted to 300,000. Suppose the same 15 sample measurements are drawn in a stratified random sample with $n_1 = 8$ and $n_2 = 7$. Note that this shifts the 280 value from stratum 2 to stratum 1. (This would not be likely to happen in practice and is only used here for illustrative purposes.) Find $\bar{y}_{st}$ and calculate the estimated variance of $\bar{y}_{st}$. The numerical answer should indicate the superiority of the cumulative square root of frequencies method.

Exercises

5.17 If no information is available on the variable of primary interest, say y, then optimal stratification can be approximated by looking at a variable, say x, that is highly correlated with y. Suppose it is desired to estimate the average number of days of sick leave granted by a certain group of firms in a given year. No information on sick leave is available, but data on the number of employees per firm can be found. If it is assumed that, for these firms, total days sick leave are highly correlated with number of employees, use the frequency data in the table to optimally divide the 97 firms into $L = 4$ strata for which equal sample sizes can be used.

Number of Employees	Frequency
0–10	2
11–20	4
21–30	6
31–40	6
41–50	5
51–60	8
61–70	10
71–80	14
81–90	19
91–100	13
101–110	3
111–120	7

5.18 In using $\bar{y}_{st}$ as an estimator of μ, it is sometimes advantageous to find an allocation and sample size that minimizes the $V(\bar{y}_{st})$ for fixed cost c. That is, the cost c allowed for the survey is fixed and we want to find the best allocation of resources in terms of maximizing the information on μ. The optimum allocation in this case is still given by equation (5.9). Show that the appropriate choice for n is

$$n = \frac{(c - c_0) \sum_{i=1}^{L} N_i \sigma_i / \sqrt{c_i}}{\sum_{i=1}^{L} N_i \sigma_i \sqrt{c_i}}$$

where c_0 is a fixed overhead cost for the survey.

5.19 It is desired to estimate the average income of employees in a large firm. Records have the employees listed by seniority and, generally speaking, salary increases with seniority. Discuss the relative merits of simple random sampling versus stratified random sampling in this case. Which would you recommend and how would you set up the sampling scheme?

5. Stratified Random Sampling

EXPERIENCES WITH REAL DATA

1. Census figures for the 1960 and 1970 population of the United States are given in table 5.4. Treating the nine divisions of the country as strata, select a stratified random sample of states and estimate the total rural population in the United States in 1970, with a bound on the error. Select your own sample sizes according to some arbitrary specification of accuracy. Be careful in your allocation scheme, noting that some strata contain only three or four states.

Table 5.4 / Population of the United States, 1960–1970

Region, Division, and State	1970 Census	1960 Census	Pct. + or −	1970* Urban	1970* Rural	Pct. Urban
United States	203,235,298	179,323,175	13.3	149,324,930	53,886,996	73.5
Regions:						
Northeast	48,999,999	44,677,819	9.7	39,449,818	9,590,885	80.4
North Central	56,577,067	51,619,139	9.6	40,480,760	16,090,903	71.6
South	62,798,347	54,973,113	14.2	40,539,961	22,255,406	64.6
West	34,809,359	28,053,104	24.1	28,854,391	5,949,802	82.9
New England	11,847,186	10,509,367	12.7	9,043,517	2,798,146	76.4
Maine	993,663	969,265	2.5	504,157	487,891	50.8
New Hampshire	737,681	606,921	21.5	416,040	321,641	56.4
Vermont	444,732	389,881	14.1	142,889	301,441	32.2
Massachusetts	5,689,170	5,148,578	10.5	4,810,449	878,721	84.6
Rhode Island	949,723	859,488	10.5	824,930	121,795	87.1
Connecticut	3,023,217	2,535,234	19.6	2,345,052	686,657	77.4
Middle Atlantic	37,152,813	34,168,452	8.7	30,406,301	6,792,739	81.7
New York	18,241,266	16,782,304	8.4	15,602,486	2,634,481	85.6
New Jersey	7,168,164	6,065,782	18.2	6,373,405	794,759	88.9
Pennsylvania	11,793,909	11,319,366	4.2	8,430,410	3,363,499	71.5
East North Central	40,252,678	36,225,024	11.1	30,091,847	10,160,629	74.8
Ohio	10,652,017	9,706,397	9.7	8.025,775	2,625,242	75.3
Indiana	5,193,669	4,662,498	11.4	3,372,060	1,821,609	64.9
Illinois	11,113,976	10,081,158	10.2	9,229,821	1,884,155	83.0
Michigan	8,875,083	7,823,194	13.4	6,553,773	2,321,310	73.8
Wisconsin	4,417,933	3,951,777	11.8	2,910,418	1,507,313	65.9
West North Central	16,324,389	15,394,115	6.0	10,388,913	5,930,274	63.7
Minnesota	3,805,069	3,413,864	11.5	2,527,308	1,277,663	66.4
Iowa	2,825,041	2,757,537	2.4	1,616,405	1,207,971	57.2
Missouri	4,677,399	4,319,813	8.3	3,277,662	1,398,839	70.1
North Dakota	617,761	632,446	−2.3	273,442	344,319	44.3
South Dakota	666,257	680,514	−2.1	296,628	368,879	44.6
Nebraska	1,483,791	1,411,330	5.1	912,598	570,895	61.5
Kansas	2,249,071	2,178,611	3.2	1,484,870	761,708	66.1
South Atlantic	30,671,337	25,971,732	18.1	19,532,920	11,147,417	63.7
Delaware	548,104	446,292	22.8	395,569	152,535	72.2
Maryland	3,922,399	3,100,689	26.5	3,003,935	918,464	76.6
District Columbia	756,510	763,956	−1.0	756,510	...	100.0
Virginia	4,468,494	3,966,949	17.2	2,934,841	1,713,653	63.1
West Virginia	1,744,237	1,860,421	−6.2	679,491	1,064,746	39.0
North Carolinia	5,082,059	4,556,155	11.5	2,285,168	2,796,891	45.0
South Carolinia	2,590,516	2,382,594	8.7	1,232,195	1,358,321	47.6
Georgia	4,589,575	3,943,116	16.4	2,768,074	1,821,501	60.3
Florida	6,789,443	4,951,560	37.1	5,468,137	1,321,306	80.5

Table 5.4 (*continued*)

Region, Division and State	1970 Census	1960 Census	Pct. + or −	Urban	1970* Rural	Pct. Urban
East South Central	12,804,552	12,050,126	6.3	6,987,943	5,815,527	54.6
Kentucky	3,219,311	3,038,256	6.0	1,684,053	1,534,653	52.3
Tennessee	3,924,164	3,567,089	10.0	2,305,307	1,618,380	58.7
Alabama	3,444,165	3,266,740	5.4	2,011,941	1,432,224	58.4
Mississippi	2,216,912	2,178,141	1.8	986,642	1,230,270	44.5
West South Central	19,322,458	16,951,255	14.0	14,028,098	5,292,462	72.6
Arkansas	1,923,295	1,786,272	7.7	960,865	962,430	50.0
Louisiana	3,643,180	2,257,022	11.9	2,406,150	1,235,156	66.1
Oklahoma	2,559,253	2,328,284	9.9	1,740,137	819,092	68.0
Texas	11,196,730	9,579,677	16.9	8,920,946	2,275,784	79.7
Mountain	8,283,585	6,855,060	20.8	6,054,979	2,226,583	73.1
Montana	694,409	674,767	2.9	370,676	323,733	53.4
Idaho	713,008	667,191	6.9	385,434	327,133	54.1
Wyoming	332,416	330,066	0.7	201,111	131,305	60.5
Colorado	2,207,259	1,753,947	25.8	1,733,311	473,948	78.5
New Mexico	1,016,000	951,023	6.8	708,775	307,225	69.8
Arizona	1,772,482	1,302,161	36.1	1,408,864	362,036	79.6
Utah	1,059,273	890,627	18.9	851,472	207,801	80.4
Nevada	488,738	285,278	71.3	395,336	93,402	80.9
Pacific	26,525,774	21,198,044	25.1	22,799,412	3,723,219	86.0
Washington	3,409,169	2,853,214	19.5	2,476,468	932,701	72.6
Oregon	2,091,385	1,768,687	18.2	1,402,704	688,681	67.1
California	19,953,134	15,717,204	27.0	18,136,045	1,817,089	90.9
Alaska	302,173	226,167	33.6	145,512	154,870	48.4
Hawaii	769,913	632,772	21.7	638,683	129,878	83.1

Source: The World Almanac & Book of Facts, 1977 Edition; Copyright © Newspaper Enterprise Association, Inc., New York, 1976, p. 229.
* Urban and rural figures do not equal total 1970 population because of errors discovered by Census Bureau after tabulation.

2. Estimate the average retail price of a common grocery item (for example, coffee, bread, toothpaste, or sugar) in the city, or section of the city, in which you live. Set up three to five strata for the stores, giving some careful consideration to the best manner of stratification. Some suggestions are to stratify on type of store (large supermarket versus neighborhood convenience store), on geographic areas, or on a combination of the two. The latter method is important if you wish to compare estimates for small neighborhood stores in different sections of the city. Carefully construct a frame, looking over various possible sources for lists of stores that should be included in the population. Choose a sample size to achieve a fixed variance of the estimator at minimum cost. Produce estimates for each stratum as well as the entire population. Use a random number table in the actual selection of your samples.

6.
Ratio and Regression Estimation

6.1 INTRODUCTION

Estimation of the population mean and total in preceding chapters was based on a sample of response measurements, $y_1, y_2, \ldots, y_n$, obtained by simple random sampling (chapter 4) and stratified random sampling (chapter 5). Sometimes other variables are closely related to the response y. By measuring y and one or more subsidiary variables, we can obtain additional information for estimating the population mean. You are probably familiar with the use of subsidiary variables to estimate the mean of a response y. It is basic to the concept of correlation and provides means for development of a prediction equation relating y and x by the method of least squares. This topic is ordinarily covered in introductory courses in statistics (Mendenhall, 1975, chapter 10).

Chapters 4 and 5 presented simple estimators of population parameters utilizing the response measurements $y_1, y_2, \ldots, y_n$; however, primary emphasis was placed on the design of the sample survey (simple and stratified random sampling). In contrast, this chapter presents two new methods of estimation based on the use of a subsidiary variable x. The methods are called *ratio* and *regression estimation*. Both require the measurement of two variables, y and x, on each element of the sample. A variety of sampling designs can be employed in conjunction with ratio and regression estimation, but we will mainly discuss simple random

6. Ratio and Regression Estimation

sampling. The basic ideas of how these techniques carry over to stratified random sampling will, however, be illustrated for ratio estimation.

6.2 SURVEYS THAT REQUIRE THE USE OF RATIO ESTIMATORS

Estimating a population total sometimes requires the use of subsidiary variables. We illustrate the use of a *ratio estimator* for one of these situations. The wholesale price paid for oranges in large shipments is based on the sugar content of the load. The exact sugar content cannot be determined prior to the purchase and extraction of the juice from the entire load; however, it can be estimated. One method of estimating this quantity is to first estimate the mean sugar content per orange, μ_y, and then to multiply by the number of oranges N in the load. Thus we could randomly sample n oranges from the load to determine the sugar content y for each. The average of these sample measurements, $y_1, y_2, \ldots, y_n$, would estimate μ_y; $N\bar{y}$ would estimate the total sugar content for the load, τ_y. Unfortunately, this method is not feasible because it would be too time-consuming and costly to determine N (that is, to count the total number of oranges in the load).

We can avoid the need to know N by noting the following two facts. First, the sugar content of an individual orange, y, is closely related to its weight x; second, the ratio of the total sugar content τ_y to the total weight of the truck load τ_x is equal to the ratio of the mean sugar content per orange, μ_y, to the mean weight μ_x. Thus

$$\frac{\mu_y}{\mu_x} = \frac{N\mu_y}{N\mu_x} = \frac{\tau_y}{\tau_x}$$

Solving for the total sugar content of the load, we have

$$\tau_y = \frac{\mu_y}{\mu_x}(\tau_x)$$

We can estimate μ_y and μ_x using $\bar{y}$ and $\bar{x}$, the averages of the sugar contents and weights for the sample of n oranges. Also, we can measure τ_x, the total weight of the oranges on the truck. Then a *ratio* estimate of the total sugar content τ_y is

$$\hat{\tau}_y = \frac{\bar{y}}{\bar{x}}(\tau_x)$$

6.3 Ratio Estimation Using Simple Random Sampling

or, equivalently (multiplying numerator and denominator by n),

$$\hat{\tau}_y = \left(\frac{n\bar{y}}{n\bar{x}}\right)(\tau_x) = \frac{\sum_{i=1}^{n} y_i}{\sum_{i=1}^{n} x_i}(\tau_x)$$

In this case the number of elements in the population, N, is unknown, and therefore it is impossible to use the simple estimator $N\bar{y}$ of the population total τ_y (section 4.3). Thus a ratio estimator or its equivalent is necessary to accomplish the estimation objective. However, if N is known, we have the choice of using the estimator $N\bar{y}$ or the ratio estimator to estimate τ_y. If y and x are highly correlated, that is, x contributes information for the prediction of y, the ratio estimator should be better than $N\bar{y}$, which depends solely on $\bar{y}$.

In addition to the population total τ_y, there are often other parameters of interest. We may want to estimate the population mean μ_y using a ratio estimation procedure. For example, suppose it is necessary to estimate the average sugar content per orange in a large shipment. We could use the sample mean $\bar{y}$ to estimate μ_y. However, if x and y are correlated, a ratio estimator that uses information from the auxiliary variable x frequently provides a more precise estimator of μ_y.

The population ratio is another parameter that could be of interest to an investigator. For example, assume we want to estimate the ratio of total automobile sales for the first quarter of this year to the number of sales during the corresponding period of the previous year. Let τ_x be the total number of sales for the first quarter of last year, and let τ_y be the total number of sales for the same period this year. We are interested in estimating the ratio

$$R = \frac{\tau_y}{\tau_x}$$

In the following sections we will consider how to estimate μ_y, τ_y, and R by using a ratio estimator. Whenever appropriate, comparisons will be made to the estimators of these parameters presented in previous chapters.

6.3 RATIO ESTIMATION USING SIMPLE RANDOM SAMPLING

Let us assume that a simple random sample of size n is to be drawn from a finite population containing N elements. How then do we estimate a population mean μ_y, a total τ_y, or a ratio R, utilizing sample information on y and a subsidiary variable x?

6. *Ratio and Regression Estimation*

Estimator of the population ratio R:

$$r = \frac{\sum_{i=1}^{n} y_i}{\sum_{i=1}^{n} x_i} \qquad (6.1)$$

Estimated variance of r:

$$\hat{V}(r) = \hat{V}\left[\frac{\sum_{i=1}^{n} y_i}{\sum_{i=1}^{n} x_i}\right] = \left(\frac{N-n}{nN}\right)\left(\frac{1}{\mu_x^2}\right)\frac{\sum_{i=1}^{n}(y_i - rx_i)^2}{n-1} \qquad (6.2)$$

Bound on the error of estimation:

$$2\sqrt{\hat{V}(r)} = 2\sqrt{\left(\frac{N-n}{nN}\right)\left(\frac{1}{\mu_x^2}\right)\frac{\sum_{i=1}^{n}(y_i - rx_i)^2}{n-1}} \qquad (6.3)$$

[If the population mean for x, μ_x, is unknown, we would use $\bar{x}^2$ to approximate μ_x^2 in equations (6.2) and (6.3).]

Example 6.1
In a survey to examine trends in real estate, an investigator is interested in the relative change over a two-year period in the assessed value of homes in a particular community. A simple random sample of $n = 20$ homes is selected from the $N = 1000$ homes in the community. From tax records the investigator obtains the assessed value for this year (y) and the corresponding value for two years ago (x) for each of the $n = 20$ homes included in the sample. He wishes to estimate R, the relative change in assessed value for the $N = 1000$ homes, using information contained in the sample.

The data for the real estate survey are presented in table 6.1. We have added the x_i^2, y_i^2, and $x_i y_i$ columns, which are useful in the calculation of $\hat{V}(r)$.

Using the data in table 6.1, estimate R, the relative change in real estate valuation over the given two-year period. Place a bound on the error of estimation.

6.3 Ratio Estimation Using Simple Random Sampling

Table 6.1 / *Data and calculation for the real estate valuation survey*

Home	Assessed Value 2 Years Ago x_i	Current Value y_i	x_i^2	y_i^2	$x_i y_i$
1	20.2	24.2	408.04	585.64	488.84
2	25.4	29.9	645.16	894.00	759.46
3	26.1	31.8	681.21	1011.24	829.98
4	29.5	36.0	870.25	1296.00	1062.00
5	24.3	28.7	590.49	823.69	697.41
6	22.1	26.0	488.41	676.00	574.60
7	23.7	28.9	561.69	835.21	684.93
8	24.9	30.3	620.01	918.09	754.47
9	21.5	25.2	462.25	635.04	541.80
10	28.2	33.3	795.24	1108.89	939.60
11	28.6	34.2	817.96	1169.64	978.12
12	26.9	32.0	723.61	1024.00	860.80
13	25.2	30.3	635.04	918.09	763.56
14	24.1	29.4	580.81	864.36	708.54
15	23.9	28.2	571.21	795.24	673.98
16	23.1	28.1	533.61	789.61	649.11
17	27.5	33.2	756.25	1102.24	913.00
18	30.2	35.6	912.04	1267.36	1075.12
19	31.4	38.6	924.16	1489.96	1212.04
20	29.3	34.3	858.49	1176.49	1004.99
	516.1	618.2	13,497.73	19,380.80	16,171.81

Solution
The estimate of R using the sample data is given by

$$r = \frac{\sum_{i=1}^{20} y_i}{\sum_{i=1}^{20} x_i} = \frac{\text{total current valuation of the 20 homes}}{\text{total valuation of the 20 homes 2 years ago}}$$

Using table 6.1,

$$r = \frac{618.2}{516.1} = 1.19783$$

Hence we estimate that real estate valuation has increased approximately 20% over a two-year period in the area studied.

The bound on the error of estimation is found by using equation (6.3). A shortcut method for calculating $\sum_{i=1}^{n}(y_i - rx_i)^2$ is given by

$$\sum_{i=1}^{n}(y_i - rx_i)^2 = \sum_{i=1}^{n} y_i^2 + r^2 \sum_{i=1}^{n} x_i^2 - 2r \sum_{i=1}^{n} x_i y_i \qquad (6.4)$$

6. Ratio and Regression Estimation

These quantities can be obtained from table 6.1:

$$\sum_{i=1}^{20} (y_i - rx_i)^2 = 19{,}380.80 + (1.19783)^2(13{,}497.73)$$
$$- 2(1.19783)(16{,}171.81)$$
$$= 5.14024$$

Using equation (6.3),

$$2\sqrt{\hat{V}(r)} = 2\sqrt{\left(\frac{N-n}{nN}\right)\left(\frac{1}{\bar{x}^2}\right)\frac{\sum_{i=1}^{n}(y_i - rx_i)^2}{n-1}}$$

$$= 2\sqrt{\frac{1{,}000 - 20}{20(1{,}000)}\left[\frac{1}{(25.805)^2}\right]\left(\frac{5.14024}{19}\right)} = .00892$$

Thus we estimate the ratio of real estate valuation to be $r = 1.198$, and we are quite confident that the error of estimation is less than .00892. You will note that the bound on the error of estimation is relatively small; hence $r = 1.198$ should be a fairly accurate estimate of the population ratio R.

The large-sample confidence intervals based on normal distribution theory, as introduced in chapter 2, apply in the ratio estimation case as well. Thus, for example, an approximate 90% confidence interval for the ratio R would be of the form

$$r \pm 1.645\sqrt{\hat{V}(r)}$$

The ratio technique for estimating a population total τ_y was applied in estimating the total sugar content of a truckload of oranges. The simple estimator, $N\bar{y}$, is not applicable because we do not know N, the total number of oranges in the truck. The following ratio estimation procedure can be applied in estimating τ_y whether or not N is known.

Ratio estimator of the population total τ_y:

$$\hat{\tau}_y = \frac{\sum_{i=1}^{n} y_i}{\sum_{i=1}^{n} x_i}(\tau_x) = r\tau_x \qquad (6.5)$$

Estimated variance of $\hat{\tau}_y$:

$$\hat{V}(\hat{\tau}_y) = (\tau_x)^2 \hat{V}(r) = (\tau_x^2)\left(\frac{N-n}{nN}\right)\left(\frac{1}{\mu_x^2}\right)\frac{\sum_{i=1}^{n}(y_i - rx_i)^2}{n-1} \qquad (6.6)$$

6.3 Ratio Estimation Using Simple Random Sampling

where μ_x and τ_x are the population mean and total, respectively, for the random variable x.

Bound on the error of estimation:

$$2\sqrt{\hat{V}(\hat{\tau}_y)} = 2\sqrt{(\tau_x^2)\left(\frac{N-n}{nN}\right)\left(\frac{1}{\mu_x^2}\right)\frac{\sum_{i=1}^{n}(y_i - rx_i)^2}{n-1}} \quad (6.7)$$

You will note that although it is not necessary to know N or μ_x, we must know τ_x in order to estimate τ_y by use of the ratio estimation procedure.

Example 6.2
To estimate the total sugar content of a truckload of oranges, a random sample of n = 10 oranges was juiced and weighed (see table 6.2). The total weight of all the oranges, obtained by first weighing the truck loaded and then unloaded, was found to be 1800 pounds. Estimate τ_y, the total sugar content for the oranges, and place a bound on the error of estimation.

Solution
The sugar content of an orange is usually recorded in degrees brix, which is a measure of the number of pounds of solids (mostly sugar) per 100 pounds of juice. For our calculations we

Table 6.2/Data for example 6.2

Orange	Sugar Content (in pounds)	Weight of Orange (in pounds)
1	.021	.40
2	.030	.48
3	.025	.43
4	.022	.42
5	.033	.50
6	.027	.46
7	.019	.39
8	.021	.41
9	.023	.42
10	.025	.44
	$\sum_{i=1}^{10} y_i = .246$	$\sum_{i=1}^{10} x_i = 4.35$

6. Ratio and Regression Estimation

will use the actual pounds per orange. An estimate of τ_y can be obtained by using equation (6.5).

$$\hat{\tau}_y = r\tau_x = \frac{\sum_{i=1}^{10} y_i}{\sum_{i=1}^{10} x_i}(\tau_x) = \frac{.246}{4.35}(1800) = 101.79 \ pounds$$

A bound on the error of estimation can be found if we use a modified version of equation (6.7). Because N is unknown in this example, we assume that the finite population correction, $(N - n)/N$, is near unity. This is reasonable because we expect at least $N = 4000$ oranges even in a small truckload. The sample mean $\bar{x}$ must be used in place of μ_x in equation (6.7), because μ_x is unknown. With these adjustments equation (6.7) becomes

$$2\sqrt{\hat{V}(\hat{\tau}_y)} = 2\sqrt{\tau_x^2 \left(\frac{1}{n}\right)\left(\frac{1}{\bar{x}^2}\right) \frac{\sum_{i=1}^{n}(y_i - rx_i)^2}{n-1}}$$

Using equation (6.4), for computational ease,

$$\sum_{i=1}^{10}(y_i - rx_i)^2 = \sum_{i=1}^{10} y_i^2 + r^2 \sum_{i=1}^{10} x_i^2 - 2r \sum_{i=1}^{10} x_i y_i$$

where

$$r = \frac{\sum_{i=1}^{10} y_i}{\sum_{i=1}^{10} x_i} = \frac{.246}{4.35} = .0566$$

From the data,

$$\sum_{i=1}^{10} y_i^2 = (.021)^2 + (.030)^2 + \cdots + (.025)^2 = .006224$$

$$\sum_{i=1}^{10} x_i^2 = (.40)^2 + (.48)^2 + \cdots + (.44)^2 = 1.9035$$

$$\sum_{i=1}^{10} y_i x_i = (.021)(.40) + (.030)(.48) + \cdots + (.025)(.44) = .10839$$

$$\bar{x} = \frac{4.35}{10} = .435$$

Substituting into equation (6.4),

$$\sum_{i=1}^{10}(y_i - rx_i)^2 = \sum_{i=1}^{10} y_i^2 + r^2 \sum_{i=1}^{10} x_i^2 - 2r \sum_{i=1}^{10} x_i y_i$$
$$= .006224 + (.0566)^2(1.9035) - 2(.0566)(.10839)$$
$$= .000052285$$

6.3 Ratio Estimation Using Simple Random Sampling

Then the bound on the error of estimation is

$$2\sqrt{\hat{V}(\hat{\tau}_y)} = 2\sqrt{\tau_x^2\left(\frac{1}{n}\right)\left(\frac{1}{\bar{x}^2}\right)\frac{\sum_{i=1}^{n}(y_i - rx_i)^2}{n-1}}$$

$$= 2\sqrt{(1800)^2\left(\frac{1}{10}\right)\left[\frac{1}{(.435)^2}\right]\left(\frac{.000052285}{9}\right)} = 6.308$$

To summarize, the ratio estimate of the total sugar content of the truckload of oranges is $\hat{\tau}_y = 101.79$ pounds, with a bound on the error of estimation of 6.308. We are confident that the total sugar content τ_y lies in the interval

$$101.79 \pm 6.308$$

that is, the interval 95.482 to 108.098 pounds.

You will recall that the population size N is frequently known. Consequently, the investigator must decide under what conditions use of the ratio estimator, $\hat{\tau}_y = r\tau_x$, is better than use of the corresponding estimator $N\bar{y}$, where both estimators are based on simple random sampling (see section 6.5). Generally, $r\tau_x$ possesses a smaller variance than $N\bar{y}$ when there is a strong positive correlation between x and y (where ρ, the correlation coefficient between x and y, is greater than $1/2$). Intuitively, this makes sense because in ratio estimation we are using the additional information provided by the subsidiary variable x.

If an investigator is interested in a population mean rather than a population total, the corresponding ratio estimation procedure is shown in equations (6.8), (6.9), and (6.10).

Ratio estimator of a population mean μ_y:

$$\hat{\mu}_y = \frac{\sum_{i=1}^{n} y_i}{\sum_{i=1}^{n} x_i}(\mu_x) = r\mu_x \qquad (6.8)$$

Estimated variance of $\hat{\mu}_y$:

$$\hat{V}(\hat{\mu}_y) = \mu_x^2 \hat{V}(r) = \mu_x^2\left(\frac{N-n}{nN}\right)\left(\frac{1}{\mu_x^2}\right)\frac{\sum_{i=1}^{n}(y_i - rx_i)^2}{n-1} \qquad (6.9)$$

Bound on the error of estimation:

$$2\sqrt{\hat{V}(\hat{\mu}_y)} = 2\sqrt{\left(\frac{N-n}{nN}\right)\frac{\sum_{i=1}^{n}(y_i - rx_i)^2}{n-1}} \qquad (6.10)$$

6. Ratio and Regression Estimation

Note that we do not need to know τ_x or N to estimate μ_y using the ratio procedure; however, we must know μ_x.

Example 6.3
A company wishes to estimate the average amount of money, μ_y, paid to employees for medical expenses during the first three months of the current calendar year. Average quarterly reports are available in the fiscal reports of the previous year. A random sample of 100 employee records is taken from the population of 1,000 employees. The sample results are summarized below. Use the data to estimate μ_y and to place a bound on the error of estimation.

$$n = 100, \quad N = 1,000$$

Total for the current quarter:

$$\sum_{i=1}^{100} y_i = 1,750$$

Total for the corresponding quarter of the previous year:

$$\sum_{i=1}^{100} x_i = 1,200$$

Population total τ_x for the corresponding quarter of the previous year:

$$\tau_x = 12,500$$

$$\sum_{i=1}^{100} y_i^2 = 31,650, \quad \sum_{i=1}^{100} x_i^2 = 15,620, \quad \sum_{i=1}^{100} y_i x_i = 22,059.35$$

Solution
The estimate of μ_y is

$$\hat{\mu}_y = r\mu_x$$

where

$$\mu_x = \frac{\tau_x}{N} = \frac{12,500}{1,000} = 12.5$$

Then

$$\hat{\mu}_y = \frac{\sum_{i=1}^{100} y_i}{\sum_{i=1}^{100} x_i}(\mu_x) = \frac{1,750}{1,200}(12.5) = 18.23$$

6.3 Ratio Estimation Using Simple Random Sampling

The bound on the error of estimation can be found by using equation (6.10); however, we must first calculate

$$\sum_{i=1}^{100} (y_i - rx_i)^2 = \sum_{i=1}^{100} y_i^2 + r^2 \sum_{i=1}^{100} x_i^2 - 2r \sum_{i=1}^{100} y_i x_i$$

$$= 31{,}650 + (1.4583)^2(15{,}620) - (2.9166)(22{,}059.35)$$

$$= 441.68$$

Substituting into equation (6.10), the bound on the error of estimation is

$$2\sqrt{\hat{V}(\hat{\mu}_y)} = 2\sqrt{\left(\frac{N-n}{nN}\right)\frac{\sum_{i=1}^{n}(y_i - rx_i)^2}{n-1}}$$

$$= 2\sqrt{\frac{1{,}000 - 100}{100(1{,}000)}\left(\frac{441.68}{99}\right)} = .42$$

Thus we estimate the average amount of money paid to employees for medical expenses to be $18.23. We are very confident that the error for estimating μ_y is less than $.42.

To remember the formulas associated with ratio estimation of a population mean, total, or ratio, we make the following associations. The sample ratio r is given by the formula

$$r = \frac{\sum_{i=1}^{n} y_i}{\sum_{i=1}^{n} x_i} \tag{6.11}$$

The estimators of R, τ_y, and μ_y are then

$$\hat{R} = r \tag{6.12}$$

$$\hat{\tau}_y = r\tau_x \tag{6.13}$$

$$\hat{\mu}_y = r\mu_x \tag{6.14}$$

Thus we need know only the formula for r and its relationship to $\hat{\mu}_y$ and $\hat{\tau}_y$.

Approximate variances can be obtained if you remember the basic formula,

$$\hat{V}(r) = \left(\frac{N-n}{nN}\right)\left(\frac{1}{\mu_x^2}\right)\frac{\sum_{i=1}^{n}(y_i - rx_i)^2}{n-1} \tag{6.15}$$

6. Ratio and Regression Estimation

Thus

$$\hat{V}(\hat{\tau}_y) = \tau_x^2 \hat{V}(r) \qquad (6.16)$$

$$\hat{V}(\hat{\mu}_y) = \mu_x^2 \hat{V}(r) \qquad (6.17)$$

6.4 SELECTING THE SAMPLE SIZE

We stated previously that the amount of information contained in the sample depends upon the variation in the data (which is frequently controlled by the sample survey design) and the number of observations n included in the sample. Once the sampling procedure (design) has been chosen, the investigator must determine the number of elements to be drawn. We will consider the sample size required to estimate a population parameter R, μ_y, or τ_y to within B units for simple random sampling using ratio estimators.

Note that the procedure for choosing the sample size n is identical to that presented in section 4.4. The number of observations required to estimate R, a population ratio, with a bound on the error of estimation of magnitude B is determined by setting two standard deviations of the ratio estimator r equal to B and solving this expression for n. That is, we must solve

$$2\sqrt{V(r)} = B \qquad (6.18)$$

for n. Although we have not discussed the form of $V(r)$, you recall that $\hat{V}(r)$, the estimated variance of r, is given by the formula

$$\hat{V}(r) = \left(\frac{N-n}{nN}\right)\left(\frac{1}{\mu_x^2}\right) \sum_{i=1}^{n} \frac{(y_i - rx_i)^2}{n-1} \qquad (6.19)$$

We can rewrite equation (6.19) as

$$\hat{V}(r) = \left(\frac{N-n}{nN}\right)\left(\frac{1}{\mu_x^2}\right) s^2 \qquad (6.20)$$

In this instance we define

$$s^2 = \frac{\sum_{i=1}^{n}(y_i - rx_i)^2}{n-1}$$

An approximate population variance, $V(r)$, can be obtained from $\hat{V}(r)$ by replacing s^2 with the corresponding population variance σ^2. Thus the number of observations required to estimate R with a bound B on the

6.4 Selecting the Sample Size

error of estimation is determined by solving the following equation for n:

$$2\sqrt{V(r)} = 2\sqrt{\left(\frac{N-n}{nN}\right)\left(\frac{1}{\mu_x^2}\right)\sigma^2} = B \qquad (6.21)$$

Sample size required to estimate R with a bound on the error of estimation B:

$$n = \frac{N\sigma^2}{ND + \sigma^2} \qquad (6.22)$$

where

$$D = \frac{B^2 \mu_x^2}{4}$$

In a practical situation we are faced with a problem in determining the appropriate sample size because we do not know σ^2. If no past information is available to calculate s^2 as an estimate of σ^2, we take a preliminary sample of size n' and compute

$$\hat{\sigma}^2 = \frac{\sum_{i=1}^{n'} (y_i - rx_i)^2}{n' - 1}$$

Then we substitute this quantity for σ^2 in equation (6.22), and we find an *approximate* sample size. If μ_x is also unknown, it can be replaced by the sample mean $\bar{x}$, calculated from the n' preliminary observations.

Example 6.4
A manufacturing company wishes to estimate the ratio of change from last year to this year in the number of man-hours lost due to sickness. A preliminary study of $n' = 10$ employee records is made, and the results are given in the accompanying table. The company records show that the total number of man-hours lost because of sickness for the previous year was $\tau_x = 16{,}300$. Use the data to determine the sample size required to estimate R, the rate of change for the company, with a bound on the error of estimation of magnitude $B = 0.01$. Assume the company has 1,000 employees ($N = 1{,}000$).

6. Ratio and Regression Estimation

Employee	Man-Hours Lost in Previous Year, x	Man-Hours Lost in Current Year, y
1	12	13
2	24	25
3	15	15
4	30	32
5	32	36
6	26	24
7	10	12
8	15	16
9	0	2
10	14	12
	178	187

Solution
First, we calculate an estimate of σ^2 using the data from the preliminary study. Thus

$$\hat{\sigma}^2 = \frac{\sum_{i=1}^{10}(y_i - rx_i)^2}{9}$$

where

$$\sum_{i=1}^{10}(y_i - rx_i)^2 = \sum_{i=1}^{10} y_i^2 + r^2 \sum_{i=1}^{10} x_i^2 - 2r \sum_{i=1}^{10} x_i y_i$$

Next, from the given data we determine

$$\sum_{i=1}^{10} y_i^2 = (13)^2 + (25)^2 + \cdots + (12)^2 = 4{,}463$$

$$\sum_{i=1}^{10} x_i^2 = (12)^2 + (24)^2 + \cdots + (14)^2 = 4{,}066$$

$$\sum_{i=1}^{10} x_i y_i = (12)(13) + (24)(25) + \cdots + (14)(12) = 4{,}245$$

$$r = \frac{\sum_{i=1}^{10} y_i}{\sum_{i=1}^{10} x_i} = \frac{187}{178} = 1.05$$

Hence

$$\sum_{i=1}^{10}(y_i - rx_i)^2 = \sum_{i=1}^{10} y_i^2 + r^2 \sum_{i=1}^{10} x_i^2 - 2r \sum_{i=1}^{10} x_i y_i$$

$$= 4{,}463 + (1.05)^2(4{,}066) - 2(1.05)(4{,}245) = 31.265$$

6.4 Selecting the Sample Size

and

$$\hat{\sigma}^2 = \frac{\sum_{i=1}^{10}(y_i - rx_i)^2}{9} = \frac{31.265}{9} = 3.474$$

The required sample size can now be found by using equation (6.22). Note that

$$\mu_x = \frac{\tau_x}{N} = \frac{16,300}{1,000} = 16.3$$

and

$$D = \frac{B^2}{4}(\mu_x^2) = \frac{(.01)^2(16.3)^2}{4} = .006642$$

Thus

$$n = \frac{N\hat{\sigma}^2}{ND + \hat{\sigma}^2} = \frac{1,000(3.474)}{1,000(.006642) + 3.474} = 343.416$$

Therefore, we should sample approximately 344 employee records to estimate R, the rate of change in man-hours lost due to sickness, with a bound on the error of estimation of .01 hours.

Similarly, we can determine the number of observations n needed to estimate a population mean μ_y, with a bound on the error of estimation of magnitude B. The required sample size is found by solving the following equation for n:

$$2\sqrt{V(\hat{\mu}_y)} = B \qquad (6.23)$$

Stated differently,

$$2\mu_x\sqrt{V(r)} = B \qquad \text{[from equation (6.17)]}$$

The solution is shown in equation (6.24).

Sample size required to estimate μ_y with a bound on the error of estimation B:

$$n = \frac{N\sigma^2}{ND + \sigma^2} \qquad (6.24)$$

where

$$D = \frac{B^2}{4}$$

---

6. Ratio and Regression Estimation

Note that we need not know the value of μ_x to determine n in equation (6.24); however, we do need an estimate of σ^2, either from prior information if it is available or from information obtained in a preliminary study.

Example 6.5
An investigator wishes to estimate the average number of trees, μ_y, per acre on an $N = 1000$-acre plantation. She plans to sample n one-acre plots and count the number of trees y on each plot. She also has aerial photographs of the plantation from which she can estimate the number of trees x on each plot for the entire plantation. Hence she knows μ_x. Therefore it seems appropriate to use a ratio estimator of μ_y. Determine the sample size needed to estimate μ_y with a bound on the error of estimation of magnitude $B = 1.0$.

Solution
Assuming no prior information is available, we must conduct a preliminary study to estimate σ^2. Since an investigator can readily examine 10 one-acre plots in a day to determine the total number of trees y per plot, it is convenient to conduct a preliminary study of $n' = 10$ plots. The results of such a study are given in the accompanying table, with the corresponding aerial estimates x.

Plot	Aerial Estimate, x	Actual Number, y
1	23	25
2	14	15
3	20	22
4	25	24
5	12	13
6	18	18
7	30	35
8	27	30
9	8	10
10	31	29
	208	221

An estimate of σ^2 is given by

$$\hat{\sigma}^2 = \sum_{i=1}^{10} \frac{(y_i - rx_i)^2}{9}$$

Using equation (6.4),

$$\sum_{i=1}^{10} (y_i - rx_i)^2 = \sum_{i=1}^{10} y_i^2 + r^2 \sum_{i=1}^{10} x_i^2 - 2r \sum_{i=1}^{10} x_i y_i$$

6.4 Selecting the Sample Size

From the preliminary study,

$$\sum_{i=1}^{10} y_i^2 = (25)^2 + (15)^2 + \cdots + (29)^2 = 5469$$

$$\sum_{i=1}^{10} x_i^2 = (23)^2 + (14)^2 + \cdots + (31)^2 = 4872$$

$$\sum_{i=1}^{10} x_i y_i = (23)(25) + (14)(15) + \cdots + (31)(29) = 5144$$

$$r = \frac{\sum_{i=1}^{10} y_i}{\sum_{i=1}^{10} x_i} = \frac{221}{208} = 1.06$$

Thus

$$\sum_{i=1}^{10} (y_i - rx_i)^2 = \sum_{i=1}^{10} y_i^2 + r^2 \sum_{i=1}^{10} x_i^2 - 2r \sum_{i=1}^{10} x_i y_i$$

$$= 5469 + (1.06)^2(4872) - 2(1.06)(5144) = 37.8992$$

$$\hat{\sigma}^2 = \sum_{i=1}^{10} \frac{(y_i - rx_i)^2}{9} = \frac{37.8992}{9} = 4.21$$

We now determine n from equation (6.24), where $D = B^2/4 = 1/4$:

$$n = \frac{N\sigma^2}{ND + \sigma^2} = \frac{100(4.21)}{1000(.25) + 4.21} = 16.56$$

To summarize, we need to examine approximately 17 plots to estimate μ_y, the average number of trees per one-acre plot, with a bound on the error of estimation of $B = 1.0$. We only need 7 additional observations since we have 10 from the preliminary study.

The sample size required to estimate τ_y with a bound on the error of estimation of magnitude B can be found by solving the following expression for n:

$$2\sqrt{V(\hat{\tau}_y)} = B \tag{6.25}$$

or, equivalently,

$$2\tau_x \sqrt{V(r)} = B \quad \text{[from equation (6.16)]}$$

6. Ratio and Regression Estimation

> Sample size required to estimate τ_y with a bound on the error of estimation B:
>
> $$n = \frac{N\sigma^2}{ND + \sigma^2}$$
>
> where
>
> $$D = \frac{B^2}{4N^2} \qquad (6.26)$$

Example 6.6
An auditor wishes to compare the actual dollar value of an inventory of a hospital, τ_y, with the recorded inventory, τ_x. The recorded inventory τ_x can be summarized from computer-stored hospital records. The actual inventory τ_y could be determined by examining and counting all hospital supplies, but this process would be very time-consuming and costly. Hence the auditor plans to estimate τ_y based on a sample of n different items randomly selected from the hospital's supplies.

Records in the computer list $N = 2100$ different item types and the number of each particular item in the hospital inventory. Using these data a total value for each item, x, can be obtained by multiplying the total number of each recorded item by the unit value per item. The total dollar value of the inventory obtained from the computer is given by

$$\tau_x = \text{sum of the dollar values for the } N = 2100 \text{ items} = \sum_{i=1}^{2100} x_i$$

In this instance τ_x was found to be $950,000. Determine the sample size (number of items) needed to estimate τ_y with a bound on the error of estimation of magnitude $B = \$500$.

Solution
Because there is no prior information available, a preliminary study must be conducted to estimate σ^2. Two people can determine the actual dollar value y for each of 15 items in one day. For this example we will use the data from a single day's inventory ($n' = 15$) as a preliminary study to obtain a rough estimate of σ^2 and consequently a rough approximation of the required sample size n. Actually, the investigator would probably take a preliminary study of two or three days' inventory to provide a good approximation to σ^2 and hence n; however, to simplify computations we will consider a preliminary study of $n' = 15$ items. These data are summarized in the table along with the corresponding computer figures (entries in hundreds of dollars).

6.4 Selecting the Sample Size

Item	Dollar Value from Computer, x	Actual Dollar Value, y
1	15.0	14.0
2	9.5	9.0
3	14.2	12.5
4	20.5	22.0
5	6.7	6.3
6	9.8	8.4
7	25.7	28.5
8	12.6	10.0
9	15.1	14.4
10	30.9	28.2
11	7.3	15.5
12	28.6	26.3
13	14.7	13.1
14	20.5	19.5
15	10.9	9.8
	242.0	237.5

To determine an estimate of σ^2, we must calculate

$$\sum_{i=1}^{15}(y_i - rx_i)^2 = \sum_{i=1}^{15} y_i^2 + r^2 \sum_{i=1}^{15} x_i^2 - 2r \sum_{i=1}^{15} x_i y_i$$

Using the data from the preliminary study,

$$\sum_{i=1}^{15} y_i^2 = (14.0)^2 + (9.0)^2 + \cdots + (9.8)^2 = 4522.19$$

$$\sum_{i=1}^{15} x_i^2 = (15.0)^2 + (9.5)^2 + \cdots + (10.9)^2 = 4706.54$$

$$\sum_{i=1}^{15} x_i y_i = (15.0)(14.0) + (9.5)(9.0) + \cdots + (10.9)(9.8) = 4560.27$$

$$r = \frac{\sum_{i=1}^{15} y_i}{\sum_{i=1}^{15} x_i} = \frac{237.5}{242} = .9814 \approx .98$$

Thus

$$\sum_{i=1}^{15}(y_i - rx_i)^2 = \sum_{i=1}^{15} y_i^2 + r^2 \sum_{i=1}^{15} x_i^2 - 2r \sum_{i=1}^{15} x_i y_i$$

$$= 4522.19 + (.98)^2(4706.54) - 2(.98)(4560.27)$$

$$= 104.2218$$

$$\hat{\sigma}^2 = \sum_{i=1}^{15} \frac{(y_i - rx_i)^2}{14} = \frac{104.2218}{14} = 7.4444$$

6. Ratio and Regression Estimation

The required sample size now can be found by using equation (6.26). We have

$$D = \frac{B^2}{4N^2} = \frac{(500)^2}{4(2100)^2} = .01417$$

and hence

$$n = \frac{N\sigma^2}{ND + \sigma^2} = \frac{2100(7.4444)}{2100(.01417) + 7.4444} = 420.2326$$

Thus the auditor must sample approximately 421 items to estimate τ_y, the actual dollar value of the inventory, to within $B = \$500$.

6.5 WHEN TO USE RATIO ESTIMATION

Use of the ratio estimator is most effective when the relationship between the response y and a subsidiary variable x is linear through the origin and the variance of y is proportional to x. The following example illustrates this point. An automobile tire distributor wishes to estimate the average cash receipt for his 1570 stores ($N = 1570$) during a particular sales period. From a simple random sample of $n = 50$ stores, the corresponding cash receipts y_i ($i = 1, 2, \ldots, 50$) are observed. One possible estimator of μ_y, the average cash receipts for the company, is $\bar{y}$, the sample mean.

In addition to obtaining cash receipts y_i, suppose the distributor can also obtain x_i ($i = 1, 2, \ldots, 50$), the number of customers who made purchases in store i during the sales period. To determine the relationship between y and x, he can plot the sales and customer data for the $n = 50$ sampled stores.

If the plot is similar to the one presented in figure 6.1, we can assume that the cash receipts y are linearly related to the number of customers purchasing goods, x. In fact, we could depict this relationship with a straight line passing through the intersection of the x- and y-axes, and hence we can say it is linear through the origin. In addition, you will note from figure 6.1 that the "scatter" of y-values widens as x increases. Hence we can say that the variance of y is proportional to x. Under these conditions the ratio estimator of μ_y, the average amount of cash receipts per store, should have a smaller variance and, hence, be more precise than $\bar{y}$.

Sometimes a plot of y versus x does not clearly indicate that ratio estimation should be used. The strength of the correlation ρ between y and x is another good indicator of the effectiveness of the ratio estimator. For $\rho > 1/2$, the ratio estimator should provide a more precise estimate of μ_y or τ_y than would $\bar{y}$ or $N\bar{y}$.

6.6 Ratio Estimation in Stratified Random Sampling

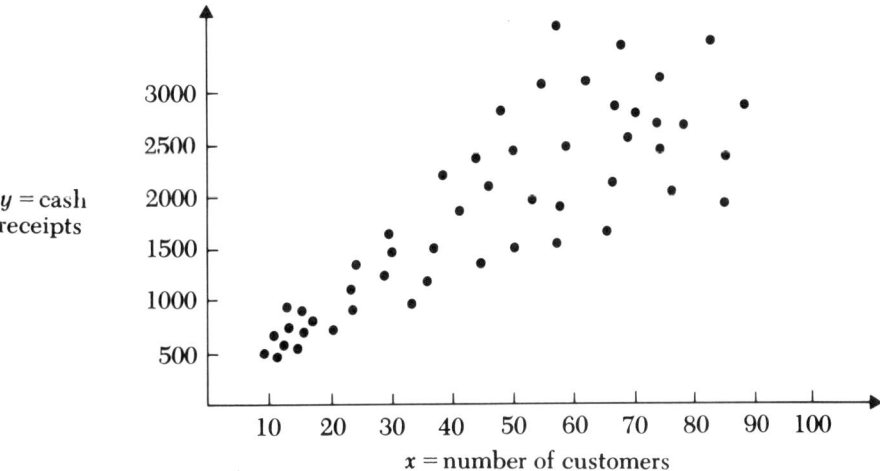

Figure 6.1/*Plot of cash receipts versus number of customers*

Unlike the estimation procedures discussed previously, ratio estimation usually leads to biased estimators. Thus we must consider the magnitude of the bias to decide which estimation procedure to use. Although there are no exact formulas to determine the bias of these estimators, it can be shown that the absolute value of the bias is less than or equal to the product of the standard deviation of the sample mean of the subsidiary variable x and the standard deviation of the ratio estimator, all divided by μ_x. That is,

$$|E(\hat{\theta}) - \theta| \le \frac{\sigma_{\bar{x}} \sigma_{\hat{\theta}}}{\mu_x} \qquad (6.27)$$

where $\hat{\theta}$ can be the ratio estimator r, $\hat{\mu}_y$, or $\hat{\tau}_y$, and θ is the corresponding parameter estimated. If estimates of $\sigma_{\bar{x}}$, $\sigma_{\hat{\theta}}$, and μ_x are known from prior experimentation, we can estimate the maximum bias for a given physical situation by using equation (6.27).

Generally, for a large sample size ($n > 30$) and for $(\sigma_{\bar{x}}/\mu_x) \le .10$, the bias is negligible. Note also that ratio estimators are unbiased when the relationship between y and x is linear through the origin.

Finally, we must consider the cost of obtaining information on the subsidiary variable x. If the physical situation suggests the use of ratio estimation, the experimenter must decide if the increased precision of the ratio estimator justifies the additional cost.

6.6 RATIO ESTIMATION IN STRATIFIED RANDOM SAMPLING

For the same reasons indicated in chapter 5, it is sometimes advantageous to stratify the population before using a ratio estimator. We will assume

6. Ratio and Regression Estimation

that we can take a large enough sample of both x's and y's in each stratum for the variance approximations to work fairly well.

Basically, there are two different methods for constructing estimators of a ratio in stratified sampling. One is to estimate the ratio of μ_y to μ_x within each stratum and then form a weighted average of these *separate* estimates as a single estimate of the population ratio. The result of this is called a *separate* ratio estimator.

The other method involves first estimating μ_y by the usual $\bar{y}_{st}$ and similarly estimating μ_x by $\bar{x}_{st}$. Then $\bar{y}_{st}/\bar{x}_{st}$ can be used as an estimator of μ_y/μ_x. This is called a *combined* ratio estimator.

We will not introduce a general (and cumbersome) notation for these estimators but will illustrate their use by a numerical example. Recall from chapter 2 that the variance of a sum of random variables is the sum of the variances, if the variables are independent. This fact will allow us to use a sum of terms similar to those in equation (6.9) for the variance of either the combined or separate ratio estimator. The next two examples illustrate the techniques used.

Example 6.7
Refer to example 6.4. Treat the 10 observations given there on man-hours lost due to sickness as a simple random sample from company A. Thus $n_A = 10$, $\bar{y}_A = 18.7$, $\bar{x}_A = 17.8$, $r_A = 1.05$, $N_A = 1,000$, and $\tau_{xA} = 16,300$.

A simple random sample of $n_B = 10$ measurements was taken from company B within the same industry. (Assume companies A and B together form the population of workers of interest in this problem.) The data are given in the accompanying table. It is known that $N_B = 1,500$ employees and $\tau_{xB} = 12,800$. Find the separate ratio estimate of μ_y and its estimated variance.

Employee	Man-Hours Lost in Previous Year, x_B	Man-Hours Lost in Current Year, y_B
1	10	8
2	8	0
3	0	4
4	14	6
5	12	10
6	6	0
7	4	2
8	0	4
9	8	4
10	16	8
	78	46

6.6 Ratio Estimation in Stratified Random Sampling

Solution
The ratio estimator of μ_{yA} is $(\bar{y}_A/\bar{x}_A)(\mu_{xA})$ [see equation (6.8)] and its estimated variance is given by equation (6.9). The corresponding estimator of μ_{yB} is $(\bar{y}_B/\bar{x}_B)(\mu_{xB})$, with a similar estimated variance.

To obtain an estimator of μ_y, the population mean of the y's, we need to average the estimators above together, choosing weights proportional to the stratum sizes, as in chapter 5. Thus, $\hat{\mu}_{yRS}$, given by

$$\hat{\mu}_{yRS} = \left(\frac{N_A}{N}\right)\left(\frac{\bar{y}_A}{\bar{x}_A}\right)(\mu_{xA}) + \left(\frac{N_B}{N}\right)\left(\frac{\bar{y}_B}{\bar{x}_B}\right)(\mu_{xB})$$

will be the estimator of μ_y, with estimated variance

$$\hat{V}(\hat{\mu}_{yRS}) = \left(\frac{N_A}{N}\right)^2 \left(\frac{N_A - n_A}{N_A n_A}\right) \frac{\sum_{i=1}^{n_A}(y_i - r_A x_i)^2}{n_A - 1}$$
$$+ \left(\frac{N_B}{N}\right)^2 \left(\frac{N_B - n_B}{N_B n_B}\right) \frac{\sum_{i=1}^{n_B}(y_i - r_B x_i)^2}{n_B - 1}$$

The observed value of $\hat{\mu}_{yRS}$ from the data given above is

$$\left(\frac{1{,}000}{2{,}500}\right)\left(\frac{18.7}{17.8}\right)(16.3) + \left(\frac{1{,}500}{2{,}500}\right)\left(\frac{4.6}{7.8}\right)(8.53) = 9.87$$

Since we already have

$$\sum_{i=1}^{n_A}(y_i - r_A x_i)^2 = 31.26$$

and by similar calculations for company B,

$$\sum_{i=1}^{n_B}(y_i - r_B x_i)^2 = 87.45$$

we can substitute into $\hat{V}(\hat{\mu}_{yRS})$ to obtain

$$\hat{V}(\hat{\mu}_{yRS}) = .40$$

Example 6.8
Refer to the data of example 6.7 and find a combined ratio estimate of μ_y.

Solution
Here we use $\bar{y}_{st}$ to estimate μ_y, $\bar{x}_{st}$ to estimate μ_x, and

$$\hat{\mu}_{yRC} = \frac{\bar{y}_{st}}{\bar{x}_{st}}(\mu_x)$$

as the combined ratio estimator of μ_y. If we denote $(\bar{y}_{st}/\bar{x}_{st})$ by r_C,

6. Ratio and Regression Estimation

the estimated variance of $\hat{\mu}_{yRC}$ looks like $\hat{V}(\hat{\mu}_{yRS})$ except that r_A and r_B are both replaced by the combined estimate r_C. Thus

$$\hat{V}(\hat{\mu}_{yRC}) = \left(\frac{N_A}{N}\right)^2 \left(\frac{N_A - n_A}{N_A n_A}\right) \frac{\sum_{i=1}^{n_A}(y_i - r_C x_i)^2}{n_A - 1}$$

$$+ \left(\frac{N_B}{N}\right)^2 \left(\frac{N_B - n_B}{N_B n_B}\right) \frac{\sum_{i=1}^{n_B}(y_i - r_C x_i)^2}{n_B - 1}$$

For the data given above,

$$\bar{y}_{st} = (.4)(18.7) + (.6)(4.6) = 10.24$$
$$\bar{x}_{st} = (.4)(17.8) + (.6)(7.8) = 11.80$$
$$\mu_x = \frac{16{,}300 + 12{,}800}{2{,}500} = 11.64$$

Hence the observed value of $\hat{\mu}_{yRC}$ is

$$\frac{10.24}{11.80}(11.64) = 10.13$$

Also,

$$\sum_{i=1}^{n_A}(y_i - r_C x_i)^2 = 154.25$$

$$\sum_{i=1}^{n_B}(y_i - r_C x_i)^2 = 192.56$$

and upon substitution into $\hat{V}(\hat{\mu}_{yRC})$, we have

$$\hat{V}(\hat{\mu}_{yRC}) = 1.04$$

On comparing examples 6.7 and 6.8, we see that the combined ratio estimator gives the larger estimated variance. This is generally the case and so we should employ the separate ratio estimator most of the time. However, the separate ratio estimator may have a larger bias since each stratum ratio estimate contributes to that bias. In summary, if the stratum sample sizes are large enough (say 20 or so) so that the separate ratios do not have large biases and so that the variance approximations work adequately, then use the separate ratio estimator. If stratum sample sizes are very small, or if the within-stratum ratios are all approximately equal, then the combined ratio estimator may perform better.

Of course, an estimator of the population total can be found by multiplying either of the estimators above by the population size N, and the variances can be adjusted accordingly. Thus we might use the notation

$$\hat{\tau}_{yRS} = N\hat{\mu}_{yRS}$$

6.7 REGRESSION ESTIMATION

We saw in section 6.5 that the ratio estimator is most appropriate when the relationship between y and x is linear through the origin. If there is evidence of a linear relationship between the observed y's and x's, but not necessarily one that would pass through the origin, then this extra information provided by the auxiliary variable x may be taken into account through a regression estimator of the mean μ_y. It will still be necessary to have knowledge of μ_x before the estimator can be employed, as it was in the case of ratio estimation of μ_y.

The underlying line that shows the basic relationship between the y's and x's is sometimes referred to as the *regression* line of y upon x. Thus the subscript L in the ensuing formulas is used to denote *linear regression*.

The estimator given below assumes the x's to be fixed in advance and the y's to be random variables. We can think of the x-value as something that has already been observed, like last year's first-quarter earnings, and the y response as a random variable yet to be observed, such as the current quarterly earnings of a company for which x is already known. The probabilistic properties of the estimator then depend only on y for a given set of x's.

Regression estimator of a population mean μ_y:

$$\hat{\mu}_{yL} = \bar{y} + b(\mu_x - \bar{x}) \quad (6.28)$$

where

$$b = \frac{\sum_{i=1}^{n}(y_i - \bar{y})(x_i - \bar{x})}{\sum_{i=1}^{n}(x_i - \bar{x})^2}$$

Estimated variance of $\hat{\mu}_{yL}$:

$$\hat{V}(\hat{\mu}_{yL}) = \left(\frac{N-n}{Nn}\right)\left(\frac{1}{n-2}\right)\left[\sum_{i=1}^{n}(y_i - \bar{y})^2 - b^2 \sum_{i=1}^{n}(x_i - \bar{x})^2\right] \quad (6.29)$$

Bound on the error of estimation:

$$2\sqrt{\hat{V}(\hat{\mu}_{yL})}$$

$$= 2\sqrt{\left(\frac{N-n}{Nn}\right)\left(\frac{1}{n-2}\right)\left[\sum_{i=1}^{n}(y_i - \bar{y})^2 - b^2 \sum_{i=1}^{n}(x_i - \bar{x})^2\right]} \quad (6.30)$$

6. Ratio and Regression Estimation

When calculating b from observed pairs $(y_1, x_1), \ldots, (y_n, x_n)$, we may use the fact that

$$\frac{\sum_{i=1}^{n}(y_i - \bar{y})(x_i - \bar{x})}{\sum_{i=1}^{n}(x_i - \bar{x})^2} = \frac{\sum_{i=1}^{n} y_i x_i - n\bar{x}\bar{y}}{\sum_{i=1}^{n} x_i^2 - n\bar{x}^2}$$

Example 6.9
A mathematics achievement test was given to 486 students prior to entering a certain college. From these students a simple random sample of $n = 10$ students was selected and their progress in calculus observed. Final calculus grades were then reported, as given in the table. If it is known that $\mu_x = 52$ for all 486 students taking the achievement test, estimate μ_y for this population and place a bound on the error of estimation.

Student	Achievement Test Score, x	Final Calculus Grade, y
1	39	65
2	43	78
3	21	52
4	64	82
5	57	92
6	47	89
7	28	73
8	75	98
9	34	56
10	52	75

Solution
Calculations yield $\bar{y} = 76$, $\bar{x} = 46$,

$$b = \frac{\sum_{i=1}^{n} x_i y_i - n\bar{x}\bar{y}}{\sum x_i^2 - n\bar{x}^2} = \frac{36{,}854 - 10(46)(76)}{23{,}634 - 10(46)^2} = .766$$

$$\sum_{i=1}^{n}(y_i - \bar{y})^2 = \sum_{i=1}^{n} y_i^2 - n\bar{y}^2 = 2{,}056$$

$$\sum_{i=1}^{n}(x_i - \bar{x})^2 = \sum_{i=1}^{n} x_i^2 - n\bar{x}^2 = 2{,}474$$

The observed value of $\hat{\mu}_{yL}$ is then

$$\bar{y} + b(\mu_x - \bar{x}) = 76 + (.766)(52 - 46) = 80.596$$

6.8 Difference Estimation

Also

$$\hat{V}(\hat{\mu}_{yL}) = \frac{N-n}{Nn}\left(\frac{1}{n-2}\right)\left[\sum_{i=1}^{n}(y_i - \bar{y})^2 - b^2 \sum_{i=1}^{n}(x_i - \bar{x})^2\right]$$

$$= \frac{486 - 10}{486(10)}\left(\frac{1}{8}\right)[2{,}056 - (.766)^2(2{,}474)] = 7.397$$

and the bound on the error of estimation is

$$2\sqrt{\hat{V}(\hat{\mu}_{yL})} = 5.440$$

Notice that the regression estimator of μ_y inflates the value of $\bar{y}$ since $\bar{x}$ turns out to be less than μ_x and b is positive.

6.8 DIFFERENCE ESTIMATION

The difference method of estimating a population mean or total is similar to the regression method in that it adjusts the $\bar{y}$-value up or down by an amount depending on the difference $(\mu_x - \bar{x})$. However, the regression coefficient b is not computed. In effect, b is set equal to unity.

The difference method is, then, easier to employ then the regression method and frequently works just as well. It is commonly employed in auditing procedures, and we will consider such an example below.

The following formulas hold provided that simple random sampling was employed.

Difference estimator of a population mean μ_y:

$$\hat{\mu}_{yD} = \bar{y} + (\mu_x - \bar{x}) = \mu_x + \bar{d} \tag{6.31}$$

where

$$\bar{d} = \bar{y} - \bar{x}$$

Estimated variance of $\hat{\mu}_{yD}$:

$$\hat{V}(\hat{\mu}_{yD}) = \left(\frac{N-n}{Nn}\right)\frac{\sum_{i=1}^{n}(d_i - \bar{d})^2}{n-1} \tag{6.32}$$

where

$$d_i = y_i - x_i$$

Bound on the error of estimation:

$$2\sqrt{\hat{V}(\hat{\mu}_{yD})} = 2\sqrt{\left(\frac{N-n}{Nn}\right)\frac{\sum_{i=1}^{n}(d_i - \bar{d})^2}{n-1}} \tag{6.33}$$

6. Ratio and Regression Estimation

Example 6.10
Auditors are often interested in comparing the audited value of items with the book value. Generally, book values are known for every item in the population of interest, and audit values are obtained for a sample of these items. The book values can then be used to obtain a good estimate of the total or average audit value for the population.

Suppose a population contains 180 inventory items with a stated book value of $13,320. Let x_i denote the book value and y_i the audit value of the ith item. A simple random sample of $n = 10$ items yields the results shown in the table. Estimate the mean audit value μ_y by the difference method and estimate the variance of $\hat{\mu}_{yD}$.

Sample	Audit Value, y_i	Book Value, x_i	d_i
1	9	10	−1
2	14	12	+2
3	7	8	−1
4	29	26	+3
5	45	47	−2
6	109	112	−3
7	40	36	+4
8	238	240	−2
9	60	59	+1
10	170	167	+3

Solution
Since $\bar{y} = 72.1$, $\bar{x} = 71.7$ and $\mu_x = 74.0$,

$$\hat{\mu}_{yD} = \mu_x + \bar{d} = 74.0 + (72.1 - 71.7) = 74.40$$

Also,

$$\left(\frac{1}{n-1}\right) \sum_{i=1}^{n} (d_i - \bar{d})^2 = \left(\frac{1}{n-1}\right)\left[\sum_{i=1}^{n} d_i^2 - n\bar{d}^2\right]$$

$$= \frac{58 - 10(0.4)^2}{9} = 6.27$$

Thus

$$\hat{V}(\hat{\mu}_{yD}) = \left(\frac{N-n}{Nn}\right)\frac{\sum_{i=1}^{n}(d_i - \bar{d})^2}{n-1} = \left[\frac{180-10}{(180)10}\right](6.27) = .59$$

The type of problems that difference estimators are designed to solve can also be solved by regression and ratio estimators. We will first compare the calculations for the three estimators, and then we will talk about how to choose one over another for certain situations.

6.8 Difference Estimation

Example 6.11
Refer to the problem of example 6.10. Estimate μ_y by using a regression estimator and a ratio estimator. Calculate an estimate of the variance in each case.

Solution
Starting with the regression estimator, we have

$$b = \frac{\sum_{i=1}^{n} y_i x_i - n\bar{x}\bar{y}}{\sum_{i=1}^{n} x_i^2 - n\bar{x}^2} = \frac{105{,}881 - 10(71.7)(72.1)}{106{,}003 - 10(71.7)^2} = .99$$

Thus
$$\hat{\mu}_{yL} = \bar{y} + b(\mu_x - \bar{x}) = 72.1 + .99(74.0 - 71.7) = 74.38$$

Using equation (6.29) and following the computations through yields
$$\hat{V}(\hat{\mu}_{yL}) = 2.24$$

For the ratio estimation of μ_y, equation (6.8) yields

$$\hat{\mu}_y = \frac{\sum_{i=1}^{n} y_i}{\sum_{i=1}^{n} x_i}(\mu_x) = \left(\frac{721}{717}\right)(74) = 74.41$$

Figure 6.2/*Plot of y versus x for example 6.10*

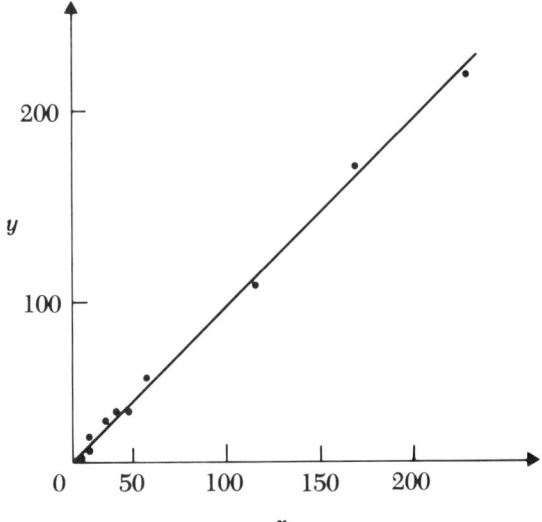

6. Ratio and Regression Estimation

Following equation (6.9),

$$\hat{V}(\hat{\mu}_y) = .66$$

Note that all three estimates of μ_y are very close together, but, in this case, the difference estimator has the smallest estimated variance, with the regression estimator having by far the largest.

How do you choose the best estimator in a given situation? The difference estimator will work well when the plot of y versus x shows the points falling along a straight line with unit slope. Checking such a plot for the data of example 6.10 (see figure 6.2) reveals that the data do indeed lie close to a straight line with a slope of unity. Thus the difference estimator is the best of the three for this case.

We have already seen in section 6.5 that the ratio estimator is very good in cases for which the dispersion of points becomes greater as the x and y values increase. (See figure 6.1.) In the terms of the auditing example, the ratio method is preferable if the differences between audit and book values are proportional to the book values.

What, then, can be said about the regression estimator? If the plot of y versus x falls along a straight line with slope far different from unity, then the regression estimator may pay big dividends. To dramatize the point in an overly simplified example, suppose that the y-value is always two times the x-value, as in the following five points:

y_i	x_i	d_i
2	1	1
4	2	2
6	3	3
8	4	4
10	5	5

Then the regression estimator will yield $\hat{V}(\hat{\mu}_{yL}) = 0$ [following equation (6.29) with $b = 2$]. The difference estimator, on the other hand, will have an estimated variance based on

$$\sum_{i=1}^{n} (d_i - \bar{d})^2 = 10$$

and certainly far greater than zero.

Of course, an estimated variance of zero will almost never occur in practice, but if the plot of y versus x is linear with a slope different from one, it may be worth the extra effort to calculate the regression estimate and its variance.

A caution is in order here, as well as in other places where more than one estimation method could be employed. The method to be used should be decided upon based on the theoretical considerations of the problem and perhaps some preliminary sampling. The experimenter should not collect data and then look for an estimator that gives small variance computations.

6.9 SUMMARY

This chapter has briefly presented ratio estimation of a population mean, total, and ratio for simple random sampling. By measuring a variable y and a subsidiary variable x on each element in the sample, we obtain additional information for estimating the population parameter of interest. When a strong positive correlation exists between the variables x and y, the ratio estimation procedure usually provides more precise estimators of μ_y and τ_y than do the standard techniques presented in chapter 4.

Sample-size requirements are presented for estimating μ_y, τ_y, and R with a bound on the error of estimation equal to B. In each case it is necessary to obtain an estimate of σ^2 from prior information or from a preliminary study to approximate the required sample size.

Regression estimation is another technique for incorporating information on a subsidiary variable. This method is usually better than ratio estimation if the relationship between the y's and the x's is a straight line, not through the origin.

Although these methods can be employed with any sampling design, we have concentrated on simple random sampling, while mentioning stratified random sampling for the ratio case.

The method of difference estimation is similar in principle to regression estimation. It works well when the plot of y versus x reveals points lying uniformly close to a straight line with unit slope.

REFERENCES

Cochran, W. G. *Sampling Techniques.* 3d ed. New York: Wiley, 1977.

Hansen, M. H.; Hurwitz, W. N.; and Madow, W. G. *Sample Survey Methods and Theory*, vol. 1. New York: Wiley, 1953.

Kish, L. *Survey Sampling.* New York: Wiley, 1965.

Mendenhall, W. *Introduction to Probability and Statistics.* 4th ed. N. Scituate, Mass.: Duxbury Press, 1975.

EXERCISES

6.1 A forester is interested in estimating the total volume of trees in a timber sale. He records the volume for each tree in a simple random sample. In addition he measures the basal area for each tree marked for sale. He then uses a ratio estimator of total volume.

6. Ratio and Regression Estimation

The forester decides to take a simple random sample of $n = 12$ from the $N = 250$ trees marked for sale. Let x denote basal area and y the cubic-foot volume for a tree. The total basal area for all 250 trees, τ_x, is 75 square feet. Use the data in the table to estimate τ_y, the total cubic-foot volume for those trees marked for sale, and place a bound on the error of estimation.

Tree Sampled	Basal Area x	Cubic-Foot Volume y
1	.3	6
2	.5	9
3	.4	7
4	.9	19
5	.7	15
6	.2	5
7	.6	12
8	.5	9
9	.8	20
10	.4	9
11	.8	18
12	.6	13

6.2 Use the y data in exercise 6.1 to compute an estimate of τ_y, using $N\bar{y}$. Place a bound on the error of estimation. Compare your results to those obtained in exercise 6.1.

6.3 A consumer survey was conducted to determine the ratio of the money spent on food to the total income per year for households in a small community. A simple random sample of 14 households was selected from 150 in the community. Sample data are given in the table. Estimate R, the population ratio, and place a bound on the error of estimation.

Household	x_i, Total Income	y_i, Amount Spent on Food
1	5,010	990
2	12,240	2,524
3	9,600	1,935
4	15,600	3,123
5	14,400	2,760
6	6,500	1,337
7	8,700	1,756
8	8,200	2,132
9	14,600	3,504
10	12,700	2,286
11	11,500	2,875
12	10,600	2,226
13	7,700	1,463
14	8,500	1,905

Exercises

6.4 A corporation is interested in estimating the total earnings from sales of color television sets at the end of a given three-month period. The total earnings figures are available for all districts within the corporation for the corresponding three-month period of the previous year. A simple random sample of 13 district offices is selected from the 123 offices within the corporation. Using a ratio estimator, estimate τ_y and place a bound on the error of estimation. Use the data in the table and take $\tau_x = 128{,}200$.

Office	Three-Month Data from Previous Year, x_i	Three-Month Data from Current Year, y_i
1	550	610
2	720	780
3	1500	1600
4	1020	1030
5	620	600
6	980	1050
7	928	977
8	1200	1440
9	1350	1570
10	1750	2210
11	670	980
12	729	865
13	1530	1710

6.5 Use the data in exercise 6.4 to estimate the mean earnings for offices within the corporation. Place a bound on the error of estimation.

6.6 An investigator has a colony of $N = 763$ rats which have been subjected to a standard drug. The average length of time to thread a maze correctly under influence of the standard drug was found to be $\mu_x = 17.2$ seconds. The investigator now would like to subject a random sample of 11 rats to a new drug. Estimate the average time required to thread the maze while under the influence of the new drug. (See the data in the table.) Place a bound on the error of estimation. (Hint: It is reasonable to employ a ratio estimator for μ_y if we assume that the rats will react to the new drug in much the same way as they did the standard drug.)

Rat	Standard Drug, x_i	New Drug, y_i
1	14.3	15.2
2	15.7	16.1
3	17.8	18.1
4	17.5	17.6
5	13.2	14.5
6	18.8	19.4
7	17.6	17.5
8	14.3	14.1
9	14.9	15.2
10	17.9	18.1
11	19.2	19.5

6. Ratio and Regression Estimation

6.7 A group of 100 rabbits is being used in a nutrition study. A prestudy weight is recorded for each rabbit. The average of these weights is 3.1 pounds. After two months the experimenter wants to obtain a rough approximation of the average weight of the rabbits. She selects $n = 10$ rabbits at random and weighs them. The original weights and current weights are presented in the table. Estimate the average current weight, and place a bound on the error of estimation.

Rabbit	1	2	3	4	5	6	7	8	9	10
Original Weight	3.2	3.0	2.9	2.8	2.8	3.1	3.0	3.2	2.9	2.8
Current Weight	4.1	4.0	4.1	3.9	3.7	4.1	4.2	4.1	3.9	3.8

6.8 A social worker wants to estimate the ratio of the average number of rooms per apartment to the average number of people per apartment in an urban ghetto area. He selects a simple random sample of 25 apartments from the 275 in the ghetto area. Let x_i denote the number of people in apartment i, and let y_i denote the number of rooms in apartment i. From a count of the number of rooms and number of people in each apartment, the following data are obtained:

$$\bar{x} = 9.2 \qquad \bar{y} = 2.6$$

$$\sum_{i=1}^{25} x_i^2 = 2240 \qquad \sum_{i=1}^{25} x_i y_i = 522 \qquad \sum_{i=1}^{25} y_i^2 = 169.0$$

Estimate the ratio of average number of rooms to average number of people for this area, and place a bound on the error of estimation.

6.9 A forest resource manager is interested in estimating the number of dead fir trees in a 300-acre area of heavy infestation. Using an aerial photo, he divides the area into 200 one-and-a-half-acre plots. Let x denote the photo count of dead firs and y the actual ground count for a simple random sample of $n = 10$ plots. The total number of dead fir trees obtained from the photo count is $\tau_x = 4200$. Use the sample data in the table to estimate τ_y, the total number of dead firs in the 300-acre area. Place a bound on the error of estimation.

Plot Sampled	Photo Count, x_i	Ground Count, y_i
1	12	18
2	30	42
3	24	24
4	24	36
5	18	24
6	30	36
7	12	14
8	6	10
9	36	48
10	42	54

Exercises

6.10 Members of a teachers' association are concerned about the salary increases given to high school teachers in a particular school system. A simple random sample of $n = 15$ teachers is selected from an alphabetical listing of all high school teachers in the system. All 15 teachers are interviewed to determine their salaries for this year and the previous year (see the table). Use these data to estimate R, the rate of change, for $N = 750$ high school teachers in the community school system. Place a bound on the error of estimation.

Teacher	Past Year's Salary	Present Year's Salary	Teacher	Past Year's Salary	Present Year's Salary
1	5,400	5,600	9	5,416	5,622
2	6,700	6,940	10	5,397	5,597
3	7,792	8,084	11	8,152	8,437
4	9,956	10,275	12	6,436	6,700
5	6,355	6,596	13	9,192	9,523
6	5,108	5,322	14	7,006	7,279
7	7,891	8,167	15	7,311	7,582
8	5,216	5,425			

6.11 An experimenter was investigating a new food additive for cattle. Midway through the two-month study, she was interested in estimating the average weight for the entire herd of $N = 500$ steers. A simple random sample of $n = 12$ steers was selected from the herd and weighed. These data and prestudy weights are presented in the table for all cattle sampled. Assume μ_x, the prestudy average, was 880 pounds. Estimate μ_y, the average weight for the herd, and place a bound on the error of estimation.

Steer	Prestudy Weight (in pounds)	Present Weight (in pounds)	Steer	Prestudy Weight (in pounds)	Present Weight (in pounds)
1	815	897	7	1323	1428
2	919	992	8	1067	1152
3	690	752	9	789	875
4	984	1093	10	573	642
5	200	768	11	834	909
6	260	828	12	1049	1122

6.12 An advertising firm is concerned about the effect of a new regional promotional campaign on the total dollar sales for a particular product. A simple random sample of $n = 20$ stores is drawn from the $N = 452$ regional stores in which the product is sold. Quarterly sales data are obtained for the current three-month period and the three-month period prior to the new campaign. Use these data to estimate τ_y, the total sales for the current period, and place a bound on the error of estimation. Assume $\tau_x = 216{,}256$.

6. Ratio and Regression Estimation

Store	Precampaign Sales	Present Sales	Store	Precampaign Sales	Present Sales
1	208	239	11	599	626
2	400	428	12	510	538
3	440	472	13	828	888
4	259	276	14	473	510
5	351	363	15	924	998
6	880	942	16	110	171
7	273	294	17	829	889
8	487	514	18	257	265
9	183	195	19	388	419
10	863	897	20	244	257

6.13 Use the data of exercise 6.12 to determine the sample size required to estimate τ_y, with a bound on the error of estimation equal to $3800.

6.14 Refer to exercises 6.4 and 6.5. By using a regression estimator, estimate the mean earning μ_y, and place a bound on the error of estimation. Compare your answer to that of exercise 6.5. Are there any advantages to using the regression estimator here?

6.15 Show how to adjust equation (6.28) and (6.29) for estimating a total τ_y rather than a mean μ_y.

6.16 Refer to exercise 6.9. Estimate τ_y by using a regression estimator, and place a bound on the error of estimation. Do you think the regression estimator is better than the ratio estimator for this problem?

6.17 Traders on the futures market are interested in relative prices of certain commodities rather than specific price levels. These relative prices can be presented in terms of a ratio. One such important ratio in agriculture is the cattle/hog ratio. From 64 trading days in the first quarter of 1977, the cattle and hog prices were sampled on 18 days, with the results as shown in the table. Estimate the true value of (μ_y/μ_x) for this period, and place a bound on the error of estimation.

Cattle, y_i	Hogs, x_i	Cattle, y_i	Hogs, x_i
42.40	47.80	39.65	49.40
41.40	48.60	38.45	44.30
39.60	48.20	37.80	43.90
39.45	46.75	37.20	42.70
37.00	46.50	37.60	43.25
37.80	45.40	37.50	44.55
38.55	47.30	36.90	45.10
38.60	48.20	37.30	45.00
38.80	49.40	38.60	45.25

6.18 A certain manufacturing firm produces a product that is packaged under two brand names, for marketing purposes. These two brands serve as strata for estimating potential sales volume for the next quarter. A simple

Exercises

random sample of customers for each brand is contacted and asked to provide a potential sales figure y (in number of units) for the coming quarter. Last year's true sales figure, for the same quarter, is available for each of the sampled customers and is denoted by x. The data are given in the table. The sample for brand I was taken from a list of 120 customers, for whom the total sales in the same quarter of last year was 24,500 units. The brand II sample came from 180 customers with a total quarterly sales last year of 21,200 units. Find a ratio estimate of the total potential sales for next quarter. Estimate the variance of your estimator.

Brand I		Brand II	
x_i	y_i	x_i	y_i
204	210	137	150
143	160	189	200
82	75	119	125
256	280	63	60
275	300	103	110
198	190	107	100
		159	180
		63	75
		87	90

EXPERIENCES WITH REAL DATA

1. Population changes for counties in the state of Florida, over the period 1970–1974, are listed in table 6.3 (p. 137).
   (a) Treating x_i as the population in 1970 and y_i as the population in 1974 for county i, form a ratio estimate of the projected 1974 population for the state of Florida. Choose a simple random sample of at least $n = 8$ counties. Place a bound on the error of estimation.
   (b) Using the same counties as sampled in part (a), estimate the total projected population for 1974 by $N\bar{y}$ and compare the accuracy with that obtained in part (a).
   (c) Estimate the total natural increase over this period by the regression method, regressing natural increase per county upon the corresponding 1970 county population. Choose a convenient sample size. Place a bound on the error of estimation.

2. Refer to table 5.4. Using divisions as strata, form a stratified ratio estimate of the 1970 U.S. population, making use of the 1960 data for individual states and the United States as a whole. Choose an appropriate sample size and place a bound on the error of estimation.

3. It might be interesting to estimate what proportion of the money spent for entertainment by students in your community goes to a specific type of entertainment, such as movie theaters. You can obtain this estimate by listing a simple random sample of n students, calling them on the telephone (or interviewing them personally), and recording the total amount spent on entertainment (x_i) as well as the amount spent on movies (y_i).

6. Ratio and Regression Estimation

Then estimate the ratio (μ_y/μ_x) and place a bound on the error.

Think about sample size before you begin the study. Also, it may be more convenient to concentrate on students in one locality, such as an apartment building or group of fraternity houses, rather than students at large. Nonresponse is always a problem when dealing with human populations, so try to think of ways to minimize it.

Table 6.3/Components of population change, by county, in Florida; April 1, 1970, to July 1, 1974

State County	April 1, 1970 (census)	July 1, 1974 (projected)	Total Change	Components of Change		Percentage of Change Due to	
				Natural Increase	Net Migration	Natural Increase	Net Migration
Florida	6,790,929	8,248,851	1,457,922	127,945	1,329,977	8.78	91.22
Alachua	104,764	125,135	20,371	4,874	15,497	23.93	76.07
Baker	9,242	11,841	2,599	513	2,086	19.74	80.26
Bay	75,283	90,150	14,867	3,885	10,982	26.13	73.87
Bradford	14,625	15,786	1,161	434	727	37.38	62.62
Brevard	230,006	248,919	18,913	7,472	11,441	39.51	60.49
Broward	620,100	828,169	208,069	5,318	202,751	2.56	97.44
Calhoun	7,624	8,078	454	170	284	37.44	62.56
Charlotte	27,559	39,844	12,285	−1,207	13,492	0	100.00
Citrus	19,196	33,517	14,321	−340	14,661	0	100.00
Clay	32,059	45,761	13,702	1,762	11,940	12.86	87.14
Collier	38,040	58,749	20,709	1,312	19,397	6.34	93.66
Columbia	25,250	28,393	3,143	1,061	2,082	33.76	66.24
Dade	1,267,792	1,413,102	145,310	18,542	126,768	12.76	87.24
De Soto	13,060	17,660	4,600	327	4,273	7.11	92.89
Dixie	5,480	6,514	1,034	200	834	19.34	80.66
Duval	528,865	570,412	41,547	22,660	18,887	54.54	45.46
Escambia	205,334	222,414	17,080	10,722	6,358	62.78	37.22
Flagler	4,454	6,259	1,805	69	1,736	3.82	96.18
Franklin	7,065	7,752	687	103	584	14.99	85.01
Gadsden	39,184	38,780	−404	2,088	−2,492	0	100.00
Gilchrist	3,551	4,910	1,359	67	1,292	4.93	95.07
Glades	3,669	4,747	1,078	85	993	7.88	92.12

Table 6.3/(continued)

State County	April 1, 1970 (census)	July 1, 1974 (projected)	Total Change	Components of Change		Percentage of Change Due to	
				Natural Increase	Net Migration	Natural Increase	Net Migration
Gulf	10,096	10,697	601	357	244	59.40	40.60
Hamilton	7,787	8,195	408	267	141	65.44	34.56
Hardee	14,889	18,074	3,185	705	2,480	22.14	77.86
Hendry	11,859	15,098	3,239	689	2,550	21.27	78.73
Hernando	17,004	26,537	9,533	99	9,434	1.04	98.96
Highlands	29,507	40,659	11,152	139	11,013	1.25	98.75
Hillsborough	490,265	588,792	98,527	16,623	81,904	16.87	83.13
Holmes	10,720	12,283	1,563	70	1,493	4.48	95.52
Indian River	35,992	45,038	9,046	429	8,617	4.74	95.26
Jackson	34,434	40,125	5,691	722	4,969	12.69	87.31
Jefferson	8,778	9,255	477	388	89	81.34	18.66
Lafayette	2,892	3,228	336	42	294	12.50	87.50
Lake	69,305	83,473	14,168	−177	14,345	0	100.00
Lee	105,216	148,495	43,279	1,130	42,149	2.61	97.39
Leon	103,047	129,903	26,856	5,185	21,671	19.31	80.69
Levy	12,756	14,868	2,112	250	1,862	11.84	88.16
Liberty	3,379	3,822	443	80	363	18.06	81.94
Madison	13,481	14,220	739	425	314	57.51	42.49
Manatee	97,115	117,642	20,527	−1,850	22,377	0	100.00
Marion	69,030	92,522	23,492	2,018	21,474	8.59	91.41
Martin	28,035	45,097	17,062	160	16,902	0.94	99.06
Monroe	52,586	53,582	996	2,229	−1,233	0	100.00
Nassau	20,626	26,693	6,067	949	5,118	15.64	84.36
Okaloosa	88,187	101,266	13,079	6,430	6,649	49.16	50.84

Okeechobee	11,233	16,284	5,051	618	4,433	12.24	87.76
Orange	344,311	423,981	79,670	13,215	66,455	16.59	83.41
Osceola	25,267	36,889	11,622	173	11,449	1.49	98.51
Palm Beach	348,993	459,167	110,174	3,086	107,088	2.80	97.20
Pasco	75,955	123,199	47,244	−2,133	49,377	0	100.00
Pinellas	522,329	649,852	127,523	−16,632	144,155	0	100.00
Polk	228,026	268,343	40,317	6,985	33,332	17.33	82.67
Putnam	36,424	42,346	5,922	913	5,009	15.42	84.58
St. Johns	31,035	37,931	6,896	383	6,513	5.55	94.45
St. Lucie	50,836	67,034	16,198	1,505	14,693	9.29	90.71
Santa Rosa	37,741	46,685	8,944	2,252	6,692	25.18	74.82
Sarasota	120,413	157,738	37,325	−3,529	40,854	0	100.00
Seminole	83,692	134,336	50,644	4,247	46,397	8.39	91.61
Sumter	14,839	20,034	5,195	385	4,810	7.41	92.59
Suwannee	15,559	17,645	2,086	466	1,620	22.34	77.66
Taylor	13,641	14,366	725	445	280	61.38	38.62
Union	8,112	9,463	1,351	157	1,194	11.62	88.38
Volusia	169,487	206,967	37,480	−2,459	39,939	0	100.00
Wakulla	6,308	8,635	2,327	183	2,144	7.86	92.14
Walton	16,087	17,569	1,482	−13	1,495	0	100.00
Washington	11,453	13,931	2,478	222	2,256	8.96	91.04

Source: Division of Population Studies, Bureau of Economic and Business Research, *Florida Estimates of Population* (Gainesville: University of Florida), pp. 23–24.

7.
Cluster Sampling

7.1 INTRODUCTION

You will recall that the objective of sample survey design is to obtain a specified amount of information about a population parameter at minimum cost. Stratified random sampling is often better suited for this than is simple random sampling for the three reasons indicated in section 5.1. This chapter introduces a third design, cluster sampling, which sometimes gives more information per unit cost than do either simple or stratified random sampling.

Definition 7.1 A *cluster sample* is a simple random sample in which each sampling unit is a collection, or cluster, of elements.

Cluster sampling is less costly than simple or stratified random sampling if the cost of obtaining a frame that lists all population elements is very high or if the cost of obtaining observations increases as the distance separating the elements increases.

To illustrate, suppose we wish to estimate the average income per household in a large city. How should we choose the sample? If we use simple random sampling, we will need a frame listing all households (elements) in the city and this may be very costly or impossible to obtain. We cannot avoid this problem by using stratified random sampling because a frame is still required for each stratum in the population. Rather than drawing a simple random sample of *elements*, we could divide the city into regions such as blocks (or clusters of elements) and select a simple random sample of blocks from the population. This is easily accomplished using a frame that lists all city blocks. Then the income of every household within each sampled block would be measured.

To illustrate the second reason for using cluster sampling, suppose that a list of households in the city is available. We could select a simple random sample of households, which probably would be scattered throughout the city. The cost of conducting interviews in the scattered households would be large due to the interviewer travel time and other related expenses. Stratified random sampling could lower these expenses, but using cluster sampling is a more effective method of reducing travel costs. Elements within a cluster should be close to each other geographically and, hence, travel expenses should be reduced. Obviously, travel within a city block would be minimal when compared to the travel associated with simple random sampling of households within the city.

To summarize, cluster sampling is an effective design for obtaining a specified amount of information at minimum cost when

1. a good frame listing population elements either is not available or is very costly to obtain
2. the cost of obtaining observations increases as the distance separating the elements increases

7.2 HOW TO DRAW A CLUSTER SAMPLE

The first task in cluster sampling is to specify appropriate clusters. Elements within a cluster are often physically close together and hence tend to have similar characteristics. Stated another way, the measurement on one element in a cluster may be highly correlated with the measurement on another. Thus the amount of information about a population parameter may not be increased substantially as new measurements are taken within a cluster. Since measurements cost money, an experimenter would waste money by choosing too large a cluster size. However, situations may arise in which elements within a cluster are very different from one another. In such cases a sample containing a few large clusters could produce a very good estimate of a population parameter, such as the mean.

For example, suppose clusters are formed by boxes of components coming off production lines, one cluster of components per line. If all lines have approximately the same rate of defects, then the components in each cluster (box) are about as variable with respect to quality as the population as a whole. In this situation a good estimate of the proportion of defectives produced could be obtained from one or two clusters.

7.2 How to Draw a Cluster Sample

On the other hand, suppose that school districts are specified as clusters for sampling households in a city. The clusters contain many households. Consequently, the resources of the experimenter allow only a small number of clusters, say two or three, to be sampled. This sample may not be representative of the population because the households within the same school district may be relatively homogeneous with respect to the characteristic being measured. More information could be obtained by sampling a larger number of clusters of smaller size.

As another example, an experimenter wants to estimate the proportion of defective light bulbs produced by a certain factory. He or she could sample individual bulbs, packs containing a small number of bulbs, or cartons containing many packs. The experimenter must choose the appropriate cluster size to obtain the most information per unit cost. Sampling individual bulbs may be expensive and consequently not used. If the cost restrictions force the experimenter to choose between sampling a few cartons (2 or 3) or many packs (20 or 30), he or she should choose the latter scheme.

Notice the main difference between the optimal construction of strata (chapter 5) and the construction of clusters. Strata are to be as homogeneous (alike) as possible within, but one stratum should differ as much as possible from another with respect to the characteristic being measured. Clusters, on the other hand, should be as heterogeneous (different) as possible within and one cluster should look very much like another in order for the economic advantages of cluster sampling to pay off.

Once appropriate clusters have been specified, a frame that lists all clusters in the population must be composed. A simple random sample of clusters is then selected from this frame by using the methods of section 4.2. We illustrate with the following example.

Example 7.1
A sociologist wants to estimate the average income per adult male in a certain small city. No list of resident adults is available. How should he design the sample survey?

Solution
Cluster sampling seems to be the logical choice for the survey design because no lists of elements (adult males) is available. The city is marked off into rectangular blocks, except for two industrial areas and three parks that contain only a few houses. It is decided that each of the city blocks will be considered one cluster, the two industrial areas will be considered one cluster, and finally the three parks will be considered one cluster. The clusters are numbered on a city map, with the numbers from 1 to 415. The experimenter has enough time and money to sample $n = 25$ clusters and to interview every adult male living within

7. Cluster Sampling

each cluster. Hence 25 random numbers between 1 and 415 are selected from table 3 of the appendix, and the clusters having these numbers are marked on the map. Interviewers are then assigned to each of the sampled clusters.

7.3 ESTIMATION OF A POPULATION MEAN AND TOTAL

Cluster sampling is simple random sampling with each sampling unit containing a number of elements. Hence the estimators of the population mean μ and total τ are similar to those for simple random sampling. In particular, the sample mean $\bar{y}$ is a good estimator of the population mean μ. An estimator of μ and two estimators of τ are discussed in this section.

The following notation is used in this chapter:

N = the number of *clusters* in the population
n = the number of clusters selected in a simple random sample
m_i = the number of elements in cluster i, $i = 1, \ldots, N$

$$\bar{m} = \frac{1}{n} \sum_{i=1}^{n} m_i = \text{the average cluster size for the sample}$$

$$M = \sum_{i=1}^{N} m_i = \text{the number of elements in the population}$$

$$\bar{M} = \frac{M}{N} = \text{the average cluster size for the population}$$

y_i = the total of all observations in the ith cluster

The estimator of the population mean μ is the sample mean $\bar{y}$, which is given by

$$\bar{y} = \frac{\sum_{i=1}^{n} y_i}{\sum_{i=1}^{n} m_i}$$

Thus $\bar{y}$ takes the form of a ratio estimator, as developed in chapter 6, with m_i taking the place of x_i. Then the estimated variance of $\bar{y}$ has the form of the variance of a ratio estimator given by equation (6.2).

Estimator of the population mean μ:

$$\bar{y} = \frac{\sum_{i=1}^{n} y_i}{\sum_{i=1}^{n} m_i} \qquad (7.1)$$

7.3 Estimation of a Population Mean and Total

Estimated variance of $\bar{y}$:

$$\hat{V}(\bar{y}) = \left(\frac{N-n}{Nn\bar{M}^2}\right)\frac{\sum_{i=1}^{n}(y_i - \bar{y}m_i)^2}{n-1} \quad (7.2)$$

Bound on the error of estimation:

$$2\sqrt{\hat{V}(\bar{y})} = 2\sqrt{\left(\frac{N-n}{Nn\bar{M}^2}\right)\frac{\sum_{i=1}^{n}(y_i - \bar{y}m_i)^2}{n-1}} \quad (7.3)$$

$\bar{M}$ can be estimated by $\bar{m}$ if M is unknown.

The estimated variance in equation (7.2) is biased and a good estimator of $V(\bar{y})$ only if n is large, say $n \geq 20$. The bias disappears if the cluster sizes $m_1, m_2, \ldots, m_N$ are equal.

Let us illustrate the use of the formulas above with an example.

Example 7.2
Interviews are conducted in each of the 25 blocks sampled in example 7.1. The data on income for adult males are presented in table 7.1. Use the data to estimate the average income per adult male in the city, and place a bound on the error of estimation.

Table 7.1/Incomes for adult males

Cluster i	Number of Adult Males m_i	Total Income Per Cluster y_i	Cluster i	Number of Adult Males m_i	Total Income Per Cluster y_i
1	8	$ 96,000	14	10	$49,000
2	12	121,000	15	9	53,000
3	4	42,000	16	3	50,000
4	5	65,000	17	6	32,000
5	6	52,000	18	5	22,000
6	6	40,000	19	5	45,000
7	7	75,000	20	4	37,000
8	5	65,000	21	6	51,000
9	8	45,000	22	8	30,000
10	3	50,000	23	7	39,000
11	2	85,000	24	3	47,000
12	6	43,000	25	8	41,000
13	5	54,000			

$\sum_{i=1}^{25} m_i = 151 \qquad \sum_{i=1}^{25} y_i = \$1{,}329{,}000$

7. Cluster Sampling

Solution
The best estimate of the population mean μ is given by equation (7.1) and calculated as follows:

$$\bar{y} = \frac{\sum_{i=1}^{n} y_i}{\sum_{i=1}^{n} m_i} = \frac{\$1,329,000}{151} = \$8,801$$

In order to calculate $\hat{V}(\bar{y})$, we need the following quantities:

$$\sum_{i=1}^{25} y_i^2 = y_1^2 + y_2^2 + \cdots + y_{25}^2$$
$$= (96,000)^2 + (121,000)^2 + \cdots + (41,000)^2$$
$$= 82,039,000,000$$

$$\sum_{i=1}^{25} m_i^2 = m_1^2 + m_2^2 + \cdots + m_{25}^2$$
$$= (8)^2 + (12)^2 + \cdots + (8)^2 = 1,047$$

$$\sum_{i=1}^{25} y_i m_i = y_1 m_1 + y_2 m_2 + \cdots + y_{25} m_{25}$$
$$= (96,000)(8) + (121,000)(12) + \cdots + (41,000)(8)$$
$$= 8,403,000$$

The following equality is easily established:

$$\sum_{i=1}^{n} (y_i - \bar{y} m_i)^2 = \sum_{i=1}^{n} y_i^2 - 2\bar{y} \sum_{i=1}^{n} y_i m_i + \bar{y}^2 \sum_{i=1}^{n} m_i^2$$

Substituting into this equation from table 7.1,

$$\sum_{i=1}^{25} (y_i - \bar{y} m_i)^2 = 82,039,000,000 - 2(8,801)(8,403,000)$$
$$+ (8,801)^2(1,047)$$
$$= 15,227,502,247$$

Since M is not known, the $\bar{M}$ appearing in equation (7.2) must be estimated by $\bar{m}$, where

$$\bar{m} = \frac{\sum_{i=1}^{n} m_i}{n} = \frac{151}{25} = 6.04$$

Example 7.1 gives $N = 415$. Then from equation (7.2),

$$\hat{V}(\bar{y}) = \left(\frac{N-n}{Nn\bar{M}^2}\right) \frac{\sum_{i=1}^{n}(y_i - \bar{y} m_i)^2}{n-1}$$

$$= \left[\frac{415 - 25}{(415)(25)(6.04)^2}\right]\left[\frac{15,227,502,247}{24}\right] = 653,785$$

7.3 Estimation of a Population Mean and Total

Thus the estimate of μ with a bound on the error of estimation is given by

$$\bar{y} \pm 2\sqrt{\hat{V}(\bar{y})}, \quad \text{or} \quad 8{,}801 \pm 2\sqrt{653{,}785}, \quad \text{or} \quad 8{,}801 \pm 1{,}617$$

The best estimate of the average income per adult male is $8,801, and the error of estimation should be less than $1,617 with probability close to .95. This is a rather large bound on the error of estimation; it could be reduced by sampling more clusters and, consequently, increasing the sample size.

The population total τ is now $M\mu$ because M denotes the total number of elements in the population. Consequently, as in simple random sampling, $M\bar{y}$ provides an estimator of τ.

Estimator of the population total τ:

$$M\bar{y} = M \frac{\sum_{i=1}^{n} y_i}{\sum_{i=1}^{n} m_i} \tag{7.4}$$

Estimated variance of $M\bar{y}$:

$$\hat{V}(M\bar{y}) = M^2 \hat{V}(\bar{y}) = N^2 \left(\frac{N-n}{Nn}\right) \frac{\sum_{i=1}^{n} (y_i - \bar{y}m_i)^2}{n-1} \tag{7.5}$$

Bound on the error of estimation:

$$2\sqrt{\hat{V}(M\bar{y})} = 2\sqrt{N^2 \left(\frac{N-n}{Nn}\right) \frac{\sum_{i=1}^{n} (y_i - \bar{y}m_i)^2}{n-1}} \tag{7.6}$$

Note that the estimator $M\bar{y}$ is useful only if the number of elements in the population, M, is known.

Example 7.3
Use the data in table 7.1 to estimate the total income of all adult males in the city, and place a bound on the error of estimation. There are 2,500 adult males in the city.

Solution
The sample mean $\bar{y}$ is calculated to be $8,801 in example 7.2. Thus the estimate of τ is

$$M\bar{y} = 2{,}500(8{,}801) = \$22{,}002{,}500$$

7. Cluster Sampling

The quantity $\hat{V}(\bar{y})$ is calculated by the method used in example 7.2, except that M can now be used in place of $\bar{m}$. The estimate of τ with a bound on the error of estimation is

$$M\bar{y} \pm 2\sqrt{\hat{V}(M\bar{y})} = M\bar{y} \pm 2\sqrt{M^2\hat{V}(\bar{y})}$$

$$22{,}002{,}500 \pm 2\sqrt{(2{,}500)^2(653{,}785)}$$

$$22{,}002{,}500 \pm 4{,}042{,}848$$

Again, this is a large bound on the error of estimation, and it could be reduced by increasing the sample size.

Often the number of elements in the population is not known in problems for which cluster sampling is appropriate. This makes it impossible to use the estimator $M\bar{y}$, but we can form another estimator of the population total that does not depend on M. The quantity $\bar{y}_t$, given by

$$\bar{y}_t = \frac{1}{n}\sum_{i=1}^{n} y_i \tag{7.7}$$

is the average of the cluster totals for the n sampled clusters. Hence $\bar{y}_t$ is an unbiased estimator of the average of the N cluster totals in the population. By the same reasoning as employed in chapter 4, $N\bar{y}_t$ is an unbiased estimator of the sum of the cluster totals or, equivalently, of the population total τ.

For example, it is highly unlikely that the number of adult males in a city would be known, and hence the estimator $N\bar{y}_t$, rather than $M\bar{y}$, would have to be used to estimate τ.

An estimator of the population total τ, which does not depend on M:

$$N\bar{y}_t = \frac{N}{n}\sum_{i=1}^{n} y_i \tag{7.8}$$

Estimated variance of $N\bar{y}$:

$$\hat{V}(N\bar{y}_t) = N^2\hat{V}(\bar{y}_t) = N^2\left(\frac{N-n}{Nn}\right)\frac{\sum_{i=1}^{n}(y_i - \bar{y}_t)^2}{n-1} \tag{7.9}$$

Bound on the error of estimation:

$$2\sqrt{\hat{V}(N\bar{y}_t)} = 2\sqrt{N^2\left(\frac{N-n}{Nn}\right)\frac{\sum_{i=1}^{n}(y_i - \bar{y}_t)^2}{n-1}} \tag{7.10}$$

7.3 Estimation of a Population Mean and Total

If there is a large amount of variation among the cluster sizes and if cluster sizes are highly correlated with cluster totals, the variance of $N\bar{y}_t$ [equation (7.9)] is generally larger than the variance of $M\bar{y}$ [equation (7.5)]. The estimator $N\bar{y}_t$ does not use the information provided by the cluster sizes $m_1, m_2, \ldots, m_n$ and hence may be less precise.

Example 7.4
Use the data of table 7.1 to estimate the total income of all adult males in the city if M is not known. Place a bound on the error of estimation.

Solution
Example 7.1 gives $N = 415$. From equation (7.8) and table 7.1, the estimate of the total income τ is

$$N\bar{y}_t = \frac{N}{n}\sum_{i=1}^{n} y_i = \frac{415}{25}(1{,}329{,}000) = \$22{,}061{,}400$$

This figure is fairly close to the estimate given in example 7.3.
To place a bound on the error of estimation, we first calculate

$$\sum_{i=1}^{n}(y_i - \bar{y}_t)^2 = \sum_{i=1}^{n} y_i^2 - \frac{1}{n}\left(\sum_{i=1}^{n} y_i\right)^2$$

$$= 82{,}039{,}000{,}000 - \frac{1}{25}(1{,}329{,}000)^2$$

$$= 11{,}389{,}360{,}000$$

Then the estimate of the total income of all adult males in the city, with a bound on the error of estimation, is

$$N\bar{y}_t \pm 2\sqrt{\hat{V}(N\bar{y}_t)}$$

Substituting into equation (7.10), we calculate

$$N\bar{y}_t \pm 2\sqrt{N^2\left(\frac{N-n}{Nn}\right)\frac{\sum_{i=1}^{n}(y_i - \bar{y}_t)^2}{n-1}}$$

$$22{,}061{,}400 \pm 2\sqrt{(415)^2\left[\frac{415-25}{(415)(25)}\right]\frac{(11{,}389{,}360{,}000)}{24}}$$

$$22{,}061{,}400 \pm 3{,}505{,}920$$

The bound on the error of estimation is slightly smaller than the bound for the estimator $M\bar{y}$ (example 7.3). This is partly because the cluster sizes are not highly correlated with the cluster total in this example. In other words, the cluster sizes are providing little information on cluster totals; hence the unbiased estimator $N\bar{y}_t$ appears to be better than the estimator $M\bar{y}$.

7. Cluster Sampling

The estimators of μ and τ possess special properties when all cluster sizes are equal (that is, $m_1 = m_2 = \cdots = m_N$). First, the estimator $\bar{y}$, given by equation (7.1), is an unbiased estimator of the population mean μ. Second, $\hat{V}(\bar{y})$, given by equation (7.2), is an unbiased estimator of the variance of $\bar{y}$. Finally, the two estimators, $M\bar{y}$ and $N\bar{y}_t$, of the population total τ are equivalent.

Example 7.5
The circulation manager of a newspaper wishes to estimate the average number of newspapers purchased per household in a given community. Travel costs from household to household are substantial. Therefore, the 4000 households in the community are listed in 400 geographical clusters of 10 households each, and a simple random sample of 4 clusters is selected. Interviews are conducted with the results as shown in the table. Estimate the average number of newspapers per household for the community, and place a bound on the error of estimation.

Cluster	Number of Newspapers										Total
1	1	2	1	3	3	2	1	4	1	1	19
2	1	3	2	2	3	1	4	1	1	2	20
3	2	1	1	1	1	3	2	1	3	1	16
4	1	1	3	2	1	5	1	2	3	1	20

Solution
From equation (7.1)

$$\bar{y} = \frac{\sum_{i=1}^{n} y_i}{\sum_{i=1}^{n} m_i}$$

When $m_1 = m_2 = \cdots = m_n = m$, the equation becomes

$$\bar{y} = \frac{\sum_{i=1}^{n} y_i}{nm} = \frac{19 + 20 + 16 + 20}{4(10)} = 1.875$$

Also, it can be shown that

$$\sum_{i=1}^{n} (y_i - \bar{y} m_i)^2 = \sum_{i=1}^{n} y_i^2 - 2\bar{y} \sum_{i=1}^{n} y_i m_i + \bar{y}^2 \sum_{i=1}^{n} m_i^2$$

$$= \sum_{i=1}^{n} y_i^2 - nm^2 \bar{y}^2$$

7.4 Selecting the Sample Size for Estimating Population Means and Totals

Substituting, we obtain

$$\sum_{i=1}^{n} (y_i - \bar{y}m_i)^2 = (19)^2 + (20)^2 + (16)^2 + (20)^2 - 4(10)^2(1.875)^2$$

$$= 10.75$$

Thus from equation (7.2),

$$\hat{V}(\bar{y}) = \left(\frac{N-n}{Nn\bar{M}^2}\right)\frac{\sum_{i=1}^{n}(y_i - \bar{y}m_i)^2}{n-1} = \frac{(400-4)(10.75)}{400(4)(10)^2(3)} = .0089$$

Therefore, the best estimate of the average number of newspapers per household with a bound on the error of estimation is

$$\bar{y} \pm 2\sqrt{\hat{V}(\bar{y})}, \quad \text{or} \quad 1.875 \pm 2\sqrt{.0089}, \quad \text{or} \quad 1.875 \pm .188$$

Thus the estimate of the average number of newspapers per household is 1.875 with a high probability that the error of estimation is less than .188

7.4 SELECTING THE SAMPLE SIZE FOR ESTIMATING POPULATION MEANS AND TOTALS

The quantity of information in a cluster sample is affected by two factors, the number of clusters and the relative cluster size. We have not encountered the latter factor in any of the sampling procedures discussed previously. In the problem of estimating the number of homes with inadequate fire insurance in a state, the clusters could be counties, voting districts, school districts, communities, or any other convenient grouping of homes. We will assume that the relative cluster size has been selected in advance and will consider the problem of choosing the number of clusters n.

From equation (7.2) the estimated variance of $\bar{y}$ is

$$\hat{V}(\bar{y}) = \frac{N-n}{Nn\bar{M}^2}(s_c^2)$$

where

$$s_c^2 = \frac{\sum_{i=1}^{n}(y_i - \bar{y}m_i)^2}{n-1} \tag{7.11}$$

The actual variance of $\bar{y}$ is approximately

$$V(\bar{y}) = \frac{N-n}{Nn\bar{M}^2}(\sigma_c^2) \tag{7.12}$$

7. Cluster Sampling

where σ_c^2 is the population quantity estimated by s_c^2.

Because we do not know σ_c^2 or the average cluster size $\bar{M}$, choice of the sample size, that is, the number of clusters necessary to purchase a specified quantity of information concerning a population parameter, is difficult. We overcome this difficulty by using the same method as we used for ratio estimation. That is, we use an estimate of σ_c^2 and $\bar{M}$ available from a prior survey or we select a preliminary sample containing n' elements. Estimates of σ_c^2 and $\bar{M}$ can be computed from the preliminary sample and used to acquire an approximate total sample size n. Thus as in all problems of selecting a sample size, we equate two standard deviations of our estimator to a bound on the error of estimation, B. This bound is chosen by the experimenter and represents the maximum error that he or she is willing to tolerate. That is,

$$2\sqrt{V(\bar{y})} = B$$

Using equation (7.12) we can solve for n.

We obtain similar results when using $M\bar{y}$ to estimate the population total τ, because $V(M\bar{y}) = M^2 V(\bar{y})$.

The approximate sample size required to estimate μ with a bound B on the error of estimation:

$$n = \frac{N\sigma_c^2}{ND + \sigma_c^2} \qquad (7.13)$$

where σ_c^2 is estimated by s_c^2 and

$$D = \frac{B^2 \bar{M}^2}{4}$$

Example 7.6
Suppose the data in table 7.1 represent a preliminary sample of incomes in the city. How large a sample should be taken in a future survey in order to estimate the average income per adult male, μ, with a bound of $500 on the error of estimation?

Solution
To use equation (7.13), σ_c^2 must be estimated; the best estimate available is s_c^2, which can be calculated using the data in table 7.1. Using the calculations in example 7.2,

$$s_c^2 = \frac{\sum_{i=1}^{n}(y_i - \bar{y}m_i)^2}{n-1} = \frac{15{,}227{,}502{,}247}{24} = 634{,}479{,}260$$

7.4 Selecting the Sample Size for Estimating Population Means and Totals

$\bar{M}$ can be estimated by $\bar{m} = 6.04$ calculated from table 7.1. Then D is approximately

$$\frac{B^2\bar{m}^2}{4} = \frac{(500)^2(6.04)^2}{4} = (62{,}500)(6.04)^2$$

Using equation (7.13),

$$n = \frac{N\sigma_c^2}{ND + \sigma_c^2} = \frac{415(634{,}479{,}260)}{415(6.04)^2(62{,}500) + 634{,}479{,}260} = 166.58$$

Thus 167 clusters should be sampled.

The approximate size required to estimate τ, using $M\bar{y}$, with a bound B on the error of estimation:

$$n = \frac{N\sigma_c^2}{ND + \sigma_c^2} \qquad (7.14)$$

where σ_c^2 is estimated by s_c^2 and

$$D = \frac{B^2}{4N^2}$$

Example 7.7
Again using the data in table 7.1 as a preliminary sample of incomes in the city, how large a sample is necessary to estimate the total income of all adult males, τ, with a bound of $1,000,000 on the error of estimation? There are 2,500 adult males in the city ($M = 2{,}500$).

Solution
We use equation (7.14) and estimate σ_c^2 by

$$s_c^2 = 634{,}479{,}260$$

as in example 7.6. When estimating τ,

$$D = \frac{B^2}{4N^2} = \frac{(1{,}000{,}000)^2}{4(415)^2}$$

$$ND = \frac{(1{,}000{,}000)^2}{4(415)} = 602{,}409{,}00$$

Then using equation (7.14),

$$n = \frac{N\sigma_c^2}{ND + \sigma_c^2} = \frac{415(634{,}479{,}260)}{602{,}409{,}000 + 634{,}479{,}260} = 212.88$$

7. Cluster Sampling

Thus 213 clusters should be sampled to estimate the total income with a bound of $1,000,000 on the error of estimation.

The estimator $N\bar{y}_t$, shown in equation (7.8), is used to estimate τ when M is unknown. The estimated variance of $N\bar{y}_t$, shown in equation (7.9), is

$$\hat{V}(N\bar{y}_t) = N^2 \left(\frac{N-n}{Nn} \right) s_t^2$$

where

$$s_t^2 = \frac{\sum_{i=1}^{n} (y_i - \bar{y}_t)^2}{n-1} \tag{7.15}$$

Thus the population variance of $N\bar{y}_t$ is

$$V(N\bar{y}_t) = N^2 V(\bar{y}_t) = N^2 \left(\frac{N-n}{Nn} \right) \sigma_t^2 \tag{7.16}$$

where σ_t^2 is the population quantity estimated by s_t^2.

Estimation of τ with a bound of B units on the error of estimation leads to the following equation:

$$2\sqrt{V(N\bar{y}_t)} = B$$

Using equation (7.16), we can solve for n.

The approximate sample size required to estimate τ, using $N\bar{y}_t$, with a bound B on the error of estimation:

$$n = \frac{N\sigma_t^2}{ND + \sigma_t^2} \tag{7.17}$$

where σ_t^2 is estimated by s_t^2, and

$$D = \frac{B^2}{4N^2}$$

Example 7.8
Assume the data of table 7.1 are from a preliminary study of incomes in the city and M is not known. Then how large a sample must be taken to estimate the total income of all adult males, τ, with a bound of $1,000,000 on the error of estimation?

Solution
The quantity σ_t^2 must be estimated by s_t^2, which is calculated

7.5 Estimation of a Population Proportion

from the data of table 7.1. Using the calculations of example 7.4,

$$s_t^2 = \frac{\sum_{i=1}^{n}(y_i - \bar{y}_t)^2}{n-1} = \frac{11{,}389{,}360{,}000}{24} - 474{,}556{,}667$$

The bound on the error of estimation is $B = \$1{,}000{,}000$, and hence

$$D = \frac{B^2}{4N^2} = \frac{(1{,}000{,}000)^2}{4(415)^2}$$

From equation (7.17)

$$n = \frac{N\sigma_t^2}{ND + \sigma_t^2} = \frac{415(474{,}556{,}667)}{\dfrac{(415)(1{,}000{,}000)^2}{4(415)^2} + 474{,}556{,}667} = 182{,}88$$

Thus a sample of 183 clusters must be taken to have a bound of $1,000,000 on the error of estimation.

7.5 ESTIMATION OF A POPULATION PROPORTION

Suppose an experimenter wishes to estimate a population proportion, or fraction, such as the proportion of houses in a state with inadequate plumbing or the proportion of corporation presidents who are college graduates. The best estimator of the population proportion p is the sample proportion $\hat{p}$. Let a_i denote the total number of elements in cluster i that possess the characteristic of interest. Then the proportion of elements in the sample of n clusters possessing the characteristic is given by

$$\hat{p} = \frac{\sum_{i=1}^{n} a_i}{\sum_{i=1}^{n} m_i}$$

where m_i is the number of elements in the ith cluster, $i = 1, \ldots, n$. Note that $\hat{p}$ has the same form as $\bar{y}$ [see equation (7.1)], except that y_i is replaced by a_i. The estimated variance of $\hat{p}$ is similar to that of $\bar{y}$.

7. Cluster Sampling

Estimator of the population proportion p:

$$\hat{p} = \frac{\sum_{i=1}^{n} a_i}{\sum_{i=1}^{n} m_i} \quad (7.18)$$

Estimated variance of $\hat{p}$:

$$\hat{V}(\hat{p}) = \left(\frac{N-n}{Nn\bar{M}^2}\right) \frac{\sum_{i=1}^{n}(a_i - \hat{p}m_i)^2}{n-1} \quad (7.19)$$

Bound on the error of estimation:

$$2\sqrt{\hat{V}(\hat{p})} = 2\sqrt{\left(\frac{N-n}{Nn\bar{M}^2}\right)\frac{\sum_{i=1}^{n}(a_i - \hat{p}m_i)^2}{n-1}} \quad (7.20)$$

The variance formula (7.19) is a good estimator only when the sample size n is large, say $n \geq 20$. If $m_1 = m_2 = \cdots = m_N$, then $\hat{p}$ is an unbiased estimator of p, and $\hat{V}(\hat{p})$, shown in equation (7.19), is an unbiased estimator of the actual variance of $\hat{p}$ for any sample size.

Example 7.9
In addition to the information on income, the adult males in the sample survey of example 7.2 are asked whether they rent or own their homes. The results are given in table 7.2. Use the data in table 7.2 to estimate the proportion of adult males in the city who rent their homes. Place a bound on the error of estimation.

Solution
The best estimate of the population proportion of renters is $\hat{p}$, shown in equation (7.18), where

$$\hat{p} = \frac{\sum_{i=1}^{n} a_i}{\sum_{i=1}^{n} m_i} = \frac{72}{151} = 477$$

To estimate the variance of $\hat{p}$, we must calculate

$$\sum_{i=1}^{n}(a_i - \hat{p}m_i)^2 = \sum_{i=1}^{n} a_i^2 - 2\hat{p}\sum_{i=1}^{n} a_i m_i + \hat{p}^2 \sum_{i=1}^{n} m_i^2$$

and, from table 7.2,

$$\sum_{i=1}^{n}(a_i - \hat{p}m_i)^2 = 262 - 2(.477)(511) + (.477)^2(1047) = 12.729$$

7.5 Estimation of a Population Proportion

Table 7.2 / *Number of adult males who rent homes*

Cluster	Number of Adult Males m_i	Number of Renters a_i	Cluster	Number of Adult Males m_i	Number of Renters a_i
1	8	4	14	10	5
2	12	7	15	9	4
3	4	1	16	3	1
4	5	3	17	6	4
5	6	3	18	5	2
6	6	4	19	5	3
7	7	4	20	4	1
8	5	2	21	6	3
9	8	3	22	8	3
10	3	2	23	7	4
11	2	1	24	3	0
12	6	3	25	8	3
13	5	2			
				$\sum_{i=1}^{25} m_i = 151$	$\sum_{i=1}^{25} a_i = 72$
	$\sum_{i=1}^{25} a_i^2 = 262$		$\sum_{i=1}^{25} m_i^2 = 1047$	$\sum_{i=1}^{25} a_i m_i = 511$	

$\bar{M}$ is estimated by $\bar{m}$, where

$$\bar{m} = \frac{\sum_{i=1}^{n} m_i}{n} = \frac{151}{25} = 6.04$$

Then from equation (7.19),

$$\hat{V}(\hat{p}) = \left(\frac{N-n}{Nn\bar{M}^2}\right) \frac{\sum_{i=1}^{n}(a_i - \hat{p}m_i)^2}{n-1}$$

$$= \frac{(415 - 25)(12.729)}{415(25)(6.04)^2(24)} = .00055$$

The estimate of p with a bound on the error is

$\hat{p} \pm 2\sqrt{\hat{V}(\hat{p})}$,   or $.477 \pm 2\sqrt{.00055}$,   or $.477 \pm .047$

Thus the best estimate of the proportion of adult males who rent homes is .477. The error of estimation should be less than .047 with probability of approximately .95.

7. Cluster Sampling

7.6 SELECTING THE SAMPLE SIZE FOR ESTIMATING PROPORTIONS

Estimation of the population p with a bound of B units on the error of estimation implies that the experimenter wants

$$2\sqrt{V(\hat{p})} = B$$

This equation can be solved for n, and the solution is similar to equation (7.13). That is,

$$n = \frac{N\sigma_c^2}{ND + \sigma_c^2}$$

where $D = B^2 \bar{M}^2/4$, and σ_c^2 is estimated by

$$s_c^2 = \frac{\sum_{i=1}^{n}(a_i - \hat{p}m_i)^2}{n-1} \qquad (7.21)$$

Equation (7.21) is equation (7.11) with y_i replaced by a_i and $\bar{y}$ by $\hat{p}$.

Example 7.10
The data in table 7.2 are out of date. A new study will be conducted in the same city for the purpose of estimating the proportion p of adult males who rent their homes. How large a sample should be taken to estimate p with a bound of .04 on the error of estimation?

Solution
The best estimate of σ_c^2 is s_c^2, which is calculated using data from table 7.2:

$$s_c^2 = \frac{\sum_{i=1}^{n}(a_i - \hat{p}m_i)^2}{n-1} = \frac{12.729}{24} = .530$$

$\bar{M}$ is estimated by $\bar{m} = 6.04$. Also, D is approximated by

$$\frac{B^2 \bar{m}^2}{4} = \frac{(.04)^2(6.04)^2}{4} = .0146$$

Then

$$n = \frac{N\sigma_c^2}{ND + \sigma_c^2} = \frac{(415)(.530)}{(415)(.0146) + .530} = 33.40$$

Thus 34 clusters should be sampled to estimate p with a bound of .04 on the error of estimation.

7.7 CLUSTER SAMPLING COMBINED WITH STRATIFICATION

As is the case with all other sampling methods, cluster sampling can be combined with stratified sampling, in the sense that the population may be divided into L strata and a cluster sample can then be selected from each stratum.

Recall that equation (7.1) has the form of a ratio estimator and can be thought of as the ratio of an estimator of the average cluster total to an estimator of the average cluster size. Thinking in terms of ratio estimators, then, there are two ways to form the estimator of a population mean across strata, the separate estimator and the combined estimator. A little investigation will show that, if the separate estimator is employed, the total number of elements in each stratum must be known in order to assign proper stratum weights. Since these quantities are usually unknown, we will investigate only the combined form of the ratio estimator in the context of cluster sampling.

Instead of presenting formidable-looking general formulas, we will illustrate the technique with a numerical example.

Example 7.11
Let the data of table 7.1 form the sample of stratum 1, with, as in example 7.2, $N_1 = 415$ and $n_1 = 25$. A smaller neighboring city is taken to be stratum 2. For stratum 2, $n_2 = 10$ blocks are to be sampled from $N_2 = 168$. Estimate the average income per adult male in the two cities combined, and place a bound on the error of estimation, given the additional data shown in the accompanying table.

Cluster i	Number of Adult Males m_i	Total Income per Cluster y_i
1	2	$18,000
2	5	52,000
3	7	68,000
4	4	36,000
5	3	45,000
6	8	96,000
7	6	64,000
8	10	115,000
9	3	41,000
10	1	12,000

Solution
The average cluster totals in the respective samples are $\bar{y}_{t1} = 53,160$ and $\bar{y}_{t2} = 54,700$. The average cluster sizes in the

7. Cluster Sampling

respective samples are $\bar{m}_1 = 6.04$ and $\bar{m}_2 = 4.90$. The estimate of the population average cluster total is then

$$\frac{1}{N}[N_1\bar{y}_{t1} + N_2\bar{y}_{t2}]$$

while the estimate of the average cluster size is

$$\frac{1}{N}[N_1\bar{m}_1 + N_2\bar{m}_2]$$

An estimate of the population mean per element is then

$$\bar{y}^* = \frac{N_1\bar{y}_{t1} + N_2\bar{y}_{t2}}{N_1\bar{m}_1 + N_2\bar{m}_2}$$

and this does have the form of a combined ratio estimate. Analogous to that used in section 6.6, the variance of $\bar{y}^*$ can be estimated by

$$\hat{V}(\bar{y}^*) = \frac{1}{M^2}\left[N_1^2 \frac{N_1 - n_1}{N_1 n_1(n_1 - 1)} \sum_{i=1}^{n_1} (y_i - \bar{y}^* m_i)^2 + N_2^2 \frac{N_2 - n_2}{N_2 n_2(n_2 - 1)} \sum_{i=1}^{n_2} (y_i - \bar{y}^* m_i)^2\right]$$

where M is the total number of elements in the population and can be estimated by $N_1\bar{m}_1 + N_2\bar{m}_2$ if it is not known. The first sum in the variance expression is over all the sample observations from stratum 1, and the second sum is over all the observations from stratum 2.

For the data given in the table,

$$\bar{y}^* = \frac{415(53{,}160) + 168(54{,}700)}{415(6.04) + 168(4.90)} = 9{,}385.25$$

For stratum 1,

$$\left(\frac{1}{n_1 - 1}\right) \sum_{i=1}^{n_1} (y_i - \bar{y}^* m_i)^2$$

$$= \left[\sum_{i=1}^{n_1} y_i^2 - 2\bar{y}^* \sum_{i=1}^{n_1} y_i m_i + (\bar{y}^*)^2 \sum_{i=1}^{n_1} m_i^2\right]\left(\frac{1}{n_1 - 1}\right)$$

$$= 688{,}887{,}395.63$$

and for stratum 2,

$$\left(\frac{1}{n_2 - 1}\right) \sum_{i=1}^{n_2} (y_i - \bar{y}^* m_i)^2 = 159{,}272{,}377.65$$

It follows that, with $N_1\bar{m}_1 + N_2\bar{m}_2 = 3{,}329.8$

$$\hat{V}(\bar{y}^*) = 745{,}341.75$$

7.8 Summary

and

$$2\sqrt{\hat{V}(\bar{y}^*)} = 1{,}726.66$$

Thus we see a bound on the error of about the same magnitude as found in example 7.2 for stratum 1 alone.

7.8 SUMMARY

This chapter introduces a third sample survey design, cluster sampling. In this design each sampling unit is a group, or cluster, of elements. Cluster sampling may provide maximum information at minimum cost when a frame listing population elements is not available or when the cost of obtaining observations increases with increasing distance between elements.

The estimator of the population mean μ is the sample mean $\bar{y}$, given by equation (7.1). The estimated variance of $\bar{y}$ is given by equation (7.2). Two estimators of the population total τ are given with their estimated variances. The estimator $M\bar{y}$ is presented in equation (7.4); it is used when the number of elements M in the population is known. $N\bar{y}_t$ [see equation (7.8)] is used when M is unknown.

In section 7.4 we discuss an appropriate sample size for estimating μ or τ with a specified bound on the error of estimation.

In cluster sampling the estimator of a population proportion p is the sample proportion $\hat{p}$, given by equation (7.18). The estimated variance of $\hat{p}$ is given by equation (7.19). The problem of selecting a sample size for estimating a proportion is similar to the problem for estimating a mean.

Cluster sampling can also be used within strata in a stratified population, and an example of this is given in section 7.7.

REFERENCES

Cochran, W. G. *Sampling Techniques.* 3d ed. New York: Wiley, 1977.

Hansen, M. H.; Hurwitz, W. N.; and Madow, W. G. *Sample Survey Methods and Theory*, vol. 1. New York: Wiley, 1953.

Kish, L. *Survey Sampling.* New York: Wiley, 1965.

EXERCISES

7.1 An experimenter working in an urban area desires to estimate the average value of a variable highly correlated with race. She thinks she should use cluster sampling, with city blocks as clusters and adults within blocks as

7. Cluster Sampling

elements. Explain why you would, or would not, use cluster sampling in each of the following situations:
(a) Most of the adults in certain blocks are white and most in other blocks are nonwhite.
(b) The proportion of nonwhites is the same in every block and is not close to zero or one.
(c) The proportion of nonwhites differs from block to block in the manner that would be expected if the clusters were made up by randomly assigning adults in the population to clusters.

7.2 A manufacturer of band saws wants to estimate the average repair cost per month for the saws he has sold to certain industries. He cannot obtain a repair cost for each saw, but he can obtain the total amount spent for saw repairs and the number of saws owned by each industry. Thus he decides to use cluster sampling with each industry as a cluster. The manufacturer selects a simple random sample of $n = 20$ from the $N = 96$ industries he services. The data on total cost of repairs per industry and number of saws per industry are as given in the table. Estimate the average repair cost per saw for the past month, and place a bound on the error of estimation.

Industry	Number of Saws	Total Repair Cost for Past Month (dollars)
1	3	50
2	7	110
3	11	230
4	9	140
5	2	60
6	12	280
7	14	240
8	3	45
9	5	60
10	9	230
11	8	140
12	6	130
13	3	70
14	2	50
15	1	10
16	4	60
17	12	280
18	6	150
19	5	110
20	8	120

7.3 For the data in exercise 7.2, estimate the total amount spent by the 96 industries on band saw repairs. Place a bound on the error of estimation.

7.4 After checking his sales records, the manufacturer of exercise 7.2 finds that he sold a total of 710 band saws to these industries. Using this additional

Exercises

information, estimate the total amount spent on saw repairs by these industries and place a bound on the error of estimation.

7.5 The same manufacturer (exercise 7.2) wants to estimate the average repair cost per saw for next month. How many clusters should he select for his sample if he wants the bound on the error of estimation to be less than $2.00?

7.6 A political scientist developed a test designed to measure the degree of awareness of current events. She wants to estimate the average score that would be achieved on this test by all students in a certain high school. The administration at the school would not allow the experimenter to randomly select students out of classes in session, but it would allow her to interrupt a small number of classes for the purpose of giving the test to every member of the class. Thus the experimenter selects 25 classes at random from the 108 classes in session at a particular hour. The test is given to each member of the sampled classes with results as shown in the table. Estimate the average score that would be achieved on this test by all students in the school. Place a bound on the error of estimation.

Class	Number of Students	Total Score	Class	Number of Students	Total Score
1	31	1590	14	40	1980
2	29	1510	15	38	1990
3	25	1490	16	28	1420
4	35	1610	17	17	900
5	15	800	18	22	1080
6	31	1720	19	41	2010
7	22	1310	20	32	1740
8	27	1427	21	35	1750
9	25	1290	22	19	890
10	19	860	23	29	1470
11	30	1620	24	18	910
12	18	710	25	31	1740
13	21	1140			

7.7 The same political scientist of exercise 7.6 wants to estimate the average test score for a similar high school. If she wants the bound on the error of estimation to be less than 2 points, how many classes should she sample? Assume the school has 100 classes in session during each hour.

7.8 An industry is considering revision of its retirement policy and wants to estimate the proportion of employees that favor the new policy. The industry consists of 87 separate plants located throughout the United States. Since results must be obtained quickly and with little cost, the industry decides to use cluster sampling with each plant as a cluster. A simple random sample of 15 plants is selected, and the opinions of the employees in these plants are obtained by questionnaire. The results are as shown in the table. Estimate the proportion of employees in the industry who favor the new retirement policy, and place a bound on the error of estimation.

7. Cluster Sampling

Plant	Number of Employees	Number Favoring New Policy	Plant	Number of Employees	Number Favoring New Policy
1	51	42	9	73	54
2	62	53	10	61	45
3	49	40	11	58	51
4	73	45	12	52	29
5	101	63	13	65	46
6	48	31	14	49	37
7	65	38	15	55	42
8	49	30			

7.9 The industry of exercise 7.8 modified its retirement policy after obtaining the results of the survey. It now wants to estimate the proportion of employees in favor of the modified policy. How many plants should be sampled to have a bound of .08 on the error of estimation? Use the data from exercise 7.8 to approximate the results of the new survey.

7.10 An economic survey is designed to estimate the average amount spent on utilities for households in a city. Since no list of households is available, cluster sampling is used with divisions (wards) forming the clusters. A simple random sample of 20 wards is selected from the 60 wards of the city. Interviewers then obtain the cost of utilities from each household within the sampled wards; the total costs are shown in the table. Estimate the average amount a household in the city spends on utilities, and place a bound on the error of estimation.

Sampled Ward	Number of Households	Total Amount Spent on Utilities	Sampled Ward	Number of Households	Total Amount Spent on Utilities
1	55	$2210	11	73	$2930
2	60	2390	12	64	2470
3	63	2430	13	69	2830
4	58	2380	14	58	2370
5	71	2760	15	63	2390
6	78	3110	16	75	2870
7	69	2780	17	78	3210
8	58	2370	18	51	2430
9	52	1990	19	67	2730
10	71	2810	20	70	2880

7.11 In the survey of exercise 7.10, the number of households in the city is not known. Estimate the total amount spent on utilities for all households in the city, and place a bound on the error of estimation.

7.12 The economic survey of exercise 7.10 is to be performed in a neighboring city of similar structure. The objective is to estimate the total amount spent on utilities by households in the city with a bound of $5000 on the error of

Exercises

estimation. Use the data in exercise 7.10 to find the approximate number of clusters needed to achieve this bound.

7.13 An inspector wants to estimate the average weight of fill for cereal boxes packaged in a certain factory. The cereal is available to him in cartons containing 12 boxes each. The inspector randomly selects 5 cartons and measures the weight of fill for every box in the sampled cartons, with the results (in ounces) as shown in the table. Estimate the average weight of fill for boxes packaged by this factory, and place a bound on the error of estimation. Assume that the total number of cartons packaged by the factory is large enough for the finite population correction to be ignored.

Carton	Ounces of Fill
1	16.1 15.9 16.1 16.2 15.9 15.8 16.1 16.2 16.0 15.9 15.8 16.0
2	15.9 16.2 15.8 16.0 16.3 16.1 15.8 15.9 16.0 16.1 16.1 15.9
3	16.2 16.0 15.7 16.3 15.8 16.0 15.9 16.0 16.1 16.0 15.9 16.1
4	15.9 16.1 16.2 16.1 16.1 16.3 15.9 16.1 15.9 15.9 16.0 16.0
5	16.0 15.8 16.3 15.7 16.1 15.9 16.0 16.1 15.8 16.0 16.1 15.9

7.14 A newspaper wants to estimate the proportion of voters favoring a certain candidate, "candidate A," in a statewide election. Since it is very expensive to select and interview a simple random sample of registered voters, cluster sampling is used, with precincts as clusters. A simple random sample of 50 precincts is selected from the 497 precincts in the state. The newspaper wants to make the estimation on election day but before final returns are tallied. Therefore, reporters are sent to the polls of each sample precinct to obtain the pertinent information directly from the voters. The results are shown in the table. Estimate the proportion of voters favoring candidate A, and place a bound on the error of estimation.

Number of Voters	Number Favoring A	Number of Voters	Number Favoring A	Number of Voters	Number Favoring A
1290	680	1893	1143	843	321
1170	631	1942	1187	1066	487
840	475	971	542	1171	596
1620	935	1143	973	1213	782
1381	472	2041	1541	1741	980
1492	820	2530	1679	983	693
1785	933	1567	982	1865	1033
2010	1171	1493	863	1888	987
974	542	1271	742	1947	872
832	457	1873	1010	2021	1093
1247	983	2142	1092	2001	1461
1896	1462	2380	1242	1493	1301
1943	873	1693	973	1783	1167
798	372	1661	652	1461	932
1020	621	1555	523	1237	481
1141	642	1492	831	1843	999
1820	975	1957	932		

7. Cluster Sampling

7.15 The newspaper of exercise 7.14 wants to conduct a similar survey during the next election. How large a sample size will be needed to estimate the proportion of voters favoring a similar candidate with a bound of .05 on the error of estimation? Use the data in exercise 7.14.

7.16 A forester wishes to estimate the average height of trees on a plantation. The plantation is divided into quarter-acre plots. A simple random sample of 20 plots is selected from the 386 plots on the plantation. All trees on the sampled plots are measured, with the results as shown in the table. Estimate the average height of trees on the plantation, and place a bound on the error of estimation. (Hint: The total for cluster i can be found by taking m_i times the cluster average.)

Number of Trees	Average Height (in feet)	Number of Trees	Average Height (in feet)
42	6.2	60	6.3
51	5.8	52	6.7
49	6.7	61	5.9
55	4.9	49	6.1
47	5.2	57	6.0
58	6.9	63	4.9
43	4.3	45	5.3
59	5.2	46	6.7
48	5.7	62	6.1
41	6.1	58	7.0

7.17 To emphasize safety, a taxicab company wants to estimate the proportion of unsafe tires on their 175 cabs. (Ignore spare tires.) It is impractical to select a simple random sample of tires, so cluster sampling is used, with each cab as a cluster. A random sample of 25 cabs gives the following number of unsafe tires per cab:

2, 4, 0, 1, 2, 0, 4, 1, 3, 1, 2, 0, 1,
1, 2, 2, 4, 1, 0, 0, 3, 1, 2, 2, 1

Estimate the proportion of unsafe tires being used on the company's cabs, and place a bound on the error of estimation.

7.18 Accountants frequently require their business clients to provide cost inventories. Since a complete inventory is costly, quarterly inventories can conveniently be accomplished by sampling. Suppose a plumbing supply firm desires a cost inventory for many small items in stock. It would be difficult to obtain a simple random sample of items. However, the items are arranged on shelves and it is relatively easy to select a simple random sample of shelves, treating each shelf as a cluster of items. Sampling 10 of the 48 shelves gave the results shown in the table. Estimate the total dollar amount of the items on the shelves, and place a bound on the error of estimation.

Exercises

Cluster	Number of Items m_i	Total Dollar Amount y_i
1	42	83
2	27	62
3	38	45
4	63	112
5	72	96
6	12	58
7	24	75
8	14	58
9	32	67
10	41	80

7.19 A certain firm specializing in the manufacture and sale of leisure clothing has 80 retail stores in Florida and 140 in California. Treating each state as a stratum, it is desired to estimate average sick leave time per employee for the past year. Each outlet can be viewed as a cluster of employees, and total sick leave time for each store can be determined from records. Simple random samples of 8 stores from Florida and 10 stores from California gave the results shown in the table (m_i denotes number of employees and y_i denotes total days sick leave for the ith store). Estimate the average amount of sick leave per employee, and calculate an estimate of the variance of your estimator.

Florida m_i	Florida y_i	California m_i	California y_i
12	40	16	51
20	52	8	32
8	30	4	11
14	36	3	10
24	71	12	33
15	48	17	39
10	39	24	61
6	21	30	37
		21	40
		9	41

EXPERIENCES WITH REAL DATA

1. Table 7.3 shows presidential election results for 1972 and 1976. Treating each state as a cluster of votes, estimate the proportion of voters favoring Carter in 1976 by selecting a simple random sample of $n = 10$ states. Place a bound on the error of estimation, and compare your estimate with the true proportion from the final vote count listed.

Table 7.3 / Presidential election statistics, popular and electoral vote, 1972 and 1976

States	Electoral Vote 1972 Nixon	Electoral Vote 1972 McGovern	Republican Nixon	Democrat McGovern	Electoral Vote Carter	Electoral Vote Ford	Democrat Carter	Republican 1976 Ford	Indep. McCarthy	Libert. MacBride
Ala.	9		728,701	256,923	9		659,170	504,070		1,481
Alas.	3		55,349	32,967		3	44,058	71,555		6,785
Ariz.	6		402,812	198,540		6	295,602	418,642	19,229	7,647
Ark.	6		445,751	198,889	6		498,604	267,903	639	
Cal.	45		4,602,096	3,475,847		45	3,742,284	3,882,244		56,388
Col.	7		597,189	329,980		7	460,801	584,278	26,047	5,338
Conn.	8		810,763	555,498		8	647,895	719,261		
Del.	3		140,357	92,298	3		122,461	109,780	2,432	
D.C.		3	35,226	127,627	3		137,818	27,873		274
Fla.	17		1,857,759	718,117	17		1,636,000	1,469,531	23,643	
Ga.	12		881,496	289,529	12		979,409	483,743		3,923
Ha.	4		168,865	101,409	4		147,375	140,003		3,558
Ida.	4		199,384	80,826		4	126,549	204,151		8,057
Ill.	26		2,788,179	1,913,472		26	2,271,295	2,364,269	55,939	
Ind.	13		1,405,154	708,568		13	1,014,714	1,185,958		
Iowa	8		706,207	496,206		8	619,931	632,863	20,051	1,452
Kan.	7		619,812	270,287		7	430,421	502,752	13,185	3,242
Ky.	9		676,446	371,159	9		615,717	531,852	6,837	814
La.	10		686,852	298,142	10		661,365	587,446	6,490	3,134
Maine	4		256,458	160,584		4	232,279	236,320	10,874	
Md.	10		829,305	505,781	10		759,612	672,661	20,051	135
Mass.		14	1,112,078	1,332,540	14		1,429,475	1,030,276	65,637	
Mich.	21		1,961,721	1,459,435		21	1,696,714	1,893,742	47,905	5,407
Minn.	10		898,269	802,346	10		1,070,440	819,395	35,490	3,529
Miss.	7		505,125	126,872	7		381,329	366,846	4,074	2,609
Mo.	12		1,154,058	698,531	12		998,387	927,443	24,029	
Mont.	4		183,976	120,197		4	149,259	173,703		1,476
Neb.	5		406,298	169,991		5	233,293	359,219	9,383	1,519
Nev.	3		115,750	66,016		3	92,479	101,273		

State									
N.H.	4		213,724	116,435	4	147,645	185,935	4,095	936
N.J.	17		1,845,502	1,102,211	17	1,444,653	1,509,688	32,717	9,449
N.M.	4		235,606	141,084	4	201,148	211,419		1,110
N.Y.	41		4,192,778	2,951,084	41	3,389,558	3,100,791		12,197
N.C.	13		1,054,889	438,705	13	927,365	741,960		2,219
N.D.	3		174,109	100,384	3	136,078	153,684	2,952	256
Oh.	25		2,441,827	1,558,889	25	2,009,959	2,000,626	58,267	8,952
Okla.	8		759,025	247,147	8	532,442	545,708	14,101	
Ore.	6		486,686	392,760	6	490,407	492,120	40,207	
Pa.	27		2,714,521	1,796,951	27	2,328,677	2,205,604	50,584	
R.I.	4		218,290	191,981	4	227,636	181,249		715
S.C.	8		477,044	186,824	8	450,807	346,149		
S.D.	4		166,476	139,945	4	147,068	151,505		1,619
Tenn.	10		813,147	357,293	10	825,879	633,969	5,004	1,375
Tex.	26		2,298,896	1,154,289	26	2,082,319	1,953,300	20,118	
Ut.	4		323,643	126,284	4	182,110	337,908	3,907	
Vt.	3		117,149	68,174	3	77,798	100,387	4,001	2,438
Va.	11*		988,493	438,887	12	813,896	836,554		4,648
Wash.	9		837,135	568,334	8**	717,323	777,732	36,986	5,042
W.Va.	6		484,964	277,435	6	435,864	314,726		
Wis.	11		989,430	810,174	11	1,040,232	1,004,987	34,943	3,814
Wyo.	3		100,464	44,358	3	62,239	92,717	624	89
TOTAL	520	17	47,165,234	28,168,110	297	40,825,829	39,147,770	680,390	17,162,700

Source: The World Almanac & Book of Facts, 1978 Edition; Copyright © Newspaper Enterprise Association, Inc., New York, 1977, p. 256.
*One elector in Virginia for John Hospers and Theodora Nathan. **One elector in Washington for Reagan.

7. Cluster Sampling

2. Per capita personal income in the United States is given in table 7.4 by states and regions. Referring to table 5.4, population figures for the states can be found for 1970. Thus the total personal income can be obtained for each state. Treating regions as strata and states as clusters of individuals, use stratified cluster sampling to estimate the total personal income for the United States for 1970. Place a bound on the error of estimation. Keep the sample sizes small, and note that one region has only four states.

Table 7.4/*Per capita personal income, by states and regions*

State and Region	1970	1972	1973	1974	1975
United States	3966	4537	5049	5486	5902
New England	4300	4783	5227	5668	6098
Connecticut	4917	5382	5929	6487	6973
Maine	3302	3693	4158	4536	4786
Massachusetts	4340	4854	5262	5667	6114
New Hampshire	3737	4183	4633	4986	5315
Rhode Island	3959	4509	4873	5355	5841
Vermont	3468	3884	4296	4602	4960
Mideast	4471	5044	5479	5968	6433
Delaware	4524	5225	5846	6284	6748
Dist. of Columbia	5079	5924	6420	7043	7742
Maryland	4309	4970	5453	5973	6474
New Jersey	4701	5303	5718	6242	6722
New York	4712	5248	5657	6120	6564
Pennsylvania	3971	4530	4989	5485	5943
Great Lakes	4135	4751	5311	5731	6121
Illinois	4507	5131	5750	6268	6789
Indiana	3772	4370	4959	5295	5653
Michigan	4180	4950	5509	5846	6173
Ohio	4020	4568	5063	5481	5810
Wisconsin	3812	4290	4831	5281	5669
Plains	3751	4318	5115	5364	5785
Iowa	3751	4297	5344	5561	6077
Kansas	3853	4540	5276	5615	6023
Minnesota	3859	4328	5112	5469	5807
Missouri	3781	4293	4794	5065	5510
Nebraska	3789	4441	5251	5379	6087
North Dakota	3086	4015	5768	5698	5737
South Dakota	3123	3790	4957	4860	4924
Southeast	3257	3859	4346	4740	5055
Alabama	2948	3472	3905	4284	4643
Arkansas	2878	3343	3952	4379	4620
Florida	3738	4510	5107	5406	5638
Georgia	3354	3968	4441	4798	5086
Kentucky	3112	3608	4048	4565	4871
Louisiana	3090	3573	3961	4456	4904
Mississippi	2626	3186	3579	3837	4052
North Carolina	3252	3853	4300	4649	4952
South Carolina	2990	3507	3972	4390	4618

Experiences with Real Data

Table 7.4/*(continued)*

State and Region	1970	1972	1973	1974	1975
Tennessee	3119	3708	4206	4567	4895
Virginia	3712	4400	4902	5377	5785
West Virginia	3061	3602	3989	4480	4918
Southwest	3546	4051	4567	5019	5487
Arizona	3665	4333	4833	5152	5355
New Mexico	3077	3518	3927	4299	4775
Oklahoma	3387	3834	4336	4823	5250
Texas	3606	4102	4632	5106	5631
Rocky Mountain	3590	4214	4785	5222	5576
Colorado	3855	4610	5137	5549	5985
Idaho	3290	3786	4489	5140	5159
Montana	3500	4070	4781	5079	5422
Utah	3227	3741	4186	4539	4923
Wyoming	3815	4276	4945	5644	6131
Far West	4374	4924	5403	5976	6481
California	4493	5044	5497	6089	6593
Nevada	4563	5138	5742	6161	6647
Oregon	3719	4328	4848	5398	5769
Washington	4053	4558	5146	5646	6247
Alaska	4644	5192	6005	7037	9448
Hawaii	4623	5123	5570	6010	6658

Source: The World Almanac & Book of Facts, 1977 Edition; Copyright © Newspaper Enterprise Association, Inc., New York, 1976, p. 127.

3. Try an economic study, perhaps by treating households in a certain fixed geographic area (perhaps a few city blocks) as clusters of people. Sample n households and, upon gaining permission for an interview, record the total weekly amount spent on food by all individuals in the household and the number of individuals. Then estimate the average amount spent on food per person among the households in this population. Even if all the money is actually spent by one person (say, the mother), that total amount is the same as would have been recorded if each individual had purchased his or her own food. Thus the cluster total is available even though the observations per element may not be.

8.
Systematic Sampling

8.1 INTRODUCTION

The final sample survey design discussed in this text is *systematic sampling*.

Definition 8.1 A sample obtained by randomly selecting one element from the first k elements in the frame and every kth element thereafter is called a *one-in-k systematic sample*.

As in previous chapters, we present methods for estimating a population mean, total, and proportion. We will also discuss appropriate bounds on the error of estimation and sample-size requirements.

Systematic sampling provides a useful alternative to simple random sampling for the following reasons:

1. Systematic sampling is easier to perform and hence is less subject to interviewer errors than simple random sampling.

2. Systematic sampling often provides greater information per unit cost than does simple random sampling.

In general, systematic sampling involves random selection of one element from the first k elements and then selection of every kth element thereafter. This procedure is easier to perform and usually less subject to interviewer error than is simple random sampling. For example, it would

8. Systematic Sampling

be difficult to use simple random sampling to select a sample of $n = 50$ shoppers on a city street corner. The interviewer could not determine which shoppers to include in the sample, because the population size N would not be known until all shoppers had passed the corner. In contrast, the interviewer could take a systematic sample (say 1 in 20 shoppers) until the required sample size was obtained. This would be an easy procedure for even an inexperienced interviewer to follow.

In addition to being easier to perform and less subject to interviewer error, systematic sampling *frequently* provides more information per unit cost than does simple random sampling. A systematic sample is *frequently* spread more uniformly over the entire population and thus can provide more information about the population than an equivalent amount of data contained in a simple random sample. Consider the following illustration: We wish to select a 1-in-5 systematic sample of travel vouchers from a stack of $N = 1000$ (that is, sample $n = 200$ vouchers) to determine the proportion of vouchers filed incorrectly. A voucher is drawn at random from the first 5 vouchers (for example, No. 3), and every fifth voucher thereafter is included in the sample. (See the accompanying table.)

Voucher	Voucher Sampled
1	
2	
3	3
4	
5	
6	
7	
8	8
9	
10	
⋮	⋮
996	
997	
998	998
999	
1000	

Suppose that most of the first 500 vouchers have been correctly filed but, due to a change in clerks, the second 500 have all been incorrectly filed. Simple random sampling could accidentally select a large number (perhaps all) of the 200 vouchers from either the first or the second 500 vouchers and hence yield a very poor estimate of p. In

8.2 How to Draw a Systematic Sample

contrast, systematic sampling would select an equal number of vouchers from each of the two groups and would give a very accurate estimate of the fraction of vouchers incorrectly filed.

Additional examples are discussed in section 8.3 to illustrate how to choose between systematic and simple random sampling in a given situation.

8.2 HOW TO DRAW A SYSTEMATIC SAMPLE

Although simple random sampling and systematic sampling both provide useful alternatives to one another, the methods of selecting the sample data are different. A simple random sample from a population is selected by using a table of random numbers, as noted in section 4.3. In contrast, various methods are possible in systematic sampling. The investigator can select a 1-in-3, a 1-in-5, or, in general, a 1-in-k systematic sample. For example, a medical investigator is interested in obtaining information about the average number of times 15,000 specialists prescribed a certain drug in the previous year ($N = 15,000$). To obtain a simple random sample of $n = 1,600$ specialists, we would use the methods of section 4.3 and refer to a table of random numbers; however, this would require a great deal of work. Alternatively, we could select one name (specialist) at random from the first $k = 9$ names appearing on the list, and then select every ninth name thereafter until a simple size 1,600 is selected. This is called a *1-in-9 systematic sample.*

Perhaps you wonder how k is chosen in a given situation. If the population size N is known, we can determine an approximate sample size n for the survey (see section 8.5) and then choose k to achieve that sample size. There are $N = 15,000$ specialists in the population for the medical survey. Suppose the required sample size is $n = 100$. We must then choose k to be 150 or less. For $k = 150$, we would obtain exactly $n = 100$ observations, while for $k < 150$, the sample size would be greater than 100.

In general, to obtain a systematic sample of n elements from a population of size N, k must be less than or equal to N/n (that is, $k \leq N/n$). Note in the preceding example that $k \leq 15,000/100$; that is, $k \leq 150$.

We cannot accurately choose k when the population size is unknown. We can determine an approximate sample size n, but we must guess the value of k needed to achieve a sample of size n. If too large a value of k is chosen, the required sample size n will not be obtained using a 1-in-k systematic sample from the population. This presents no problem if the experimenter can return to the population and conduct another 1-in-k systematic sample until the required sample size is obtained. However, in some situations it is impossible to start a second

8. Systematic Sampling

systematic sample. For example, it would be impossible to conduct another 1-in-20 systematic sample of shoppers if the required sample of $n = 50$ shoppers is not obtained at the time they pass the corner.

8.3 ESTIMATION OF A POPULATION MEAN AND TOTAL

As we have repeatedly stressed, the objective of most sample surveys is to estimate one or more population parameters. We can estimate a population mean μ from a systematic sample using the sample mean $\bar{y}$. This is shown in equation (8.1).

Estimator of the population mean μ:

$$\hat{\mu} = \bar{y}_{sy} = \frac{\sum_{i=1}^{n} y_i}{n} \qquad (8.1)$$

where the subscript sy signifies that systematic sampling was used.

Estimated variance of $\bar{y}_{sy}$:

$$\hat{V}(\bar{y}_{sy}) = \left(\frac{N-n}{N}\right)\left(\frac{s^2}{n}\right) \qquad (8.2)$$

Bound on the error of estimation:

$$2\sqrt{\hat{V}(\bar{y}_{sy})} = 2\sqrt{\left(\frac{N-n}{N}\right)\left(\frac{s^2}{n}\right)} \qquad (8.3)$$

If N is unknown, we eliminate the *fpc*, $(N-n)/N$, in equations (8.2) and (8.3).

You will recognize that the estimated variance of $\bar{y}_{sy}$ given in equation (8.2) is identical to the estimated variance of $\bar{y}$ obtained using simple random sampling (section 4.3). This does not imply that the corresponding population variances are equal. The variance of $\bar{y}$ is given by

$$V(\bar{y}) = \frac{\sigma^2}{n}\left(\frac{N-n}{N-1}\right) \qquad (8.4)$$

Similarly, it can be shown that the variance of $\bar{y}_{sy}$ is given by

$$V(\bar{y}_{sy}) = \frac{\sigma^2}{n}[1 + (n-1)\rho] \qquad (8.5)$$

8.3 Estimation of a Population Mean and Total

where ρ is a measure of the correlation between pairs of elements within the same systematic sample. If ρ is close to one, then the elements within the sample are all quite similar with respect to the characteristic being measured, and systematic sampling will yield a higher variance of the sample mean than will simple random sampling. If ρ is negative, then systematic sampling may be better than simple random sampling. This would be the case if elements within the systematic sample tended to be extremely different. (Note that ρ cannot be so large negatively that the variance expression becomes negative.) For ρ close to zero and N fairly large, systematic sampling is roughly equivalent to simple random sampling.

Let us look briefly at the relationship between systematic sampling, cluster sampling, and stratified random sampling. Think, first, of the $N = nk$ population elements as a collection of k clusters containing n elements each. Then the systematic sample can be thought of as a cluster sampling situation in which only one cluster is sampled. As we saw in chapter 7, the clusters should be kept as heterogeneous as possible, and that same idea carries over to systematic sampling.

On the other hand, think of the $N = nk$ population elements as divided into n strata of k elements each, and the systematic sample as approximately equivalent to taking one observation from each stratum. Again, the strata should be kept homogeneous within but there should be wide variation from stratum to stratum. This would result in a sample containing highly variable elements, which is the ideal case for systematic sampling.

An unbiased estimate of $V(\bar{y}_{sy})$ cannot be obtained by using the data from only one systematic sample. This does not imply that we can never obtain an estimate of $V(\bar{y}_{sy})$. When systematic sampling is equivalent to simple random sampling, we can take $V(\bar{y}_{sy})$ to be approximately equal to the estimated variance of $\bar{y}$ based on simple random sampling.

For which populations does this relationship occur? To answer this question we must consider the following three types of populations:

1. random population
2. ordered population
3. periodic population

Definition 8.2 A population is *random* if the elements of the population are in random order.

Elements of a systematic sample drawn from a random population are expected to be heterogeneous with ρ approximately equal to zero. Thus when N is large, the variance of $\bar{y}_{sy}$ is approximately equal to the variance of $\bar{y}$ based on simple random sampling. Systematic sampling in

8. Systematic Sampling

this case is equivalent to simple random sampling. For example, an investigator wishes to determine the average number of prescriptions written by certain doctors during the previous year. If the frame consists of a current alphabetical listing of doctors, it is reasonable to assume that the names on the list are unrelated to the number of prescriptions written for a particular drug. Hence we consider the population random. A systematic sample would be equivalent to a simple random sample in this case.

Definition 8.3 A population is *ordered* if the elements within the population are ordered in magnitude according to some scheme.

In a survey to estimate the effectiveness of instruction in a large introductory course, students are asked to evaluate their instructor according to a numerical scale. A sample is then drawn from a list of evaluations that are arranged in ascending numerical order. The population of measurements from which the sample is drawn is considered an *ordered* population.

A systematic sample drawn from an ordered population is generally heterogeneous with $\rho \leq 0$. It can be shown, using equations (8.4) and (8.5), that when N is large and $\rho \leq 0$,

$$V(\bar{y}_{sy}) \leq V(\bar{y})$$

Thus a systematic sample from an ordered population provides more information per unit cost than does a simple random sample, because the variance of $\bar{y}_{sy}$ is less than the corresponding variance of $\bar{y}$.

Since we cannot obtain an estimate of $V(\bar{y}_{sy})$ from the sample data, a conservative estimate (one that is larger than we would expect) of $V(\bar{y}_{sy})$ is given by

$$\hat{V}(\bar{y}_{sy}) = \frac{s^2}{n}\left(\frac{N-n}{N}\right)$$

Definition 8.4 A population is *periodic* if the elements of the population have cyclical variation.

Suppose we are interested in determining the average daily sales volume for a chain of grocery stores. The population of daily sales is clearly periodic, with peak sales occurring towards the end of each week. The effectiveness of a 1-in-k sample depends on the value we choose for k. If we sample daily sales every Wednesday, we would probably underestimate the true average daily sales volume. Similarly, if we sample sales every Friday, we would probably overestimate the true average sales. We might sample every ninth workday to avoid consistently sampling either the low or high sales days.

8.3 Estimation of a Population Mean and Total

Elements of a systematic sample drawn from a periodic population can be homogeneous (that is, $\rho > 0$). For example, the elements within a systematic sample of daily sales taken every Wednesday would be fairly homogeneous. It can be shown, using equations (8.4) and (8.5), that when N is large and $\rho > 0$,

$$V(\bar{y}_{sy}) > V(\bar{y})$$

Thus in this case systematic sampling provides less information per unit cost than does simple random sampling. As in the preceding situations, $V(\bar{y}_{sy})$ cannot be estimated directly using a single systematic sample. We can approximate its value using $\hat{V}(\bar{y})$ as for simple random sampling. In general, this should underestimate the true variance of $\bar{y}_{sy}$.

To avoid this problem that occurs with systematic sampling from a periodic population, the investigator could change the random starting point several times. This would reduce the possibility of choosing observations from the same relative position in a periodic population. For example, when a 1-in-10 systematic sample is being drawn from a long list of file cards, a card is randomly selected from the first 10 cards (for example, No. 2) and every tenth card thereafter. This procedure can be altered by randomly selecting a card from the first 10 (for example, No. 2) and every tenth card thereafter for perhaps 15 selections to obtain the numbers

$$2, 12, 22, \ldots, 152$$

At this point another random starting point can be selected from the next 10 numbers:

$$153, 154, 155, \ldots, 162$$

If 156 is selected, we then proceed to select every tenth number thereafter for the next 15 selections. This entire process would be repeated until the desired sample size is obtained.

The process of selecting a random starting point several times throughout the systematic sample has the effect of shuffling the elements of the population and then drawing a systematic sample. Hence we can assume that the sample obtained is equivalent to a systematic sample drawn from a random population. The variance of $\bar{y}_{sy}$ can then be approximated by using

$$\hat{V}(\bar{y}_{sy}) = \frac{s^2}{n}\left(\frac{N-n}{N}\right)$$

Example 8.1
An investigator wishes to determine the quality of maple syrup contained in the sap of trees on a Vermont farm. The total number of trees N is unknown; hence it is impossible to conduct

8. Systematic Sampling

a simple random sample of trees. As an alternative procedure, the investigator decides to use a 1-in-7 systematic sample. The data from this survey are listed in the table. Entries are the percentage of sugar content (in the sap) for the trees sampled. Use these data to estimate μ, the average sugar content of maple trees on the farm. Place a bound on the error of estimation.

Tree Sampled	Sugar Content of the Sap, y	y^2
1	82	6724
2	76	5776
3	83	6889
⋮	⋮	⋮
210	84	7056
211	80	6400
212	79	6241
	$\sum_{i=1}^{212} y_i = 17,066$	$\sum_{i=1}^{212} y_i^2 = 1,486,800$

Solution
An estimate of μ is given by

$$\bar{y}_{sy} = \frac{\sum_{i=1}^{n} y_i}{n} = \frac{17,066}{212} = 80.5$$

To find a bound on the error of estimation, we must first compute s^2. Using the computational formula,

$$s^2 = \frac{\sum y_i^2 - \frac{(\sum y_i)^2}{n}}{n-1} = \frac{1,486,800 - \frac{(17,066)^2}{212}}{211} = 535.483$$

Intuitively, it is reasonable to assume that the population of trees on the farm is random. Under this assumption, the estimated variance of $\bar{y}_{sy}$ is given by equation (8.2). Having conducted the 1-in-7 sample, we know N. Assuming $N = 1,484$,

$$\hat{V}(\bar{y}_{sy}) = \frac{s^2}{n}\left(\frac{N-n}{N}\right) = \frac{535.483}{212}\left(\frac{1,484 - 212}{1,484}\right) = 2.165$$

An approximate bound on the error of estimation is given by

$$2\sqrt{\hat{V}(\bar{y}_{sy})} \approx 2\sqrt{2.165} = 2.942$$

To summarize, we estimate the average sugar content of the sap to be 80.5%. We are quite confident that the bound on the error of estimation is less than 2.942%.

8.3 Estimation of a Population Mean and Total

You will recall that estimation of a population total requires knowledge of the total number of elements N in the population when using the procedures of chapters 4, 5, and 7. For example, we use

$$\hat{\tau} = N\bar{y}$$

as an estimator of τ based on simple random sampling. Also, we use

$$\hat{\tau}_{st} = \sum_{i=1}^{L} N_i \bar{y}_i$$

where

$$\sum_{i=1}^{L} N_i = N$$

as an estimator of τ based on stratified random sampling from L strata (section 5.3). Similarly, we need to know N to estimate τ using systematic sampling.

The population size is unknown in many practical situations, which suggests using systematic sampling; however, when N is known, we can estimate τ using equations (8.6), (8.7), and (8.8).

Estimator of the population total τ:

$$\hat{\tau} = N\bar{y}_{sy} \qquad (8.6)$$

Estimated variance of $\hat{\tau}$:

$$\hat{V}(N\bar{y}_{sy}) = N^2 \hat{V}(\bar{y}_{sy}) = N^2 \left(\frac{s^2}{n}\right)\left(\frac{N-n}{N}\right) \qquad (8.7)$$

Bound on the error of estimation:

$$2\sqrt{\hat{V}(N\bar{y}_{sy})} = 2\sqrt{N^2\left(\frac{s^2}{n}\right)\left(\frac{N-n}{N}\right)} \qquad (8.8)$$

Note that the results presented in equations (8.6), (8.7), and (8.8) are identical to those presented for estimating a population total under simple random sampling. This does not imply that the variance of $N\bar{y}_{sy}$ is the same as the variance of $N\bar{y}$. Again, we cannot obtain an unbiased estimator of $V(N\bar{y}_{sy})$ from the data in a single systematic sample. However, in certain circumstances, as noted earlier, systematic sampling is equivalent to simple random sampling, and we can use the results presented in section 4.3.

Example 8.2
A Virginia horticulturist has an experimental orchard of $N = 1300$ apple trees of a new variety under study. The investigator

8. Systematic Sampling

wishes to estimate the total yield (in bushels) from the orchard, based on a 1-in-10 systematic sample of trees. The sample mean and variance for the sampled trees are found to be $\bar{y}_{sy} = 3.52$ bushels and $s^2 = .48$ bushels. Use these data to estimate τ, and place a bound on the error of estimation.

Solution
It seems reasonable to assume that the population is random; hence systematic and simple random sampling are equivalent. If the population were periodic, the experimenter could choose several random starting points in selecting the trees to be included in the sample.

An estimate of τ is given by

$$N\bar{y}_{sy} = 1300(3.52) = 4576$$

A bound on the error of estimation can be found using equation (8.8) with $n = 130$.

$$2\sqrt{\hat{V}(N\bar{y}_{sy})} = 2\sqrt{N^2\left(\frac{s^2}{n}\right)\left(\frac{N-n}{N}\right)}$$

$$= 2\sqrt{1300^2\left(\frac{.48}{130}\right)\left(\frac{1300-130}{1300}\right)} = 149.88$$

Thus we estimate that the total yield from the apple orchard is 4576 bushels with a bound on the error of estimation of 149.88 bushels.

If it is advantageous to stratify the populations, systematic sampling can be used within each stratum in place of simple random sampling. Using the estimator of equation (8.1) with its estimated variance (8.2) within each stratum, the resulting estimator of the population mean would look similar to equation (5.1), with an estimated variance given by equation (5.2). Such a situation might arise if we were to stratify an industry by plants and then take a systematic sample of the records within each plant to estimate average accounts receivable, time lost to accidents, and so on.

8.4 ESTIMATION OF A POPULATION PROPORTION

An investigator frequently wishes to use data from a systematic sample to estimate a population proportion. For example, to determine the proportion of registered voters in favor of an upcoming bond issue, it would be convenient to use a 1-in-k systematic sample from the voter registration list.

8.4 Estimation of a Population Proportion

The estimator of the population proportion p obtained from systematic sampling is denoted by $\hat{p}_{sy}$. As in simple random sampling (section 4.5), the properties of $\hat{p}_{sy}$ parallel those of the sample mean $\bar{y}_{sy}$ if the response measurements are defined as follows: let $y_i = 0$ if the ith element sampled does not possess the specified characteristic and $y_i = 1$ if it does. The estimator $\hat{p}_{sy}$ is then the average of the 0 and 1 values from the sample.

Estimator of the population proportion p:

$$\hat{p}_{sy} = \bar{y}_{sy} = \frac{\sum_{i=1}^{n} y_i}{n} \tag{8.9}$$

Estimated variance of $\hat{p}_{sy}$:

$$\hat{V}(\hat{p}_{sy}) = \frac{\hat{p}_{sy}\hat{q}_{sy}}{n-1}\left(\frac{N-n}{N}\right) \tag{8.10}$$

where $\hat{q}_{sy} = 1 - \hat{p}_{sy}$.

Bound on the error of estimation:

$$2\sqrt{\hat{V}(\hat{p}_{sy})} = 2\sqrt{\frac{\hat{p}_{sy}\hat{q}_{sy}}{n-1}\left(\frac{N-n}{N}\right)} \tag{8.11}$$

We can ignore the *fpc*, $(N - n)/N$, in equations (8.10) and (8.11) if the population size N is unknown but can be assumed large relative to n.

We again note that the estimated variance of $\hat{p}_{sy}$ (or $\bar{y}_{sy}$) is identical to the estimated variance of $\hat{p}$ (or $\bar{y}$) using simple random sampling (section 4.5). This does not imply that the corresponding population variances are equal; however, if N is large, and if the observations within a systematic sample are unrelated (that is, $\rho = 0$), the two population variances will be equal.

Example 8.3
A 1-in-6 systematic sample is obtained from a voter registration list to estimate the proportion of voters in favor of the proposed bond issue. Several different random starting points are used to insure that the results of the sample are not affected by periodic variation in the population. The coded results of this preelection survey are as shown in the table. Estimate p, the proportion of the 5775 registered voters in favor of the proposed bond issue ($N = 5775$). Place a bound on the error of estimation.

8. Systematic Sampling

Voter	Response
4	1
10	0
16	1
⋮	⋮
5760	0
5766	0
5772	1
$\sum_{i=1}^{962} y_i = 652$	

Solution
The sample proportion is given by

$$\hat{p}_{sy} = \frac{\sum_{i=1}^{962} y_i}{962} = \frac{652}{962} = .678$$

Since N is large and several random starting points were chosen in drawing the systematic sample, we can assume that

$$\hat{V}(\hat{p}_{sy}) = \frac{\hat{p}_{sy}\hat{q}_{sy}}{n-1}\left(\frac{N-n}{N}\right)$$

provides a good estimate of $V(\hat{p}_{sy})$.
The bound on the error of estimation is

$$2\sqrt{\hat{V}(\hat{p}_{sy})} = 2\sqrt{\frac{\hat{p}_{sy}\hat{q}_{sy}}{n-1}\left(\frac{N-n}{N}\right)}$$

$$= 2\sqrt{\frac{(.678)(.322)}{961}\left(\frac{5775-962}{5775}\right)} \approx .0275$$

Thus we estimate .678 (67.8%) of the registered voters favor the proposed bond issue. We are relatively confident that the error of estimation is less than .0275 (2.75%).

8.5 SELECTING THE SAMPLE SIZE

Now let us determine the number of observations necessary to estimate μ to within B units. The required sample size is found by solving the following equation for n:

$$2\sqrt{V(\bar{y}_{sy})} = B \quad (8.12)$$

The solution to equation (8.12) involves both σ^2 and ρ, which must be known (at least approximately) in order to solve for n. Although these

8.5 Selecting the Sample Size

parameters sometimes can be estimated if data from a prior survey are available, we do not discuss this method in this text. Instead we use the formula for n based on simple random sampling. This formula could give an extra large sample for ordered populations and too small a sample for periodic populations. As noted earlier, the variances of $\bar{y}_{sy}$ and $\bar{y}$ are equivalent if the population is random.

The sample size required to estimate μ with a bound B on the error of estimation:

$$n = \frac{N\sigma^2}{(N-1)D + \sigma^2} \qquad (8.13)$$

where

$$D = \frac{B^2}{4}$$

Example 8.4

The management of a large utility company is interested in the average amount of time delinquent bills are overdue. A systematic sample will be drawn from an alphabetical list of $N = 2500$ overdue customer accounts. In a similar survey conducted the previous year, the sample variance was found to be $s^2 = 100$ days. Determine the sample size required to estimate μ, the average amount of time utility bills are overdue, with a bound on the error of estimation of $B = 2$ days.

Solution

It is reasonable to assume that the population of interest is random; hence $\rho \approx 0$. Then we can use equation (8.13) to find the approximate sample size. Replacing σ^2 by s^2 and setting

$$D = \frac{B^2}{4} = \frac{4}{4} = 1$$

we have

$$n = \frac{N\sigma^2}{(N-1)D + \sigma^2} = \frac{2500(100)}{2499(1) + 100} = 96.19$$

Thus management must sample approximately 97 accounts to estimate the average amount of time delinquent bills are overdue, to within 2 days.

To determine the sample size required to estimate τ with a bound on the error of estimation of magnitude B, we use the corresponding method presented in section 4.4.

8. Systematic Sampling

The sample size required to estimate p to within B units is found by using the sample-size formula for estimating p under simple random sampling.

Sample size required to estimate p with a bound B on the error of estimation:

$$n = \frac{Npq}{(N-1)D + pq} \qquad (8.14)$$

where

$$q = 1 - p \quad \text{and} \quad D = \frac{B^2}{4}$$

In a practical situation we do not know p. We can find an approximate sample size by replacing p with an estimated value. If no prior information is available to estimate p, we can obtain a conservative sample size by setting $p = .5$.

Example 8.5
An advertising firm is starting a promotion campaign for a new product. The firm wants to sample potential customers in a small community to determine customer acceptance.

To eliminate some of the costs associated with personal interviews, the investigators decide to run a systematic sample from $N = 5000$ names listed in a community registry and collect the data via telephone interviews. Determine the same size required to estimate p, the proportion of people who consider the product "acceptable," with a bound on the error of estimation of magnitude $B = .03$ (that is, 3%).

Solution
The required sample size can be found by using equation (8.14). Although no previous data are available on this new product, we can still find an approximate sample size. Set $p = .5$ in equation (8.14) and

$$D = \frac{B^2}{4} = \frac{(.03)^2}{4} = .000225$$

Then the required sample size is

$$n = \frac{Npq}{(N-1)D + pq} = \frac{5000(.5)(.5)}{4999(.000225) + (.5)(.5)} = 909.240$$

Hence the firm must interview 910 people to determine consumer acceptance to within 3%.

8.6 REPEATED SYSTEMATIC SAMPLING

We state in section 8.3 that it is impossible to estimate the variance of $\bar{y}_{sy}$ based on information contained in a single systematic sample unless the systematic sampling generates, for all practical purposes, a random sample. When this occurs we can use the random sampling estimation procedures outlined in section 4.3. However, in most cases systematic random sampling is not equivalent to simple random sampling. An alternate method must be used to estimate $V(\bar{y}_{sy})$. Repeated systematic sampling is one such method.

As the name implies, repeated systematic sampling requires the selection of more than one systematic sample. For example, ten 1-in-50 systematic samples, each containing six measurements, could be acquired in approximately the same time as a 1-in-5 systematic sample containing 60 measurements. Both procedures yield 60 measurements for estimating the population mean μ, but the repeated sampling procedure allows us to estimate $V(\bar{y}_{sy})$ by using the square of the deviations of the $n_s = 10$ individual sample means about their mean. The average, $\hat{\mu}$, of the 10 sample means will estimate the population mean μ.

To select n_s repeated systematic samples, we must space the elements of each sample further apart. Thus ten 1-in-50 samples ($n_s = 10$, $k' = 50$) of six measurements each contain the same number of measurements as does a single 1-in-5 sample ($k = 5$) containing $n = 60$ measurements. The starting point for each of the n_s systematic samples is randomly selected from the first k' elements. The remaining elements in each sample are acquired by adding k', $2k'$, and so forth, to the starting point until the total number per sample, n/n_s, is obtained.

A population consists of $N = 960$ elements, which we can number consecutively. To select a systematic sample of size $n = 60$, we choose $k = N/n = 16$ and a random number between 1 and 16 as a starting point. What procedure do we follow to select 10 repeated systematic samples in place of the one systematic sample? First, we choose $k' = 10k = 10(16) = 160$. Next, we select 10 random numbers between 1 and 160. Finally, the constant 160 is added to each of these random starting points to obtain 10 numbers between 161 and 320; the process of adding the constant is continued until 10 samples of size 6 are obtained.

A random selection of ten integers between 1 and 160 gives the following:

$$73, 42, 81, 145, 6, 21, 86, 17, 112, 102$$

These numbers form the random starting points for 10 systematic samples, as shown in table 8.1. The second element in each sample is found by adding 160 to the first, the third by adding 160 to the second, and so forth.

8. Systematic Sampling

Table 8.1 / Selection of repeated systematic samples

Random Starting Point	Second Element in Sample	Third Element in Sample		Sixth Element in Sample
6	166	326	...	806
17	177	337	...	817
21	181	341	...	821
42	202	362	...	842
73	233	393	...	873
81	241	401	...	881
86	246	406	...	886
102	262	422	...	902
112	272	432	...	912
145	305	465	...	945

We frequently select $n_s = 10$ to allow us to obtain enough sample means to acquire a satisfactory estimate of $V(\hat{\mu})$. We choose k' to give the same number of measurements as would be obtained in a single 1-in-k systematic sample; thus

$$k' = kn_s$$

The formulas for estimating μ from n_s systematic samples are shown in equations (8.15), (8.16), and (8.17).

Estimator of the population mean μ using n_s one-in-k' systematic samples:

$$\hat{\mu} = \sum_{i=1}^{n_s} \frac{\bar{y}_i}{n_s} \qquad (8.15)$$

where $\bar{y}_i$ represents the average of the ith systematic sample.

Estimated variance of $\hat{\mu}$:

$$\hat{V}(\hat{\mu}) = \left(\frac{N-n}{N}\right) \frac{\sum_{i=1}^{n_s}(\bar{y}_i - \hat{\mu})^2}{n_s(n_s - 1)} \qquad (8.16)$$

Bound on the error of estimation:

$$2\sqrt{\hat{V}(\hat{\mu})} = 2\sqrt{\left(\frac{N-n}{N}\right) \frac{\sum_{i=1}^{n_s}(\bar{y}_i - \hat{\mu})^2}{n_s(n_s - 1)}} \qquad (8.17)$$

8.6 Repeated Systematic Sampling

We can also use repeated systematic sampling to estimate a population total τ, if N is known. The necessary formulas are given in equations (8.18), (8.19), and (8.20).

Estimator of the population total τ using n_s one-in-k' systematic samples:

$$\hat{\tau} = N\hat{\mu} = N \sum_{i=1}^{n_s} \frac{\bar{y}_i}{n_s} \qquad (8.18)$$

Estimated variance of $\hat{\tau}$:

$$\hat{V}(\hat{\tau}) = N^2 \hat{V}(\hat{\mu}) = N^2 \left(\frac{N-n}{N}\right) \frac{\sum_{i=1}^{n_s}(\bar{y}_i - \hat{\mu})^2}{n_s(n_s - 1)} \qquad (8.19)$$

Bound on the error of estimation:

$$2\sqrt{\hat{V}(\hat{\tau})} = 2\sqrt{N^2\left(\frac{N-n}{N}\right)\frac{\sum_{i=1}^{n_s}(\bar{y}_i - \hat{\mu})^2}{n_s(n_s - 1)}} \qquad (8.20)$$

Example 8.6

A state park charges admission by carload rather than by person, and a park official wants to estimate the average number of persons per car for a particular summer holiday. She knows from past experience that there should be about 400 cars entering the park, and she wants to sample 80 cars. To obtain an estimate of the variance, she uses repeated systematic sampling with 10 samples of 8 cars each. Using the data given in table 8.2, estimate the average number of persons per car and place a bound on the error of estimation.

Solution

For one systematic sample,

$$k = \frac{N}{n} = \frac{400}{80} = 5$$

hence for $n_s = 10$ samples,

$$k' = 10k = 10(5) = 50$$

The following ten random numbers between 1 and 50 are drawn:

$$13, 35, 2, 40, 26, 7, 31, 45, 5, 46$$

Cars with these numbers form the random starting points for the systematic samples.

8. Systematic Sampling

Table 8.2/*Data on number of persons per car (the responses, y_i, are in parentheses)*

Random Starting Point	Second Element	Third Element	Fourth Element	Fifth Element	Sixth Element	Seventh Element	Eighth Element	$\bar{y}_i$
2 (3)	52 (4)	102 (5)	152 (3)	202 (6)	252 (1)	302 (4)	352 (4)	3.75
5 (5)	55 (3)	105 (4)	155 (2)	205 (4)	255 (2)	305 (3)	355 (4)	3.38
7 (2)	57 (4)	107 (6)	157 (2)	207 (3)	257 (2)	307 (1)	357 (3)	2.88
13 (6)	63 (4)	113 (6)	163 (7)	213 (2)	263 (3)	313 (2)	363 (7)	4.62
26 (4)	76 (5)	126 (7)	176 (4)	226 (2)	276 (6)	326 (2)	376 (6)	4.50
31 (7)	81 (6)	131 (4)	181 (4)	231 (3)	281 (6)	331 (7)	381 (5)	5.25
35 (3)	85 (3)	135 (2)	185 (3)	235 (6)	285 (5)	335 (6)	385 (8)	4.50
40 (2)	90 (6)	140 (2)	190 (5)	240 (5)	290 (4)	340 (4)	390 (5)	4.12
45 (2)	95 (6)	145 (3)	195 (6)	245 (4)	295 (4)	345 (5)	395 (4)	4.25
46 (6)	96 (5)	146 (4)	196 (6)	246 (3)	296 (3)	346 (5)	396 (3)	4.38

For table 8.2, the quantity $\bar{y}_1$ is the average for the first row, $\bar{y}_2$ the average for the second row, and so forth. The estimate of μ is

$$\hat{\mu} = \frac{1}{n_s} \sum_{i=1}^{n_s} \bar{y}_i = \frac{1}{10}(3.75 + 3.38 + \cdots + 4.38) = 4.163$$

The following identity can be established:

$$\sum_{i=1}^{n_s} (\bar{y}_i - \hat{\mu})^2 = \sum_{i=1}^{n_s} \bar{y}_i^2 - \frac{1}{n_s}\left(\sum_{i=1}^{n_s} \bar{y}_i\right)^2$$

Substituting, we obtain

$$\sum_{i=1}^{10} (\bar{y}_i - \hat{\mu})^2 = 177.410 - \frac{1}{10}(1733.06) = 4.104$$

Thus the estimated variance of $\hat{\mu}$ becomes

$$\hat{V}(\hat{\mu}) = \left(\frac{N-n}{N}\right) \frac{\sum_{i=1}^{n_s}(\bar{y}_i - \hat{\mu})^2}{n_s(n_s - 1)} = \left(\frac{400 - 80}{400}\right)\left(\frac{4.104}{10(9)}\right) = .0365$$

The estimate of μ with a bound on the error of estimation is

$$\hat{\mu} \pm 2\sqrt{\hat{V}(\hat{\mu})}, \quad \text{or} \quad 4.163 \pm 2\sqrt{.0365}, \quad \text{or} \quad 4.163 \pm .382$$

Therefore, our best estimate of the average of persons per car is 4.163. The error of estimation should be less than .382 with probability approximately .95.

8.7 SUMMARY

Systematic sampling is the final sample survey design presented in this text. It is presented as an alternative to simple random sampling. Systematic sampling is easier to perform and, therefore, is less subject to interviewer errors than simple random sampling. In addition, systematic

Exercises

sampling often provides more information per unit cost than does simple random sampling.

We consider estimation of a population mean, total, and proportion using the estimators $\bar{y}_{sy}$, $N\bar{y}_{sy}$, and $\hat{p}_{sy}$, respectively. The corresponding bounds on the errors of estimation are given for these estimators.

We must first consider the type of population under investigation in order to choose between systematic and simple random sampling. For example, when N is large and $\rho < 0$, the variance of $\bar{y}_{sy}$ is smaller than the corresponding variance of $\bar{y}$ based on simple random sampling. A systematic sample is preferable when the population of interest is ordered and N is large. When the population is random, the two sampling procedures are equivalent and either design can be used. Care must be used in applying systematic sampling to periodic populations.

Sample-size requirements for estimating μ, τ, and p are determined using formulas presented for simple random sampling.

Repeated systematic sampling is discussed in section 8.6; it allows the experimenter to estimate the population mean or total and the variance of the estimator without making any assumptions about the nature of the population.

REFERENCES

Cochran, W. G. *Sampling Techniques.* 3d ed. New York: Wiley, 1977.

Deming, W. E. *Sample Design in Business Research.* New York: Wiley, 1960.

Jones, H. L. "Investigation of the Properties of a Sample Mean by Employing Random Subsample Means." *Journal of the American Statistical Association*, vol. 51 (1956), pp. 54–83.

Kish, L. *Survey Sampling.* New York: Wiley, 1965.

EXERCISES

8.1 Suppose that a home mortgage company has N mortgages numbered serially in the order that they were granted over a period of 20 years. There is a generally increasing trend in the unpaid balances because of the rising cost of housing over the years. It is desired to estimate the total amount of unpaid balances. Would you employ a systematic or a simple random sample? Why?

8.2 A corporation lists employees by income brackets (alphabetically within brackets) from highest to lowest. If the objective is to estimate average income per employee, should systematic, stratified, or simple random sampling be used? Assume that costs are equivalent for the three methods and that you can stratify on income brackets. Discuss the advantages and disadvantages of the three methods.

8. Systematic Sampling

8.3 A retail store with four departments has charge accounts arranged by department, with past-due accounts at the front of each departmental list. Suppose the departments average around 10 accounts each, with approximately 40% past due. On a given day, the accounts might appear as shown in the accompanying table (with account numbers 1 through 40). It is desired to estimate the proportion of past-due accounts by systematic sampling.

	Department			
Account Numbers	1–11	12–20	21–28	29–40
Delinquent Accounts	1, 2, 3, 4	12, 13, 14	21, 22, 23, 24, 25	29, 30, 31, 32

(a) List all possible 1-in-10 systematic samples, and compute the exact variance of the sample proportion. (Note that there are 10 possible values, not all distinct, for the sample proportion, each with probability 1/10 of occurring.)

(b) List all possible 1-in-5 systematic samples, and compute the exact variance of the sample proportion.

(c) Compare the result in part (a) with an approximate variance that would have been obtained in a simple random sample of size $n = 4$ from this population. Similarly, compare the result in part (b) with what would have been obtained from a simple random sample with $n = 8$. What general conclusions can you make?

8.4 The management of a particular company is interested in estimating the proportion of employees favoring a new investment policy. A 1-in-10 systematic sample is obtained from employees leaving the building at the end of a particular workday. Use the data in the table to estimate p, the proportion in favor of the new policy, and place a bound on the error of estimation. Assume $N = 2000$.

Employee Sampled	Response
3	1
13	0
23	1
⋮	⋮
1993	1
	$\sum_{i=1}^{200} y_i = 132$

8.5 For the situation outlined in exercise 8.4, determine the sample size required to estimate p to within .01 units. What type of systematic sample should be run?

8.6 The quality control section of an industrial firm uses systematic sampling to estimate the average amount of fill in 12-ounce cans coming off an

Exercises

assembly line. The data in the table represent a 1-in-50 systematic sample of the production in one day. Estimate μ and place a bound on the error of estimation. Assume $N = 1800$.

Amount of Fill (in ounces)					
12.00	11.97	12.01	12.03	12.01	11.80
11.91	11.98	12.03	11.98	12.00	11.83
11.87	12.01	11.98	11.87	11.90	11.88
12.05	11.87	11.91	11.93	11.94	11.89
11.72	11.93	11.95	11.97	11.93	12.05
11.85	11.98	11.87	12.05	12.02	12.04

8.7 Use the data of exercise 8.6 to determine the sample size required to estimate μ to within .03 units.

8.8 Soil experts want to determine the amount of exchangeable calcium (in parts per million) in a plot of ground. To simplify the sampling scheme, a rectangular grid is superimposed on the field. Soil samples are taken at each point of intersection on the grid (see diagram). Use the following data to determine the average amount of exchangeable calcium on the plot of ground. Place a bound on the error of estimation.

$$n = 45$$

$$\sum y_i = 90{,}320 \quad \text{exchangeable calcium}$$

$$\sum y_i^2 = 148{,}030{,}000$$

8.9 The highway patrol of a particular state is concerned about the proportion of motorists who carry their licenses. A checkpoint is set up on a major highway and the driver of every seventh car is questioned. Use the data in the table to estimate the proportion of drivers carrying their licenses. Place a bound on the error of estimation. Assume that $N = 2800$ cars pass the checkpoint during the sampling period.

Car	Response, y_i
1	1
2	1
3	0
⋮	⋮
400	1
	$\sum y_i = 324$

8. Systematic Sampling

8.10 If the highway patrol expects at least $N = 3000$ cars to pass the checkpoint, determine the sample size required to estimate p to within $B = .015$ units.

8.11 A college is concerned about improving its relations with a neighboring community. A 1-in-150 systematic sample of the $N = 4500$ students listed in the directory is taken to estimate the total amount of money spent on clothing during one quarter of the school year. The results of the sample are listed in the table. Use these data to estimate τ, and place a bound on the error of estimation.

Student	Amount Spent (in dollars)	Student	Amount Spent (in dollars)
1	30	16	32
2	22	17	14
3	10	18	29
4	62	19	48
5	28	20	50
6	31	21	9
7	40	22	15
8	29	23	6
9	17	24	93
10	51	25	21
11	29	26	20
12	21	27	13
13	13	28	12
14	15	29	29
15	23	30	38

8.12 What sample size is needed to estimate τ in exercise 8.11 with a bound on the error of estimation approximately equal to $10,000? What systematic sampling scheme would you recommend?

8.13 A census is conducted in a particular community. In addition to the usual population information, the surveyors question the occupants of every twentieth household to determine how long they have occupied their present home. These results are summarized below.

$$n = 115 \qquad \sum y_i^2 = 2011.15$$
$$\sum y_i = 407.1 \text{ (years)} \qquad N = 2300$$

Use these data to estimate the average amount of time people have lived in their present home. Place a bound on the error of estimation.

8.14 A group of guidance counselors are concerned about the average yearly tuition for out-of-state students in 371 junior colleges. From an alphabetical list of these colleges, a 1-in-7 systematic sample is drawn. Data concerning out-of-state tuition expenses for an academic year (September to June) are obtained for each college sampled. Let y_i be the amount of

Exercises

tuition required for the ith college sampled. Use the data below to estimate μ, and place a bound on the error of estimation.

$$\sum_{i=1}^{53} y_i = \$11{,}950 \qquad \sum_{i=1}^{53} y_i^2 = \$2{,}731{,}037$$

8.15 Museum officials are interested in the total number of persons who visit their museum during a 180-day period when an expensive antique collection is on display. Since it is too costly to monitor the museum traffic each day, officials decide to obtain these data every tenth day. The information from this 1-in-10 systematic sample is summarized in the table. Use these data to estimate τ, the total number of persons visiting the museum during the specified period. Place a bound on the error of estimation.

Day	Number of People Visiting the Museum
3	160
13	350
23	225
⋮	⋮
173	290

$$\sum_{i=1}^{18} y_i = 4{,}868$$

$$\sum_{i=1}^{18} y_i^2 = 1{,}321{,}450$$

8.16 Foresters are interested in determining the mean timber volume per acre for 520 one-acre plots ($N = 520$). A 1-in-25 systematic sample is conducted. Using the data presented in the table, estimate μ, the average timber volume per plot, and place a bound on the error of estimation.

Plot Sampled	Volume (in board feet)	Plot Sampled	Volume (in board feet)
4	7030	279	7540
29	6720	304	6720
54	6850	329	6900
79	7210	354	7200
104	7150	379	7100
129	7370	404	6860
154	7000	429	6800
179	6930	454	7050
204	6570	479	7420
229	6910	504	7090
254	7380		

8. Systematic Sampling

8.17 The officers of a certain professional society wish to determine the proportion of the membership that favors several proposed revisions in refereeing practices. They conduct a 1-in-10 systematic sample from an alphabetical list of the $N = 650$ registered members. Let $y_i = 1$ if the ith person sampled favors the proposed changes and $y_i = 0$ if he opposes the changes. Use the sample data summarized below to estimate p, the proportion of members in favor of the proposed changes. Place a bound on the error of estimation.

$$\sum_{i=1}^{65} y_i = 48$$

8.18 In a sociological survey, a 1-in-50 systematic sample is drawn from city tax records to determine the total number of families in the city who rent their homes. Let $y_i = 1$ if the family in the ith household sampled rents and let $y_i = 0$ if the family does not. If there are $N = 15{,}200$ households in the community, use the data below to estimate τ, the total number of families who rent. Place a bound on the error of estimation.

$$\sum_{i=1}^{304} y_i = 88$$

[Hint: If $\hat{p}$ = estimated fraction who rent, then $N\hat{p}$ would be an estimate of the total number who rent. $\hat{V}(N\hat{p}) = N^2 \hat{V}(\hat{p})$.]

8.19 It is desired to estimate the total weight of fruit to be produced in a field of zucchini (squash) by sampling just prior to harvest. The plot consists of 20 rows with 400 plants per row. The manufacturer of the seeds says that each plant can yield up to 8 pounds of fruit. Outline an appropriate systematic sampling plan for this problem so as to estimate the total weight of fruit to within 2000 pounds.

EXPERIENCES WITH REAL DATA

1. The stock prices for the week ending August 26, 1977, are listed in table 8.3 for selected firms. Also listed are the differences between the high and low prices for the week, and the difference between the closing price for this week and that of the previous week (between-week change).
   (a) Select a systematic sample from the list and estimate the average high price for the week among the firms listed. Place a bound on the error of estimation.
   (b) It is sometimes of interest to compare within-week fluctuations to between-week fluctuations. Select a systematic sample of firms [you can use the same sample as in part (a)] and estimate the proportion of firms for which the within-week change is greater in magnitude than the between-week change, placing a bound on the error of estimation. (In fact, 56 of the 81 firms listed have larger within-week fluctuations.)

Table 8.3/*Stock prices for week ending August 26, 1977*

Fund	High	Low	Last	Within-Week Change	Between-Week Change
AetnaIncSh	13.18	13.13	13.18	.05	+.06
AmEquityFd	4.96	4.86	4.86	.13	−.09
American Funds:					
CapitFd	6.48	6.39	6.39	.09	−.07
WshMutInv	6.44	6.38	6.38	.06	−.06
Amer General:					
EquityGrth	6.55	6.44	6.44	.11	−.07
AmInvest	5.73	5.64	5.64	.09	−.07
Anchor Group:					
Income Fd	7.45	7.41	7.41	.04	−.02
Axe Houghton:					
FundB	7.84	7.76	7.76	.08	−.07
BabsonInvmt	9.26	9.12	9.13	.14	−.09
BerkshireCap	7.82	7.69	7.70	.13	−.10
Calvin Bullock:					
DividendSh	3.00	2.95	2.95	.05	−.04
CG IncomeFd	8.73	8.68	8.73	.05	+.05
Chase Gr Bos:					
Fund	6.17	6.07	6.08	.10	−.08
ChemicalFund	7.09	7.00	7.00	.09	−.05
Colonial:					
Fund	9.15	9.09	9.09	.06	−.03
ComwthTrA B	.99	.98	.98	.01	−.01
ConsolivInv	9.62	9.62	9.62	.00	.00
deVeghtMut	30.82	30.36	30.36	.46	−.32
DirectorsCap	4.24	4.15	4.18	.09	−.03
Dreyfus Grp:					
Leverage	15.95	15.79	15.79	.16	−.16
ThirdCentry	13.01	12.66	12.66	.35	−.31
Eaton&Howard:					
IncomeFund	6.16	6.14	6.16	.02	+.02
Egret Fund	10.53	10.41	10.42	.12	−.09
Federated Funds:					
FourthEmpir	17.60	17.34	17.34	.26	−.26
Fidelity Group:					
ContraFund	10.23	10.08	10.08	.15	−.06
MuniBond	10.62	10.60	10.62	.02	+.02
Trend	21.49	21.03	21.06	.46	−.21
First Investors:					
FundGrowth	6.49	6.56	6.56	.07	−.11
Found Growth	3.80	3.78	3.78	.02	.00
Founders Group:					
Special	9.40	9.28	9.28	.12	−.10
Franklin Group					
Income Stk	1.75	1.74	1.74	.01	−.01
Fundpack	8.30	8.16	8.16	.15	−.15
GenEISSP	25.67	25.24	25.24	.43	−.31

8. *Systematic Sampling*

Table 8.3/*(continued)*

Fund	High	Low	Last	Within-Week Change	Between-Week Change
Hamilton					
Income	7.68	7.60	7.60	.08	−.07
HoraceMannFd	15.01	14.71	14.71	.30	−.23
IndustryFund	2.97	2.91	2.91	.06	−.05
Inv Counsel:					
CapitShrsInc	6.05	5.90	5.90	.15	−.15
Investors Group:					
TaxExempt	5.05	5.03	5.05	.02	+.02
IvyFund	6.14	6.04	6.04	.10	−.06
JohnstnMut	19.33	19.08	19.13	.25	−.17
Kemper Funds:					
SummitFd	10.76	10.57	10.57	.19	−.14
Keystone Funds:					
DiscBd B4	8.58	8.57	8.57	.01	−.01
Polaris	3.26	3.20	3.20	.06	−.05
Lincoln Natl:					
SelectAm	7.09	7.04	7.04	.05	−.04
Lord Abbett:					
Income	3.55	3.53	3.53	.02	−.02
Massachusett Co:					
IndependFd	7.46	7.31	7.32	.15	−.11
Mass Financ I:					
MCD	14.01	13.84	13.84	.17	−.13
Merrill Lynch:					
RdyAsset	1.00	1.00	1.00	.00	.00
MIF Fund	8.25	8.06	8.06	.19	−.17
MutualShrs	29.69	29.47	29.47	.22	−.15
Nat Secur Ser:					
Growth	5.63	5.63	5.54	.10	−.07
NE Life Fund:					
Income	14.12	14.06	14.12	.06	+.07
NewWrldFd	10.98	10.83	10.83	.15	−.12
NuveenFd	9.82	9.75	9.82	.07	+.08
Oppenheimer Fd:					
TaxFreeBd	10.61	10.57	10.61	.04	+.05
PennMutual	3.97	3.93	3.93	.04	.00
Pilgrim Grp:					
MagnaCap	3.35	3.29	3.29	.06	−.05
PligrowthFnd	10.59	10.46	10.46	.13	−.15
Price Funds:					
TaxFree	10.37	10.35	10.37	.02	+.02
Putnam Funds:					
George	13.16	13.05	13.05	.11	−.08
Vista	10.20	10.01	10.02	.19	−.13
SafecoGrowth	9.21	9.09	9.09	.12	−.11
ScudStevClk:					
ManageRes	10.01	10.01	10.01	.00	.00

Experiences with Real Data

Table 8.3/*(continued)*

Fund	High	Low	Last	Within-Week Change	Between-Week Change
Security Funds:					
Ultra	10.37	10.07	10.07	.30	−.31
Shareholders Gp:					
ComstockFd	6.20	6.12	6.12	.08	−.07
Shearson Funds:					
Appreciation	16.54	16.25	16.25	.29	−.28
Sigma Funds:					
Invest	10.27	10.13	10.13	.14	−.13
SouthwstnInv	7.97	7.85	7.86	.12	−.08
State Bond Gr:					
ProgressFd	3.85	3.78	3.78	.07	−.04
Steadman Funds:					
Invest	1.41	1.38	1.39	.03	−.01
Surveyor Fund	8.81	8.71	8.71	.10	−.06
TudorHedge	14.14	13.92	13.92	.22	−.15
USAACapGth	7.70	7.61	7.61	.09	−.07
UnifMutual	8.16	8.09	8.09	.07	−.04
United Funds:					
Accumultiv	6.16	6.10	6.10	.06	−.04
Municpl	10.24	10.19	10.24	.05	+.05
Value Line Fd:					
Income	5.15	5.09	5.09	.06	−.05
Vance Sanders:					
Common	6.44	6.32	6.32	.12	−.11
Vanguard Group:					
MorganFdn	12.02	11.82	11.82	.20	−.14
WindsorFnd	10.29	10.16	10.16	.13	−.09
WisconsinIncm	5.18	5.16	5.17	.02	.00

2. From a list of names, like those in a student directory, select a systematic sample and interview the selected persons to find out if they favor a certain issue of current importance (such as a proposed government action or pending campus decision). Estimate the population proportion favoring the issue, and place a bound on the error of estimation.

Repeat the procedure outlined above three more times, so that four independent systematic samples are available. Compare the results from the individual samples with the combined result of the four samples analyzed according to the methods of section 8.6. If you prefer to work with something other than lists of people, use other listed records in a similar way. For example, you could systematically sample names of employees from a file and estimate average age, income, and so on.

9.
Two-Stage Cluster Sampling

9.1 INTRODUCTION

Two-stage cluster sampling is an extension of the concept of cluster sampling. You will recall from the discussion of cluster sampling in chapter 7 that a cluster is usually a convenient or natural collection of elements, such as blocks of households or cartons of flashbulbs. A cluster often contains too many elements to obtain a measurement on each, or it contains elements so nearly alike that measurement of only a few elements provides information on an entire cluster. When either situation occurs, the experimenter can select a simple random sample of clusters and then take a simple random sample of elements within each cluster. The result is a two-stage cluster sample.

Definition 9.1 A *two-stage cluster sample* is obtained by first selecting a simple random sample of clusters and then selecting a simple random sample of elements from each sampled cluster.

For example, a national survey of university student opinions could be conducted by selecting a simple random sample of universities from all those in the country and then selecting a simple random sample of students from each university. Thus a university would correspond to a cluster of students. Similarly, the total amount of accounts receivable for a chain store could be estimated by first taking a simple random sample of stores and then selecting a simple random sample of accounts from each. Thus each chain store provides a cluster of accounts.

There is a certain similarity between cluster sampling and stratified random sampling. Think of a population being divided into nonoverlapping groups of elements. If these groups are considered to be strata, then a simple random sample is selected from *each* group. If these groups are considered to be clusters, then a simple random sample of *groups* is selected, and the sampled groups are then subsampled. Stratified random sampling provides estimators with small variance when there is little variation among elements within each group. Cluster sampling does well when the elements within each group are highly variable, and all groups are quite similar to one another.

The advantages of two-stage cluster sampling over other designs are the same as those listed in chapter 7 for cluster sampling. First, a frame listing all elements in the population may be impossible or costly to obtain, whereas it may be easy to obtain a list of all clusters. For example, it would be expensive and time-consuming to compile a list of all university students in the country, but a list of universities could be readily acquired. Second, the cost of obtaining data may be inflated by travel costs if the sampled elements are spread over a large geographic area. Thus it is often economical to sample clusters of elements that are physically close together.

9.2 HOW TO DRAW A TWO-STAGE CLUSTER SAMPLE

The first problem in selecting a two-stage cluster sample is the choice of appropriate clusters. Two conditions are desirable: (1) geographic proximity of the elements within a cluster and (2) cluster sizes that are convenient to administer.

The selection of appropriate clusters also depends on whether we want to sample a few clusters and many elements from each or many clusters and a few elements from each. Ultimately the choice is based on costs. Large clusters tend to possess heterogeneous elements and, hence a large sample is required from each in order to acquire accurate estimates of population parameters. In contrast, small clusters frequently contain relatively homogeneous elements, in which case accurate information on the characteristics of a cluster can be obtained by selecting a small sample from each cluster.

Consider the problem of sampling personal incomes in a large city. The city could be divided into large clusters, for example precincts, which contain a heterogeneous assortment of incomes. Thus a small number of precincts might yield a representative cross section of incomes within the city, but a fairly large sample of elements from each cluster

9.3 Unbiased Estimation of a Population Mean and Total

would be required in order to accurately estimate its mean (due to the heterogeneity of incomes within the cluster). In contrast, the city could be divided into small, relatively homogeneous clusters, say city blocks. Then a small sample of people from each block would give adequate information on each cluster's mean, but it would require many blocks to obtain accurate information on the mean income for the entire city.

For another example, consider the university student opinion poll. If students within a university hold similar opinions on the question of interest but opinions differ widely from university to university, then the sample should contain a few representatives from many different universities. If the opinions vary greatly within each university, then the survey should include many representatives from each of a few universities.

To select the sample, we first obtain a frame listing all clusters in the population. We then draw a simple random sample of clusters, using the random sampling procedures presented in chapter 4. Third, we obtain frames that list all elements in each of the sampled clusters. Finally, we select a simple random sample of elements from each of these frames.

9.3 UNBIASED ESTIMATION OF A POPULATION MEAN AND TOTAL

As in previous chapters, we are interested in estimating a population mean μ or a population total τ and placing a bound on the error of estimation. The following notation is used:

N = the number of clusters in the population

n = the number of clusters selected in a simple random sample

M_i = the number of elements in cluster i

m_i = the number of elements selected in a simple random sample from cluster i

$M = \sum_{i=1}^{N} M_i$ = the number of elements in the population

$\bar{M} = \dfrac{M}{N}$ = the average cluster size for the population

y_{ij} = the jth observation in the sample from the ith cluster

$\bar{y}_i = \dfrac{1}{m_i} \sum_{j=1}^{m_i} y_{ij}$ = the sample mean for the ith cluster

9. Two-Stage Cluster Sampling

Unbiased estimator of the population mean μ:

$$\hat{\mu} = \left(\frac{N}{M}\right)\frac{\sum\limits_{i=1}^{n} M_i \bar{y}_i}{n} \tag{9.1}$$

Estimated variance of $\hat{\mu}$:

$$\hat{V}(\hat{\mu}) = \left(\frac{N-n}{N}\right)\left(\frac{1}{n\bar{M}^2}\right)s_b^2 + \frac{1}{nN\bar{M}^2}\sum_{i=1}^{n} M_i^2\left(\frac{M_i - m_i}{M_i}\right)\left(\frac{s_i^2}{m_i}\right) \tag{9.2}$$

where

$$s_b^2 = \frac{\sum\limits_{i=1}^{n}(M_i\bar{y}_i - \bar{M}\hat{\mu})^2}{n-1} \tag{9.3}$$

and

$$s_i^2 = \frac{\sum\limits_{j=1}^{m_i}(y_{ij} - \bar{y}_i)^2}{m_i - 1} \qquad i = 1,\ldots,n \tag{9.4}$$

Bound on the error of estimation:

$$2\sqrt{\hat{V}(\hat{\mu})} \tag{9.5}$$

The estimator, $\hat{\mu}$, shown in equation (9.1), depends on M, the number of elements in the population. A method of estimating μ when M is unknown is given in the next section.

Note that s_i^2 is the sample variance for the sample selected from cluster i.

Example 9.1
A garment manufacturer has 90 plants located throughout the United States and wants to estimate the average number of hours that the sewing machines were down for repairs in the past months. Because the plants are widely scattered, she decides to use cluster sampling, specifying each plant as a cluster of machines. Each plant contains many machines, and it would be time-consuming to check the repair record for each machine. Therefore, it seems appropriate to use two-stage sampling. Enough time and money are available to sample $n = 10$ plants and approximately 20% of the machines in each plant.

9.3 Unbiased Estimation of a Population Mean and Total

Table 9.1 / *Downtime for sewing machines*

Plant	M_i	m_i	Downtime (in hours)	$\bar{y}_i$	s_i^2
1	50	10	5, 7, 9, 0, 11, 2, 8, 4, 3, 5	5.40	11.38
2	65	13	4, 3, 7, 2, 11, 0, 1, 9, 4, 3, 2, 1, 5	4.00	10.67
3	45	9	5, 6, 4, 11, 12, 0, 1, 8, 4	5.67	16.75
4	48	10	6, 4, 0, 1, 0, 9, 8, 4, 6, 10	4.80	13.29
5	52	10	11, 4, 3, 1, 0, 2, 8, 6, 5, 3	4.30	11.12
6	58	12	12, 11, 3, 4, 2, 0, 0, 1, 4, 3, 2, 4	3.83	14.88
7	42	8	3, 7, 6, 7, 8, 4, 3, 2	5.00	5.14
8	66	13	3, 6, 4, 3, 2, 2, 8, 4, 0, 4, 5, 6, 3	3.85	4.31
9	40	8	6, 4, 7, 3, 9, 1, 4, 5	4.88	6.13
10	56	11	6, 7, 5, 10, 11, 2, 1, 4, 0, 5, 4	5.00	11.80

Using the data in table 9.1, estimate the average downtime per machine and place a bound on the error of estimation. The manufacturer knows she has a combined total of 4500 machines in all plants.

Solution
The best estimate of μ is $\hat{\mu}$, shown in equation (9.1), which yields

$$\hat{\mu} = \frac{N}{Mn} \sum_{i=1}^{n} M_i \bar{y}_i$$

$$= \frac{90}{(4500)(10)}[(50)(5.40) + (65)(4.00) + \cdots + (56)(5.00)]$$

$$= \frac{90}{(4500)(10)}(2400.59) = 4.80$$

In order to estimate the variance of $\hat{\mu}$, we must calculate

$$s_b^2 = \frac{1}{n-1} \sum_{i=1}^{n} (M_i \bar{y}_i - \bar{M}\hat{\mu})^2$$

$$= \frac{1}{n-1}\left[\sum_{i=1}^{n}(M_i\bar{y}_i)^2 - 2\bar{M}\hat{\mu}\sum_{i=1}^{n} M_i\bar{y}_i + n(\bar{M}\hat{\mu})^2\right]$$

$$= \tfrac{1}{9}[583,198.6721 - 2(50)(4.80)(2400.59) + 10(240)^2]$$

$$= 768.38$$

$$\sum_{i=1}^{n} M_i^2 \left(\frac{M_i - m_i}{M_i}\right)\left(\frac{s_i^2}{m_i}\right)$$

$$= (50)^2\left(\frac{50-10}{50}\right)\left(\frac{11.38}{10}\right) + \cdots + (56)^2\left(\frac{56-11}{56}\right)\left(\frac{11.80}{11}\right)$$

$$= 21,990.96$$

9. Two-Stage Cluster Sampling

Then from equation (9.2),

$$\hat{V}(\hat{\mu}) = \left(\frac{N-n}{N}\right)\left(\frac{1}{n\bar{M}^2}\right)s_b^2 + \frac{1}{nN\bar{M}^2}\sum_{i=1}^{n} M_i^2\left(\frac{M_i - m_i}{M_i}\right)\left(\frac{s_i^2}{m_i}\right)$$

$$= \left(\frac{90-10}{90}\right)\left[\frac{1}{(10)(50)^2}\right](768.38)$$

$$+ \frac{1}{(10)(90)(50)^2}(21{,}990.96)$$

$$= .037094$$

The estimate of μ with a bound on the error of estimation is given by

$\hat{\mu} \pm 2\sqrt{\hat{V}(\hat{\mu})}$, or $4.80 \pm 2\sqrt{.037094}$, or $4.80 \pm .38$

Thus the average downtime is estimated to be 4.80 hours. The error of estimation should be less than .38 hours with a probability of approximately .95.

An unbiased estimator of a population total can be found by taking an unbiased estimator of the population mean and multiplying by the number of elements in the population in a manner similar to that used in simple random sampling. Thus $M\hat{\mu}$ is an unbiased estimator of τ for two-stage cluster sampling.

Estimation of the population total τ:

$$\hat{\tau} = M\hat{\mu} = N \frac{\sum_{i=1}^{n} M_i \bar{y}_i}{n} \qquad (9.6)$$

Estimated variance of $\hat{\tau}$:

$$\hat{V}(\hat{\tau}) = M^2 \hat{V}(\hat{\mu})$$

$$= \left(\frac{N-n}{N}\right)\left(\frac{N^2}{n}\right)s_b^2 + \frac{N}{n}\sum_{i=1}^{n} M_i^2\left(\frac{M_i - m_i}{M_i}\right)\left(\frac{s_i^2}{m_i}\right) \qquad (9.7)$$

where s_b^2 is given by equation (9.3) and s_i^2 is given by equation (9.4).

Bound on the error of estimation:

$$2\sqrt{\hat{V}(\hat{\tau})} = 2\sqrt{M^2 \hat{V}(\hat{\mu})} \qquad (9.8)$$

9.4 Ratio Estimation of a Population Mean

Note that we do not need to know M in order to calculate $\hat{\tau}$ or the estimated variance of $\hat{\tau}$, since the M's cancel out in the formula for $\hat{\tau}$ and s_b^2 [see equations (9.6) and (9.7)].

Example 9.2
Estimate the total amount of downtime during the past month for all machines owned by the manufacturer in example 9.1. Place a bound on the error of estimation.

Solution
The best estimate of τ is

$$\hat{\tau} = M\hat{\mu} = \frac{N}{n}\sum_{i=1}^{n} M_i \bar{y}_i = \frac{90}{10}(2400.59) = 21{,}605.31$$

The estimated variance of $\hat{\tau}$ is found by using the value of $\hat{V}(\hat{\mu})$ calculated in example 9.1 and substituting as follows:

$$\hat{V}(\hat{\tau}) = M^2 \hat{V}(\hat{\mu}) = (4{,}500)^2(.037094)$$

The estimate of τ with a bound on the error of estimation is

$$\hat{\tau} \pm 2\sqrt{\hat{V}(\hat{\tau})}, \quad \text{or} \quad 21{,}605.31 \pm 2\sqrt{(4{,}500)^2(.037094)}$$

$$21{,}605.31 \pm 1{,}733.4$$

Thus the estimate of total downtime is 21,605.31 hours. We are fairly confident that the error of estimation is less than 1,733.4 hours.

9.4 RATIO ESTIMATION OF A POPULATION MEAN

The estimator $\hat{\mu}$, given by equation (9.1), depends on the total number of elements in the population, M. When M is unknown, as is frequently the case, it must be estimated from the sample data. We obtain an estimator of M by multiplying the average cluster size, $\sum_{i=1}^{n} M_i/n$, by the number of clusters in the population, N. If we replace M by its estimator, we obtain a ratio estimator, denoted by $\hat{\mu}_r$, because the numerator and denominator are both random variables.

9. Two-Stage Cluster Sampling

Ratio estimator of the population mean μ:

$$\hat{\mu}_r = \frac{\sum\limits_{i=1}^{n} M_i \bar{y}_i}{\sum\limits_{i=1}^{n} M_i} \qquad (9.9)$$

Estimated variance of $\hat{\mu}_r$:

$$\hat{V}(\hat{\mu}_r) = \left(\frac{N-n}{N}\right)\left(\frac{1}{n\bar{M}^2}\right)s_r^2 + \frac{1}{nN\bar{M}^2}\sum_{i=1}^{n} M_i^2\left(\frac{M_i - m_i}{M_i}\right)\left(\frac{s_i^2}{m_i}\right) \qquad (9.10)$$

where

$$s_r^2 = \frac{\sum\limits_{i=1}^{n} M_i^2(\bar{y}_i - \hat{\mu}_r)^2}{n-1} \qquad (9.11)$$

and

$$s_i^2 = \frac{\sum\limits_{j=1}^{m_i}(y_{ij} - \bar{y}_i)^2}{m_i - 1} \qquad i = 1, \ldots, n \qquad (9.12)$$

Bound on the error of estimation:

$$2\sqrt{\hat{V}(\hat{\mu}_r)} \qquad (9.13)$$

The estimator $\hat{\mu}_r$ is biased, but the bias is negligible when n is large.

Example 9.3

Using the data in table 9.1, estimate the average downtime per machine and place a bound on the error of estimation. Assume the manufacturer does not know how many machines there are in all plants combined.

Solution

Because M is unknown, we must use $\hat{\mu}_r$, given by equation (9.9), to estimate μ. Our calculations yield

$$\hat{\mu}_r = \frac{\sum\limits_{i=1}^{n} M_i \bar{y}_i}{\sum\limits_{i=1}^{n} M_i} = \frac{(50)(5.40) + (65)(4.00) + \cdots + (56)(5.00)}{50 + 65 + \cdots + 56}$$

$$= \frac{2{,}400.59}{522} = 4.60$$

9.5 Estimation of a Population Proportion

To find the estimated variance of $\hat{\mu}_r$, we must calculate

$$s_r^2 = \frac{1}{n-1} \sum_{i=1}^{n} M_i^2 (\bar{y}_i - \hat{\mu}_r)^2$$

$$= \frac{1}{n-1} \left[\sum_{i=1}^{n} (M_i \bar{y}_i)^2 - 2\hat{\mu}_r \sum_{i=1}^{n} M_i^2 \bar{y}_i + (\hat{\mu}_r)^2 \sum_{i=1}^{n} M_i^2 \right]$$

$$= \tfrac{1}{9}[583{,}198.6721 - 2(4.60)(126{,}530.87) + (4.6)^2(27{,}978)]$$

$$= 1{,}236.57$$

Note that, as in example 9.1,

$$\sum_{i=1}^{n} M_i^2 \left(\frac{M_i - m_i}{M_i} \right) \left(\frac{s_i^2}{m_i} \right) = 21{,}990.96$$

We can estimate $\bar{M}$ by using the average cluster size for the sample:

$$\frac{\sum_{i=1}^{n} M_i}{n} = \frac{522}{10} = 52.2$$

Substituting into equation (9.10), the estimated variance of $\hat{\mu}_r$ is

$$\hat{V}(\hat{\mu}_r) = \left(\frac{N-n}{N}\right)\left(\frac{1}{n\bar{M}^2}\right) s_r^2 + \frac{1}{nN\bar{M}^2} \sum_{i=1}^{n} M_i^2 \left(\frac{M_i - m_i}{M_i}\right)\left(\frac{s_i^2}{m_i}\right)$$

$$= \left(\frac{90-10}{90}\right)\left[\frac{1}{(10)(52.2)^2}\right](1236.57)$$

$$+ \frac{1}{10(90)(52.2)^2}(21{,}990.96)$$

$$= .049306$$

The estimate of the average downtime with a bound on the error of estimation is

$$\hat{\mu}_r \pm 2\sqrt{\hat{V}(\hat{\mu}_r)}, \quad \text{or} \quad 4.60 \pm 2\sqrt{.049306}, \quad \text{or} \quad 4.60 \pm .44$$

Thus the estimated mean downtime per machine is 4.60 hours with a bound on the error of estimation of .44 hours.

9.5 ESTIMATION OF A POPULATION PROPORTION

Consider the problem of estimating a population proportion p such as the proportion of university students in favor of a certain law or the proportion of machines that have had no downtime for the past month. An

9. Two-Stage Cluster Sampling

estimate of p can be obtained by using $\hat{\mu}$, given in equation (9.1), or $\hat{\mu}_r$, given in equation (9.9), and letting $y_{ij} = 1$ or 0 depending on whether or not the jth element in the ith cluster falls into the category of interest.

Because M is usually unknown, we present the formulas for estimating p with a ratio estimator analogous to $\hat{\mu}_r$, given in equation (9.9). Let $\hat{p}_i$ denote the proportion of sampled elements from cluster i that fall into the category of interest.

Estimator of a population proportion p:

$$\hat{p} = \frac{\sum_{i=1}^{n} M_i \hat{p}_i}{\sum_{i=1}^{n} M_i} \tag{9.14}$$

Estimated variance of $\hat{p}$:

$$\hat{V}(\hat{p}) = \left(\frac{N-n}{N}\right)\left(\frac{1}{n\bar{M}^2}\right)s_r^2 + \frac{1}{nN\bar{M}^2}\sum_{i=1}^{n} M_i^2\left(\frac{M_i - m_i}{M_i}\right)\left(\frac{\hat{p}_i \hat{q}_i}{m_i - 1}\right) \tag{9.15}$$

where

$$s_r^2 = \frac{\sum_{i=1}^{n} M_i^2 (\hat{p}_i - \hat{p})^2}{n - 1} \tag{9.16}$$

and

$$\hat{q}_i = 1 - \hat{p}_i$$

Bound on the error of estimation:

$$2\sqrt{\hat{V}(\hat{p})} \tag{9.17}$$

Example 9.4
The manufacturer in example 9.1 wants to estimate the proportion of machines that have been shut down for major repairs (those requiring parts from stock outside the factory). The sample proportions of machines requiring major repairs are given in table 9.2. The data are for the machines sampled in example 9.1. Estimate p, the proportion of machines involved in major repairs for all plants combined, and place a bound on the error of estimation.

9.5 Estimation of a Population Proportion

Table 9.2 / *Proportion of sewing machines requiring major repairs*

Plant	M_i	m_i	Proportion of Machines Requiring Major Repairs, $\hat{p}_i$
1	50	10	.40
2	65	13	.38
3	45	9	.22
4	48	10	.30
5	52	10	.50
6	58	12	.25
7	42	8	.38
8	66	13	.31
9	40	8	.25
10	56	11	.36

Solution
The best estimate of p is given by

$$\hat{p} = \frac{\sum_{i=1}^{n} M_i \hat{p}_i}{\sum_{i=1}^{n} M_i} = \frac{50(.40) + 65(.38) + \cdots + 56(.36)}{50 + 65 + \cdots + 56}$$

$$= \frac{176.08}{522} = .34$$

To estimate the variance of $\hat{p}$, we calculate

$$s_r^2 = \frac{1}{n-1} \sum_{i=1}^{n} M_i^2 (\hat{p}_i - \hat{p})^2$$

$$= \frac{1}{n-1}\left[\sum_{i=1}^{n} (M_i \hat{p}_i)^2 - 2\hat{p} \sum_{i=1}^{n} M_i^2 \hat{p}_i + (\hat{p})^2 \sum_{i=1}^{n} M_i^2\right]$$

$$= \tfrac{1}{9}[3{,}381.4688 - 2(.34)(9{,}484.84) + (.34)^2(27{,}978)]$$

$$= 18.4482$$

$$\sum_{i=1}^{n} M_i^2 \left(\frac{M_i - m_i}{M_i}\right)\left(\frac{\hat{p}_i \hat{q}_i}{m_i - 1}\right)$$

$$= (50)^2\left(\frac{50-10}{50}\right)\left[\frac{(.4)(.6)}{9}\right] + \cdots + (56)^2\left(\frac{56-11}{56}\right)\left[\frac{(.36)(.64)}{10}\right]$$

$$= 509.4881$$

9. Two-Stage Cluster Sampling

Then the estimated variance of $\hat{p}$ when $\bar{M}$ is estimated by the sample average, 52.2, is

$$\hat{V}(\hat{p}) = \left(\frac{N-n}{N}\right)\left(\frac{1}{n\bar{M}^2}\right)s_r^2 + \frac{1}{nN\bar{M}^2}\sum_{i=1}^{n} M_i^2\left(\frac{M_i - m_i}{M_i}\right)\left(\frac{\hat{p}_i\hat{q}_i}{m_i - 1}\right)$$

$$= \left(\frac{90-10}{90}\right)\left[\frac{1}{(10)(52.2)^2}\right](18.4482)$$

$$+ \frac{1}{(10)(90)(52.2)^2}(509.4881)$$

$$= .00081$$

The best estimate of the proportion of machines that have undergone major repairs is

$$\hat{p} \pm 2\sqrt{\hat{V}(\hat{p})}, \quad \text{or} \quad .34 \pm 2\sqrt{.00081}, \quad \text{or} \quad .34 \pm .056$$

We estimate the proportion of machines involved in major repairs to be .34, with a bound of .056 on the error of estimation.

9.6 SUMMARY

The concept of cluster sampling can be extended to two-stage sampling by taking a simple random sample of elements from each sampled cluster. Two-stage cluster sampling is advantageous when it is desirable to have sample elements in geographic proximity because of travel costs.

Two-stage cluster sampling eliminates the need to sample all elements in each sampled cluster. Thus the cost of sampling can often be reduced with little loss of information.

An unbiased estimator of μ is presented for the case when M, the total number of elements in the population, is known. When M is unknown, a ratio estimator is employed. Estimators are also given for a population total τ and for a population proportion p.

REFERENCES

Cochran, W. G. *Sampling Techniques*. 3d ed. New York: Wiley, 1977.
Hansen, M. H.; Hurwitz, W. N.; and Madow, W. G. *Sampling Survey Methods and Theory*, vol. 1. New York: Wiley, 1953.
Kish, L. *Survey Sampling*. New York: Wiley, 1965.

EXERCISES

9.1 Suppose a large retail store has its accounts receivable listed by department. It is desired to estimate the total accounts receivable on a given day

Exercises

by sampling. Discuss the relative merits of stratified random sampling, single-stage cluster sampling, systematic sampling, and two-stage cluster sampling. What extra information would you like to have on these accounts before selecting the sampling design?

9.2 A nurseryman wants to estimate the average height of seedlings in a large field that is divided into 50 plots that vary slightly in size. He believes the heights are fairly constant throughout each plot but may vary considerably from plot to plot. Therefore, it is decided to sample 10% of the trees within each of 10 plots using a two-stage cluster sample. The data are as given in

Plot	Number of Seedlings	Number of Seedlings Sampled	Heights of Seedlings (in inches)
1	52	5	12, 11, 12, 10, 13
2	56	6	10, 9, 7, 9, 8, 10
3	60	6	6, 5, 7, 5, 6, 4
4	46	5	7, 8, 7, 7, 6
5	49	5	10, 11, 13, 12, 12
6	51	5	14, 15, 13, 12, 13
7	50	5	6, 7, 6, 8, 7
8	61	6	9, 10, 8, 9, 9, 10
9	60	6	7, 10, 8, 9, 9, 10
10	45	6	12, 11, 12, 13, 12, 12

the table. Estimate the average height of seedlings in the field, and place a bound on the error of estimation.

9.3 In exercise 9.2 assume that the nurseryman knows there are approximately 2600 seedlings in the field. Use this additional information to estimate the average height, and place a bound on the error of estimation.

9.4 A supermarket chain has stores in 32 cities. A company official wants to estimate the proportion of stores in the chain that do not meet a specified cleanliness criterion. Stores within each city appear to possess similar characteristics; therefore it is decided to select a two-stage cluster sample containing one-half of the stores within each of 4 cities. Cluster sampling is desirable in this situation because of travel costs. The data collected are

City	Number of Stores in City	Number of Stores Sampled	Number of Stores Not Meeting Criterion
1	25	13	3
2	10	5	1
3	18	9	4
4	16	8	2

given in the table. Estimate the proportion of stores not meeting the cleanliness criterion, and place a bound on the error of estimation.

9. Two-Stage Cluster Sampling

9.5 Repeat exercise 9.4 given that the chain contains 450 stores.

9.6 To improve telephone service, an executive of a certain company wants to estimate the total number of phone calls placed by secretaries in the company during one day. The company contains 12 departments, each making approximately the same number of calls per day. Each department employs approximately 20 secretaries, and the number of calls made varies considerably from secretary to secretary. It is decided to employ two-stage cluster sampling, using a small number of departments (clusters) and selecting a fairly large number of secretaries (elements) from each. Ten secretaries are sampled from each of 4 departments. The data are sum-

Department	Number of Secretaries	Number of Secretaries Sampled	Mean $\bar{y}_i$	Variance s_i^2
1	21	10	15.5	2.8
2	23	10	15.8	3.1
3	20	10	17.0	3.5
4	20	10	14.9	3.4

marized in the table. Estimate the total number of calls placed by the secretaries in this company, and place a bound on the error of estimation.

9.7 A city zoning commission wants to estimate the proportion of property owners in a certain section of a city who favor a proposed zoning change. The section is divided into 7 distinct residential areas, each containing similar residents. Because the results must be obtained in a short period of time, two-stage cluster sampling is used. Three of the 7 areas are selected at random and 20% of the property owners in each area selected are sampled. The figure of 20% seems reasonable because the people living within each area seem to be in the same socioeconomic class and hence they tend to hold similar opinions on the zoning question. The results are

Area	Number of Property Owners	Number of Property Owners Sampled	Number in Favor of Zoning Change
1	46	9	1
2	67	13	2
3	93	20	2

given in the table. Estimate the proportion of property owners who favor the proposed zoning change, and place a bound on the error of estimation.

9.8 A forester wants to estimate the total number of trees in a certain county that are infected with a particular disease. There are 10 well-defined forest areas in the county; these areas can be subdivided into plots of approximately the same size. Four crews are available to conduct the survey, which must be completed in one day. Hence two-stage cluster sampling is used. Four areas (clusters) are chosen with 6 plots (elements) randomly selected from each. (Each crew can survey 6 plots in one day.) The data are

Exercises

given in the table. Estimate the total number of infected trees in the county, and place a bound on the error of estimation.

Area	Number of Plots	Number of Plots Sampled	Number of Infected Trees per Plot
1	12	6	15, 14, 21, 13, 9, 10
2	15	6	4, 6, 10, 9, 8, 5
3	14	6	10, 11, 14, 10, 9, 15
4	21	6	8, 3, 4, 1, 2, 5

9.9 A new bottling machine is being tested by a company. During a test run, the machine fills 24 cases, each containing 12 bottles. It is desired to estimate the average number of ounces of fill per bottle. A two-stage cluster sample is employed using 6 cases (clusters), with 4 bottles (elements) randomly selected from each. The results are given in the table.

Case	Average Ounces of Fill for Sample, $\bar{y}_i$	Sample Variance, s_i^2
1	7.9	.15
2	8.0	.12
3	7.8	.09
4	7.9	.11
5	8.1	.10
6	7.9	.12

Estimate the average number of ounces per bottle, and place a bound on the error of estimation.

9.10 A certain manufacturing plant contains 40 machines, all producing the same product (say, boxes of cereal). It is desired to estimate the proportion of defective products (say, boxes underfilled) for a given day. Discuss the relative merits of two-stage cluster sampling (machines as clusters of boxes) versus stratified random sampling (machines as strata) as possible designs for this study.

EXPERIENCES WITH REAL DATA

1. Refer to table 5.4. Construct a two-stage cluster sampling estimate of the total rural population in the United States for 1970 by first sampling divisions and then sampling states within divisions. Sample 4 of the 9 divisions and at least 2 states within each sampled division. Compute an estimate of the variance attached to your estimator. Would you recommend this procedure over stratified random sampling? Why?

2. When sampling people, the naturally occurring frames typically involve people grouped in clusters. Hence two-stage cluster sampling is commonly employed as a matter of economic convenience. For example, try

9. Two-Stage Cluster Sampling

estimating the total number of library books currently checked out by students on your campus. (Any other numerical variable of interest to you can be substituted for the number of library books.) Some naturally occurring clusters of students are those in residence halls, classrooms, fraternities and sororities, and pages of a student directory. (Can you think of others?) Estimate the total of interest, and place a bound on the error of estimation, by

(a) sampling residences and students within residences
(b) sampling classrooms in use and students within classrooms
(c) sampling pages of the student directory and students' names within pages

Whichever method you choose, think carefully about the relative sample sizes for the first and second stages. If the experiment with students is not applicable to your situation, a simpler problem to carry out is to estimate the number of words in this (or any other) book by randomly sampling pages and then sampling lines within a page. Should the two-stage sampling scheme for a statistics book with formulas and tables differ from the scheme for a novel?

10.
Sampling from Wildlife Populations

10.1 INTRODUCTION

The estimation of population sizes is very important in the study of growth, evolution, and maintenance of many wildlife populations. Various techniques for sampling wildlife populations have been used for many years. We will discuss two procedures for obtaining an estimate of N, the total size of a wildlife population.

The first method is *direct sampling*. Basically, this procedure entails drawing a random sample from a wildlife population of interest, tagging each animal sampled, and returning the tagged animals to the population. At a later date another random sample (of a fixed size) is drawn from the same population, and the number of tagged animals is observed. If N represents the total population size, t represents the number of animals tagged in the initial sample, and p represents the proportion of tagged animals in the population, then

$$\frac{t}{N} = p$$

Consequently, $N = t/p$. We can obtain an estimate of N because t is known and p can be estimated by $\hat{p}$, the proportion of tagged animals in the second sample. Thus

$$\hat{N} = \frac{\text{the number of animals tagged}}{\text{the proportion of tagged animals in the second sample}}$$

10. Sampling from Wildlife Populations

or, equivalently,

$$\hat{N} = \frac{t}{\hat{p}}$$

The second technique is *inverse sampling*. It is similar to direct sampling, but the second sample size is not fixed. That is, we sample until a fixed number of tagged animals is observed. Using this procedure, we can also obtain an estimate of N, the total population size, using

$$\hat{N} = \frac{t}{\hat{p}}$$

10.2 ESTIMATION OF A POPULATION SIZE USING DIRECT SAMPLING

Direct sampling can be used to estimate the size of a mobile population. First, a random sample size t is drawn from the population of interest. At a later date a second sample of size n is drawn. For example, suppose a conservationist is concerned about the apparent decline in the number of seals in Alaska. Estimates of the population size are available from previous years. To determine whether or not there has been a decline, a random sample of $t = 200$ seals is caught, tagged, and then released. A month later a second sample of size $n = 100$ is obtained. Using these data (often called recapture data) we can estimate N, the population size.

Let s be the number of tagged individuals observed in the second sample. The proportion of tagged individuals in the sample is

$$\hat{p} = \frac{s}{n}$$

An estimate of N is given by

$$\hat{N} = \frac{t}{\hat{p}} = \frac{nt}{s}$$

Estimator of N:

$$\hat{N} = \frac{nt}{s} \quad (10.1)$$

Estimated variance of $\hat{N}$:

$$\hat{V}(\hat{N}) = \frac{t^2 n(n-s)}{s^3} \quad (10.2)$$

10.2 Estimation of a Population Size Using Direct Sampling

Bound on the error of estimation:

$$2\sqrt{\hat{V}(\hat{N})} = 2\sqrt{\frac{t^2 n(n-s)}{s^3}} \qquad (10.3)$$

Note that s must be greater than 0 for equations (10.1), (10.2), and (10.3) to hold. We will assume that n is large enough so that s is greater than 0 with high probability.

You should also realize that $\hat{N}$, which is presented in equation (10.1), is not an unbiased estimator of N. For $s > 0$

$$E(\hat{N}) \approx N + \frac{N(N-t)}{nt}$$

Hence for fairly large sample sizes, that is, t and n large, the term

$$\frac{N(N-t)}{nt}$$

is small and the bias of the estimator $\hat{N}$ approaches 0. $\hat{N}$ tends to overestimate the true value of N. Chapman (1952) gives another estimator of N, along with its approximate variance, which is nearly unbiased for most direct sampling situations.

Example 10.1
Before posting a schedule for the upcoming hunting season, the game commission for a particular county wishes to estimate the size of the deer population. A random sample of 300 deer is captured ($t = 300$). The deer are tagged and released. A second sample of 200 is taken two weeks later ($n = 200$). If 62 tagged deer are recaptured in the second sample ($s = 62$), estimate N and place a bound on the error of estimation.

Solution
Using equation (10.1), we have

$$\hat{N} = \frac{nt}{s} = \frac{200(300)}{62} = 967.74$$

or $\hat{N} = 968$.

A bound on the error of estimation is given by

$$2\sqrt{\hat{V}(\hat{N})} = 2\sqrt{\frac{t^2 n(n-s)}{s^3}} = 2\sqrt{\frac{(300)^2(200)(138)}{(62)^3}} = 204.18$$

Thus the game commission estimates the total number of deer is 968 with a bound on the error of estimation of approximately 205 deer.

10. Sampling from Wildlife Populations

You may be concerned about the magnitude of the bound on the error of estimation in this example. As might be expected, we can obtain a more accurate estimator of N by increasing the two sample sizes (n and t). Further information on the choice of t and n is given in section 10.4.

10.3 ESTIMATION OF A POPULATION SIZE USING INVERSE SAMPLING

Inverse sampling is the second method for estimating N, the total size of a population. We again assume that an initial sample of t individuals is drawn, tagged, and released. Later, random sampling is conducted until exactly s tagged animals are recaptured. If the sample contains n individuals, the proportion of tagged individuals in the sample is given by $\hat{p} = s/n$. We use this sample proportion to estimate the proportion of tagged individuals in the population.

Again, the estimator of N is given by

$$\hat{N} = \frac{t}{\hat{p}} = \frac{nt}{s}$$

but it is important to note that s is fixed and n is random.

Estimator of N:

$$\hat{N} = \frac{nt}{s} \qquad (10.4)$$

Estimated variance of $\hat{N}$:

$$\hat{V}(\hat{N}) = \frac{t^2 n(n-s)}{s^2(s+1)} \qquad (10.5)$$

Bound on the error of estimation:

$$2\sqrt{\hat{V}(\hat{N})} = 2\sqrt{\frac{t^2 n(n-s)}{s^2(s+1)}} \qquad (10.6)$$

Note that equations (10.4), (10.5), and (10.6) hold only for $s > 0$. This restriction offers no difficulty; we simply specify that s must be greater than 0, and we sample until s tagged individuals are recaptured. The estimator $\hat{N} = nt/s$, obtained using inverse sampling, provides an unbiased estimator of N, and the variance given by equation (10.5) is an unbiased estimator of the true variance of $\hat{N}$.

10.4 Choosing Sample Sizes for Direct and Inverse Sampling

Variance (10.5) for the inverse case looks very much like variance (10.2) for the direct case, and the estimators $\hat{N}$ appear to be identical. However, the inverse method offers the advantages that s can be fixed in advance, $\hat{N}$ is unbiased, and an unbiased estimator of the true variance of $\hat{N}$ is available.

Example 10.2
Authorities of a large wildlife preserve are interested in the total number of birds of a particular species that inhabit the preserve. A random sample of $t = 150$ birds is trapped, tagged, and then released. In the same month a second sample is drawn until 35 tagged birds are recaptured ($s = 35$). In total, 100 birds are recaptured in order to find 35 tagged ones ($n = 100$). Estimate N and place a bound on the error of estimation.

Solution
Using equation (10.4), we estimate N by

$$\hat{N} = \frac{nt}{s} = \frac{100(150)}{35} = 428.57$$

A bound on the error of estimation is found by using equation (10.6) as follows:

$$2\sqrt{\hat{V}(\hat{N})} = 2\sqrt{\frac{t^2 n(n-s)}{s^2(s+1)}} = 2\sqrt{\frac{(150)^2(100)(65)}{(35)^2(36)}} = 115.173$$

Hence we estimate that 429 birds of the particular species inhabit the preserve. We are quite confident that our estimate is within approximately 116 birds of the true population size.

10.4 CHOOSING SAMPLE SIZES FOR DIRECT AND INVERSE SAMPLING

We have been discussing direct sampling and inverse sampling techniques. You probably wonder which is the better to use. Either method can be used. Inverse sampling yields more precise information than does direct sampling, provided the second sample size n required to recapture s tagged individuals is small relative to the population size N. However, if nothing is known about the size of N, a poor choice of t could make n quite large when inverse sampling is used. For example, if $N = 10{,}000$ and a first sample of $t = 50$ individuals is drawn, it would take a large second sample to obtain exactly $s = 10$ tagged animals.

Table 10.1 is useful in determining the sample sizes (t and n) required to estimate $\hat{N}$ with a fixed bound on the error of estimation. However, to use these data requires some prior knowledge concerning

10. Sampling from Wildlife Populations

the magnitude of N. Entries in table 10.1 are $V(\hat{N})/N$ for direct sampling. If you know the approximate size of N, you can determine the variance of the estimator for fixed values of the sample sizes t and n. In table 10.1 these sample sizes are expressed as fractions of N. These fractions, given by

$$p_1 = \frac{t}{N} \quad \text{and} \quad p_2 = \frac{n}{N}$$

are called sampling fractions.

Table 10.1/Values of $\dfrac{V(\hat{N})}{N}$ **for direct sampling**

$p_2 = \dfrac{n}{N}$	\multicolumn{6}{c}{$p_1 = \dfrac{t}{N}$}					
	.001	.01	.1	.25	.50	1.0
.001	999,000	99,000	9,000	3,000	1,000	0
.01	99,900	9,900	900	300	100	0
.1	9,990	990	90	30	10	0
.25	3,996	396	36	12	4	0
.50	1,998	198	18	6	2	0
1.0	999	99	9	3	1	0

It would be convenient to have a graph of the entries in this table. However, the numbers are so large that we can only display a portion of table 10.1. In figure 10.1 we display the values of $V(\hat{N})/N$ for various values of the sampling fractions $p_1 = t/N$ and $p_2 = n/N$. Note that as either p_1 or p_2 increases, the variance of $\hat{N}$ divided by N decreases; consequently $V(\hat{N})$ decreases for a fixed value of N. Intuitively this makes sense since we should obtain a more accurate estimate of N by taking large sample sizes.

Example 10.3
The game commission in example 10.1 believes that the size of the deer population is approximately the same as in the preceding year, when there were between 800 and 1,000 deer. Determine the bound on the error of estimation associated with the sampling fractions of $p_1 = .25$ and $p_2 = .25$.

Solution
We take the larger of the two figures (N approximately 1,000) to obtain a conservative estimate of $V(\hat{N})$ (one that is larger than would be expected). We see from figure 10.1 (or table 10.1) that the sampling fractions of $p_1 = t/N = .25$ and $p_2 = s/N = .25$ yield

$$\frac{V(\hat{N})}{N} = 12$$

10.4 Choosing Sample Sizes for Direct and Inverse Sampling

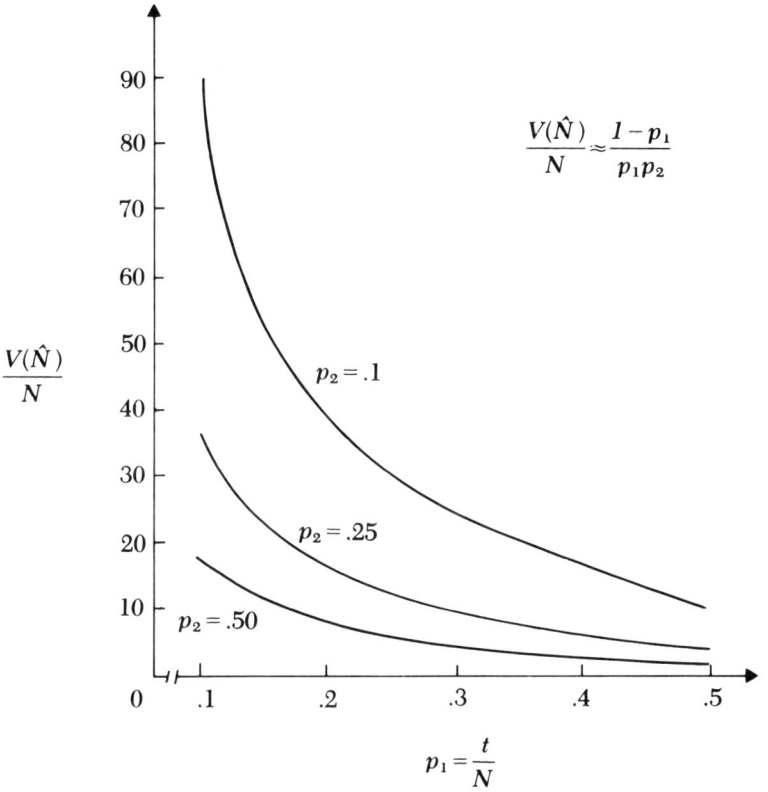

Figure 10.1/*Graph of values of table 10.1*

Taking $N = 1{,}000$ we have
$$V(\hat{N}) = 1{,}000(12) = 12{,}000$$
$$\sqrt{V(\hat{N})} = \sqrt{12{,}000} = 109.541$$

The corresponding bound on the error of estimation is
$$2\sqrt{V(\hat{N})} = 2(109.541) = 219.082$$

An investigator could use this information to plan his survey. If this bound on the error of estimation is acceptable, he could run a survey using $p_1 = .25$ and $p_2 = .25$; that is, he could draw an initial sample of
$$t = p_1 N = (.25)(1000) = 250$$
and a second sample of
$$n = p_2 N = (.25)(1000) = 250$$

He could then estimate N using the data from the survey. The bound on the error of estimation should be approximately equal to 220, provided the original range for N is accurate.

10. Sampling from Wildlife Populations

If the bound on the error for $\hat{N}$ is not acceptable using the sampling fractions of $p_1 = p_2 = .25$, the investigator can work with table 10.1 (or figure 10.1) to determine the sampling fractions required to achieve an acceptable bound on the error of estimation.

We can examine $V(\hat{N})$ for inverse sampling in the same manner as

Table 10.2 / Values of $\dfrac{V(\hat{N})}{N}$ for inverse sampling

	\multicolumn{6}{c}{$p_1 = \dfrac{t}{N}$}					
$p_2 = \dfrac{s}{N}$	.001	.01	.1	.25	.5	1.0
.001	999	990	900	750	500	0
.01		99	90	75	50	0
.1			9	7.5	5	0
.25				3	2	0
.5					1	0
1.0						0

for direct sampling. Entries in table 10.2 are the values of $V(\hat{N})/N$ for various sampling fractions $p_1 = t/N$ and $p_2 = s/N$ when inverse sampling is used. You recall that in inverse sampling we fix s rather than n; hence the second sampling fraction is in terms of s. A graphical representation of these data would be helpful, but again the numbers are too large to plot conveniently. A portion of table 10.2 is presented in figure 10.2.

Note that $V(\hat{N})/N$ [or equivalently, $V(\hat{N})$ for a given value of N] decreases as p_1 and p_2 increase. If the experimenter has an approximate range for N, he or she could use either figure 10.2 or table 10.2 to determine the sampling fractions $(p_1 = t/N, p_2 = s/N)$ necessary to achieve a reasonable bound. Then the experimenter could conduct a survey with an initial sample of

$$t = p_1 N$$

The experimenter would begin a second sample at a future time and continue until

$$s = p_2 N$$

tagged animals are recaptured. The corresponding bound on the error of estimation for N would be acceptable provided the original estimate for N was reasonable.

The preceding tag-recapture techniques can be extended to more than two stages. At the second stage the $(n - s)$ untagged animals can be tagged and all n returned to the population. At a later time a third sample can be taken, and the counting and tagging operation repeated. This

10.5 Summary

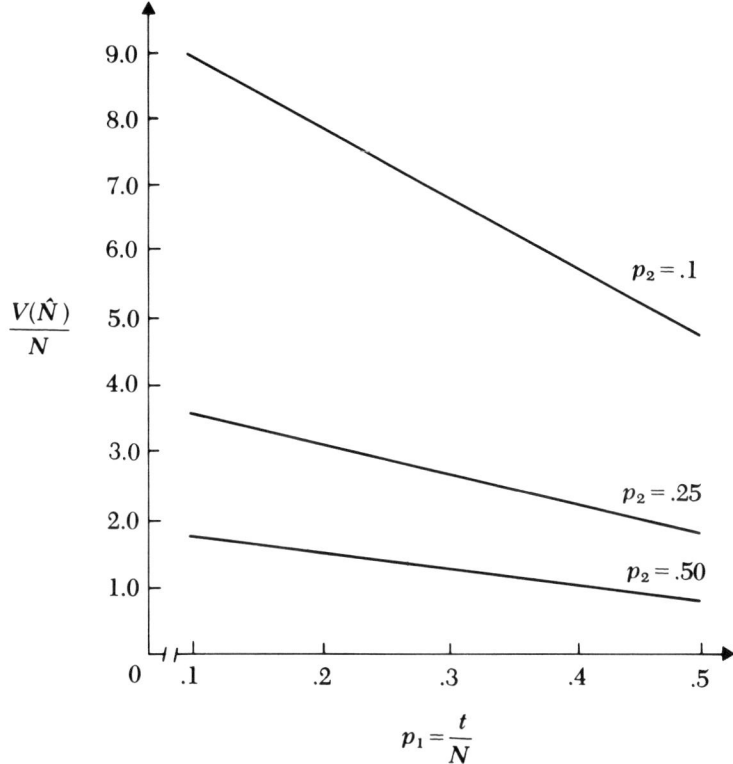

Figure 10.2/*Graph of values of table 10.2*

multiple-stage approach will result in an improved estimator of N and is especially useful in ongoing studies where samples might be taken every week or so.

Many other techniques for estimating population size and other characteristics of animal populations are available but will not be surveyed here. An excellent reference is the manual of wildlife investigational techniques listed in the references at the end of this chapter.

10.5 SUMMARY

Estimation of the size of a population is often very important when studying mobile animal populations. This chapter presents two procedures for estimating the total population size N.

The first technique is direct sampling. A random sample of t individuals is drawn from a population and tagged. At a later date a fixed random sample of size n is drawn and the number of tagged individuals is observed. Using these data, we can estimate N and place a bound on the error of estimation.

10. Sampling from Wildlife Populations

The second technique, inverse sampling, is similar to direct sampling with the exception that we continue sampling until a fixed number s of tagged individuals is recaptured in the second sample. The sample data are then used to estimate N and to place a bound on the error of estimation.

When a choice is available between inverse and direct sampling procedures, inverse procedure appears to provide more accurate results. However, in some instances, particularly when little or nothing is known concerning the relative size of N, the direct sampling procedure is the better choice.

REFERENCES

Bailey, N. T. J. "On Estimating the Size of Mobile Populations from Recapture Data." *Biometrika*, vol. 38 (1951), pp. 292–306.

Chapman, D. G. "Inverse, Multiple and Sequential Sample Censuses." *Biometrics*, vol. 8 (1952), pp. 286–306.

Lovelace, C. M. "The Mobility and Composition of Bobwhite Quail Populations in South Florida." Florida Game and Fresh Water Fish Commission Technical Report No. 4 (1958).

Mosby, H. S., ed. *Wildlife Investigational Techniques*. 3d ed. Washington, D.C.: Wildlife Society, 1969.

EXERCISES

10.1 Discuss the differences between direct and inverse sampling.

10.2 Name the restriction implicit in the use of (a) direct sampling, or (b) inverse sampling. How can this restriction be satisfied in each case?

10.3 Assuming the cost of sampling is not significant, how can you improve the bound on the error of estimation using either direct or inverse sampling?

10.4 A particular sportsmen's club is concerned about the number of brook trout in a certain stream. During a period of several days, $t = 100$ trout are caught, tagged, and then returned to the stream. Note that the sample represents 100 different fish; hence any fish caught during these dates that had already been tagged was immediately released. Several weeks later a second sample of $n = 120$ trout is caught and observed. If 27 in the second sample were tagged ($s = 27$), estimate N, the total size of the population, and place a bound on the error of estimation.

10.5 Wildlife biologists wish to estimate the total size of the bobwhite quail population in a section of southern Florida. A series of 50 traps is used. In the first sample $t = 320$ quail are caught. After being captured each bird is removed from the trap and tagged with a metal band on its left leg. All birds are then released.

Exercises

Several months later a second sample of $n = 515$ quail is obtained. If $s = 91$ of these birds have tags, estimate N, and place a bound on the error of estimation.

10.6 A game commission is interested in estimating the number of large-mouth bass in a reservoir. A random sample of $t = 2876$ bass is caught. Each bass is marked and released. One month later a second sample of $n = 2562$ is caught. If $s = 678$ have tags in the second sample, estimate the total population size. Place a bound on the error of estimation.

10.7 A team of conservationists is interested in estimating the size of the pheasant population in a particular area prior to the hunting season. The team believes that the true population size is between 2000 and 3000. Assuming $N \approx 3000$, the sampling fractions of p_1 and p_2 equal to .25 should give a bound on the error of estimation approximately equal to $2(189.74) = 379.48$ (figure 10.1). The conservationists feel that this bound on the error is reasonable and so decide to choose $t = 750$ and $n = 750$. By using traps they catch 750 pheasants for the first sample. Each of these pheasants is tagged and released. Several weeks later the second sample of $n = 750$ is obtained. If 168 of these pheasants have tags ($s = 168$), estimate the population size and place a bound on the error of estimation.

10.8 City officials are concerned about the nuisance caused by pigeons around city hall. To emphasize the problem, they hire a team of investigators to estimate the number of pigeons occupying the building. Using several different traps a sample of $t = 60$ pigeons is captured, tagged, and released. One month later the process is repeated, using $n = 60$. If $s = 18$ tagged pigeons are observed in the second sample, estimate N, and place a bound on the error of estimation.

10.9 Animal resource experts on a particular game preserve are concerned about an apparent decline in the rabbit population. In a study conducted two years ago, the population size was estimated to be $N = 2500$. Assume the population size is still of this magnitude and use figure 10.1 to determine the approximate sample sizes (t and n) required to estimate N with a bound equal to 356.

10.10 A zoologist wishes to estimate the size of the turtle population in a given geographical area. She believes that the turtle population size is between 500 and 1000; hence an initial sample of 100 (10%) appears to be sufficient. The $t = 100$ turtles are caught, tagged, and released. A second sampling is begun one month later and it is decided to continue sampling until $s = 15$ tagged turtles are recaptured. If it takes 160 turtles to obtain 15 tagged turtles ($n = 160$, $s = 15$), estimate N, and place a bound on the error of estimation.

10.11 Due to a particularly harsh winter, state park officials are concerned about the number of squirrels inhabiting their parks. An initial sample of $t = 100$ squirrels is trapped, tagged, and released. As soon as the first sample is completed, the officials begin working on a second sample of $n = 75$. They trap 10 squirrels that were tagged previously. Estimate N, and place a bound on the error of estimation.

10.12 Assume the costs of taking an observation in the first sample and in the

10. Sampling from Wildlife Populations

second sample are the same. Determine which is the most desirable: to have $t > n$, $t = n$, or $t < n$ for a fixed cost of conducting the two samples. (Hint: Consult figures 10.1 and 10.2.)

10.13 A team of wildlife ecologists is interested in the effectiveness of an antifertility drug in controlling the growth of pigeon populations. To measure effectiveness, they will estimate the size of the population this year and compare it to the estimated size for a previous year. A large trap was constructed for the experiment. The trap was then baited with a corn feed containing a fixed amount of the drug. An initial sample of $t = 120$ pigeons is trapped and allowed to eat the medicated feed. Each bird is then tagged on its leg and released. At a later date a second sample of $n = 100$ pigeons is trapped. If 48 of these birds have tags ($s = 48$), estimate the size of the pigeon population, and place a bound on the error of estimation.

EXPERIENCES WITH REAL DATA

1. Simulate the tag-recapture technique for animal populations by conducting the following experiment. Put a known number, N, of beads in a jar. Mark t of them in some distinguishable manner and thoroughly mix the beads. Then sample n beads, record the number of "tags," and estimate N by the direct method, placing a bound on the error of estimation. Does the resulting interval include your known N?

    Replace the n beads and repeat the sampling using the inverse method (sample until you have s tagged beads), and place a bound on the error. Does this interval include N?

    You might try various sample sizes and various degrees of mixing. How would you choose an appropriate sample size? What do you think would happen if the marked beads were not thoroughly mixed with the others? Does this suggest a realistic difficulty with the tag-recapture method?

2. The structure of the problems discussed in this chapter require that there be t marked objects (tags) randomly distributed among the N objects in a population. If t is known, a random sample of size n will supply information to estimate N, provided that some marked objects show up in the sample. The marked objects could be entered into the population without taking an initial sample.

    Try the following technique for estimating the size of a crowd at a sporting event, lecture, movie, or other similar event. Obtain the names and descriptions of t people that you know will be attending the event. Ask them to distribute themselves somewhat randomly in the crowd. Then sample n people at random, perhaps as people leave the building. Count the number of original t "tagged" individuals who appear in your sample, and estimate N. (You could use the inverse sample method here also.)

11.

Supplemental Topics

11.1 INTRODUCTION

Four sample survey designs, simple and stratified random sampling, cluster sampling, and systematic sampling, have been discussed in preceding chapters. For each design it was assumed that the data were correctly recorded and provided an accurate representation of the n elements sampled from the population of interest. Under these assumptions we were able to estimate certain population parameters and place a bound on the error of estimation.

There are many situations in which the assumptions underlying these designs are not fulfilled. First, the recorded measurements are not always accurate representations of the desired data, because of biases of the interviewers or measuring equipment. Second, the frame is not always adequate and hence the sample might not have been selected from the complete population of interest. Third, accurate sample data might be impossible to obtain because of the sensitive nature of the questions.

In this chapter we give some methods for analyzing data when measurement errors are present or an inadequate frame is used.

11.2 INTERPENETRATING SUBSAMPLES

An experimenter is interested in obtaining information from a simple random sample of n persons selected from a population size N. She has k

interviewers available to do the field work, but the interviewers differ in their manner of interviewing and hence they obtain slightly different responses from identical subjects. For example, suppose the interviewer is to rate the health of a respondent on a scale from 0 to 5, with 0 denoting poor health. Obtaining this type of data requires skill in interviewing and a subjective judgment by the interviewer. One interviewer might not obtain enough information and might tend to rate the health of an individual too high, while another might obtain detailed information and tend to rate the health too low.

A good estimate of the population mean can be obtained by using the following technique. Randomly divide the n sampled elements into k subsamples of m elements each, and assign one interviewer to each of the k subsamples. Note that $m = n/k$ and n can always be chosen so that m is an integer. We consider the first subsample to be a simple random sample of size m selected from the n elements in the total sample. The second subsample is then a simple random sample of size m selected from the $n - m$ remaining elements. This process is continued until the n elements have been randomly divided into k subsamples. The k subsamples are sometimes called *interpenetrating subsamples.*

We expect some interviewers to give measurements that are too small and some too large, but the average of all sample measurements should be close to the population mean. That is, we expect the biases of the investigators to possess an average that is very near zero. Thus the sample mean $\bar{y}$ is the best estimator of the population mean μ, even though the measurements are biased.

We use the following notation. Let y_{ij} denote the jth observation in the ith subsample, $j = 1, \ldots, m, i = 1, \ldots, k$. Then $\bar{y}_i$, given by

$$\bar{y}_i = \frac{1}{m} \sum_{j=1}^{m} y_{ij} \tag{11.1}$$

is the average of all observations in the ith subsample. The sample mean $\bar{y}$ is the average of the k subsample means.

Estimator of the population mean μ:

$$\bar{y} = \frac{1}{k} \sum_{i=1}^{k} \bar{y}_i \tag{11.2}$$

Estimated variance of $\bar{y}$:

$$\hat{V}(\bar{y}) = \left(\frac{N-n}{N}\right) \frac{\sum_{i=1}^{k}(\bar{y}_i - \bar{y})^2}{k(k-1)} \tag{11.3}$$

11.2 Interpenetrating Subsamples

Bound on the error of estimation:

$$2\sqrt{\hat{V}(\bar{\bar{y}})} = 2\sqrt{\left(\frac{N-n}{n}\right)\frac{\sum_{i=1}^{k}(\bar{y}_i - \bar{\bar{y}})^2}{k(k-1)}} \qquad (11.4)$$

The technique of interpenetrating subsamples gives an estimate of the variance of $\bar{\bar{y}}$, given in equation (11.3), which accounts for interviewer biases. That is, the estimated variance given in equation (11.3) is usually larger than the standard estimate of the variance of a sample mean obtained in simple random sampling because of the biases present in the measurements.

Example 11.1
A sociologist wants to estimate the average height of adult males in a community containing 800 men. He has 10 assistants, each with his or her own equipment, to acquire the measurements. Since the experimenter believes the assistants will produce slightly biased measurements, he decides to take a simple random sample of n = 80 males from the population and randomly divide the sample into 10 subsamples of 8 persons each. Each assistant is then assigned to one subsample. The measurements produce the following subsample means (measurements in feet):

$$\begin{array}{ll}
\bar{y}_1 = 5.9 & \bar{y}_6 = 5.7 \\
\bar{y}_2 = 5.8 & \bar{y}_7 = 5.8 \\
\bar{y}_3 = 6.1 & \bar{y}_8 = 5.6 \\
\bar{y}_4 = 6.0 & \bar{y}_9 = 5.9 \\
\bar{y}_5 = 6.1 & \bar{y}_{10} = 6.0
\end{array}$$

Estimate the mean height of adult males in the community, and place a bound on the error of estimation.

Solution
The best estimate of the population mean is the sample mean $\bar{\bar{y}}$. Thus from equation (11.2),

$$\bar{\bar{y}} = \frac{1}{k}\sum_{i=1}^{k}\bar{y}_i = \frac{1}{10}(5.9 + 5.8 + \cdots + 6.0) = 5.89$$

We must now estimate the variance of $\bar{\bar{y}}$ using equation (11.3). The following identity can be established:

$$\sum_{i=1}^{k}(\bar{y}_i - \bar{\bar{y}})^2 = \sum_{i=1}^{k}\bar{y}_i^2 - \frac{\left(\sum_{i=1}^{k}\bar{y}_i\right)^2}{k}$$

Substituting, we obtain

$$\sum_{i=1}^{k} (\bar{y}_i - \bar{y})^2 = 347.17 - \frac{(58.9)^2}{10} = .25$$

Then

$$\hat{V}(\bar{y}) = \left(\frac{N-n}{N}\right) \frac{\sum_{i=1}^{k}(\bar{y}_i - \bar{y})^2}{k(k-1)} = \left(\frac{800-80}{800}\right)\left(\frac{.25}{10(9)}\right) = .0025$$

The estimate of the mean height of adult males with a bound on the error of estimation is given by

$$\bar{y} \pm 2\sqrt{\hat{V}(\bar{y})}, \quad \text{or} \quad 5.89 \pm 2\sqrt{.0025}, \quad \text{or} \quad 5.89 \pm .10$$

To summarize, the best estimate of the mean height is 5.89 feet and we are reasonably confident that our error of estimation is less than .10 feet.

11.3 ESTIMATION OF MEANS AND TOTALS OVER SUBPOPULATIONS

It is often impossible to obtain a frame that lists only those elements in the population of interest. For example, we may wish to sample households containing children, but the best frame available may be a list of all households in a city. We may be interested in a firm's overdue accounts, but the only frame available may list all the firm's accounts receivable. In situations of this type, we wish to estimate parameters of a subpopulation of the population represented in the frame. Sampling is complicated because we do not know whether an element belongs to the subpopulation until after it has been sampled.

The problem of estimating a subpopulation mean is solved essentially in the same manner as in chapter 4. Let N denote the number of elements in the population and N_1 the number of elements in the subpopulation of interest. A simple random sample of n elements is selected from the population of N elements. Let n_1 denote the number of sampled elements that are from the subpopulation of interest. Let y_{1j} denote the jth sampled observation that falls in the subpopulation. Then the sample mean for elements from the subpopulation, denoted by $\bar{y}_1$, is given by

$$\bar{y}_1 = \frac{1}{n_1} \sum_{j=1}^{n_1} y_{1j}$$

The sample mean $\bar{y}_1$ is an unbiased estimate of the subpopulation mean μ_1.

11.3 Estimation of Means and Totals over Subpopulations

Estimator of the subpopulation mean μ_1:

$$\bar{y}_1 = \frac{1}{n_1} \sum_{j=1}^{n_1} y_{1j} \qquad (11.5)$$

Estimated variance of $\bar{y}_1$:

$$\hat{V}(\bar{y}_1) = \left(\frac{N_1 - n_1}{N_1}\right) \frac{\sum_{j=1}^{n_1} (y_{1j} - \bar{y}_1)^2}{n_1(n_1 - 1)} \qquad (11.6)$$

Bound on the error of estimation:

$$2\sqrt{\hat{V}(\bar{y}_1)} = 2\sqrt{\left(\frac{N_1 - n_1}{N_1}\right) \frac{\sum_{j=1}^{n_1} (y_{1j} - \bar{y}_1)^2}{n_1(n_1 - 1)}} \qquad (11.7)$$

The quantity $(N_1 - n_1)/N_1$ can be estimated by $(N - n)/N$ if N_1 is unknown.

Example 11.2

An economist wants to estimate the average weekly amount spent on food by families with children in a certain county known to be a poverty area. A complete list of all the 250 families in the county is available, but it is impossible to identify those families with children. The economist selects a simple random sample of $n = 50$ families and finds that $n_1 = 42$ families have at least one child. The 42 families with children are interviewed and give the following information:

$$\sum_{j=1}^{42} y_{1j} = \$1{,}720 \qquad \sum_{j=1}^{42} y_{1j}^2 = 72{,}200$$

Estimate the average weekly amount spent on food by all families with children, and place a bound on the error of estimation.

Solution

The estimator of the population mean is $\bar{y}_1$, given by equation (11.5). Calculations yield

$$\bar{y}_1 = \frac{1}{n_1} \sum_{j=1}^{n_1} y_{1j} = \frac{1}{42}(1{,}720) = 40.95$$

We have the equality

$$\sum_{j=1}^{n_1} (y_{1j} - \bar{y}_1)^2 = \sum_{j=1}^{n_1} y_{1j}^2 - \frac{1}{n_1}\left(\sum_{j=1}^{n_1} y_{1j}\right)^2$$

11. Supplemental Topics

and substituting,

$$\sum_{j=1}^{n_1}(y_{1j}-\bar{y}_1)^2 = 72{,}200 - \frac{1}{42}(1{,}720)^2 = 1{,}762$$

The quantity $(N_1 - n_1)/N_1$ must be estimated by $(N - n)/N$, since N_1 is unknown. The estimated variance of $\bar{y}_1$, given in equation (11.6), then becomes

$$\hat{V}(\bar{y}_1) = \left(\frac{N-n}{N}\right)\frac{\sum_{j=1}^{n_1}(y_{1j}-\bar{y}_1)^2}{n_1(n_1-1)} = \left(\frac{250-50}{250}\right)\left(\frac{1762}{42(41)}\right)$$

$$= .819$$

Thus the estimate of the population average with a bound on the error of estimation is given by

$$\bar{y}_1 \pm 2\sqrt{\hat{V}(\bar{y}_1)}, \quad \text{or} \quad 40.95 \pm 2\sqrt{.819}, \quad \text{or} \quad 40.95 \pm 1.81$$

Our best estimate of the average weekly amount spent on food by families with children is $40.95. The error of estimation should be less than $1.81 with probability approximately .95.

If the number of elements in the subpopulation N_1 is known, the subpopulation total τ_1 can be estimated by $N_1\bar{y}_1$.

Estimator of the subpopulation total τ_1:

$$N_1\bar{y}_1 = \frac{N_1}{n_1}\sum_{j=1}^{n_1}y_{1j} \qquad (11.8)$$

Estimated variance of $N_1\bar{y}_1$:

$$\hat{V}(N_1\bar{y}_1) = N_1^2\hat{V}(\bar{y}_1) = N_1^2\left(\frac{N_1-n_1}{N_1}\right)\frac{\sum_{j=1}^{n_1}(y_{1j}-\bar{y}_1)^2}{n_1(n_1-1)} \qquad (11.9)$$

Bound on the error of estimation:

$$2\sqrt{\hat{V}(N_1\bar{y}_1)} = 2\sqrt{N_1^2\left(\frac{N_1-n_1}{N_1}\right)\frac{\sum_{j=1}^{n_1}(y_{1j}-\bar{y}_1)^2}{n_1(n_1-1)}} \qquad (11.10)$$

11.3 Estimation of Means and Totals over Subpopulations

Example 11.3
A recent preliminary study of the county in example 11.2 reveals $N_1 = 205$ families with children. Using this information and data given in example 11.2, estimate the total weekly amount spent on food by families with children. (Note: N_1 will vary over time. We assume that the value of N_1 used in this analysis is correct.)

Solution
The best estimator of the total is $N_1 \bar{y}_1$, given in equation (11.8), which yields an estimate of

$$N_1 \bar{y}_1 = 205(40.95) = 8{,}394.75$$

The quantity $\sum_{j=1}^{n_1} (y_{1j} - \bar{y}_1)^2$ is calculated in example 11.2 to be 1,762. The estimated variance of $N_1 \bar{y}_1$ is then [from equation (11.9)]

$$\hat{V}(N_1 \bar{y}_1) = N_1^2 \left(\frac{N_1 - n_1}{N_1} \right) \frac{\sum_{j=1}^{n_1} (y_{1j} - \bar{y}_1)^2}{n_1(n_1 - 1)}$$

$$= (205)^2 \left(\frac{205 - 42}{205} \right) \left(\frac{1{,}762}{42(41)} \right) = 34{,}191.19$$

The estimate of the total weekly amount that families with children spend on food, given with a bound on the error of estimation, is

$$N_1 \bar{y}_1 \pm 2\sqrt{\hat{V}(N_1 \bar{y}_1)}$$

$$8{,}394.75 \pm 2\sqrt{34{,}191.19}$$

$$8{,}394.75 \pm 369{,}82$$

Frequently the number of elements in the subpopulation, N_1, is unknown. For example, it would be difficult to determine the exact number of households containing children in a city, whereas the total number of households could perhaps be obtained from a city directory. An unbiased estimate of τ can still be obtained even though N_1 is unknown.

11. Supplemental Topics

Estimator of the subpopulation total τ_1 when N_1 is unknown:

$$\hat{\tau}_1 = \frac{N}{n} \sum_{j=1}^{n_1} y_{1j} \tag{11.11}$$

Estimated variance of $\hat{\tau}_1$:

$$\hat{V}(\hat{\tau}_1) = N^2 \left(\frac{N-n}{N}\right) \frac{\sum_{j=1}^{n_1} y_{1j}^2 - \frac{\left(\sum_{j=1}^{n_1} y_{1j}\right)^2}{n}}{n(n-1)} \tag{11.12}$$

Bound on the error of estimation:

$$2\sqrt{\hat{V}(\hat{\tau}_1)} = 2\sqrt{N^2 \left(\frac{N-n}{N}\right) \frac{\sum_{j=1}^{n_1} y_{1j}^2 - \frac{\left(\sum_{j=1}^{n_1} y_{1j}\right)^2}{n}}{n(n-1)}} \tag{11.13}$$

Example 11.4
Suppose that the experimenter in example 11.3 doubts the accuracy of the preliminary value of N_1. Use the data of example 11.3 to estimate the total weekly amount spent on food by families with children without using the value given for N_1.

Solution
The estimator of the total that does not depend on N_1 is $\hat{\tau}_1$, given by equation (11.11). Thus

$$\hat{\tau}_1 = \frac{N}{n} \sum_{j=1}^{n_1} y_{1j} = \frac{250}{50}(1{,}720) = 8{,}600$$

Substituting into equation (11.12), the estimated variance of $\hat{\tau}_1$ is

$$\hat{V}(\hat{\tau}_1) = N^2 \left(\frac{N-n}{N}\right) \frac{\sum_{j=1}^{n_1} y_{1j}^2 - \frac{1}{n}\left(\sum_{j=1}^{n_1} y_{1j}\right)^2}{n(n-1)}$$

$$= (250)^2 \left(\frac{250-50}{250}\right) \frac{72{,}200 - \frac{1}{50}(1{,}720)^2}{50(49)} = 265{,}960$$

11.4 Random Response Model

Thus the estimate of the total weekly amount spent on food with a bound on the error of estimation is

$$\hat{\tau}_1 \pm 2\sqrt{\hat{V}(\hat{\tau}_1)}, \quad or \quad 8{,}600 \pm 2\sqrt{265{,}960}, \quad or \quad 8{,}600 \pm 1{,}031.44$$

This is a large bound on the error of estimation and should be reduced by increasing the sample size n.

Note that the variance of $\hat{\tau}_1$, calculated in example 11.4, is much larger than the variance of $N_1 \bar{y}_1$, calculated in example 11.3. This is because the information provided by N_1 is used in $N_1 \bar{y}_1$ but not in $\hat{\tau}_1$. Thus if N_1 is known, or if it can be found with little additional cost, the estimator $N_1 \bar{y}_1$ should be used.

11.4 RANDOM RESPONSE MODEL

Persons being interviewed often refuse to answer or give correct answers to sensitive questions that may embarrass them or be harmful to them in some way. For example, some persons may not respond truthfully to political questions such as, "Are you a Communist?" In this section we present a method of estimating the proportion of people who have some characteristic of interest without obtaining direct answers from the people interviewed. The method is due to S. L. Warner (see the references at the end of the chapter).

Designate the people in the population who have or do not have the characteristic of interest as groups A and B, respectively. Thus each person in the population is in either group A or group B. Let p be the proportion of people in group A. The objective is to estimate p without asking each person directly whether or not he belongs to group A. We can estimate p by using a device called a *random response model*. We start with a stack of cards that are identical except that a fraction, θ, are marked with A and the remaining fraction, $(1 - \theta)$, are marked with B. A simple random sample of n people is selected from the population. Each person in the sample is asked to randomly draw a card from the deck and to state "yes" if the letter on the card agrees with the group to which he or she belongs, or "no" if the letter on the card is different from the group to which he or she belongs. The card is replaced before the next person draws. The interviewer does not see the card and simply records whether the response is "yes" or "no." Let n_1 be the number of people in the sample who respond with "yes." An unbiased estimator, $\hat{p}$, of the population proportion p is given in equation (11.14).

Estimator of a population proportion p:

$$\hat{p} = \frac{\theta - 1}{2\theta - 1} + \frac{n_1}{(2\theta - 1)n} \qquad (11.14)$$

Estimated variance of $\hat{p}$:

$$\hat{V}(\hat{p}) = \frac{1}{n}\left[\frac{1}{16\left(\theta - \frac{1}{2}\right)^2} - \left(\hat{p} - \frac{1}{2}\right)^2\right] \qquad (11.15)$$

Bound on the error of estimation:

$$2\sqrt{\hat{V}(\hat{p})} = 2\sqrt{\frac{1}{n}\left[\frac{1}{16\left(\theta - \frac{1}{2}\right)^2} - \left(\hat{p} - \frac{1}{2}\right)^2\right]} \qquad (11.16)$$

Equations (11.14), (11.15), and (11.16) are based on the assumption that the population size is large relative to n, so that the finite population correction can be ignored. The fraction θ of cards marked A may be arbitrarily chosen by the experimenter but must not equal $1/2$. A value $\theta = 1$ must not be used, because the respondents will then realize that they are telling whether or not they belong to group A, which is exactly what they do not wish to do. A value of θ between $1/2$ and 1, for example $3/4$, is usually adequate.

Example 11.5
A study is designed to estimate the proportion of people in a certain district who give false information on income tax returns. Since respondents would not admit cheating on tax returns, a random response technique is used. The experimenter constructs a deck of cards in which 3/4 of the cards are marked F, denoting a falsified return, and 1/4 are marked C, denoting a correct return. A simple random sample of n = 400 persons is selected from the large population of taxpayers in the district. In separate interviews each sampled taxpayer is asked to draw a card from the deck and to respond "yes" if the letter agrees with the group to which he or she belongs. The experiment results in n_1 = 120 "yes" responses. Estimate p, the proportion of taxpayers in the district who have falsified returns, and place a bound on the error of estimation.

Solution
From equation (11.4)

$$\hat{p} = \frac{\theta - 1}{2\theta - 1} + \frac{n_1}{(2\theta - 1)n}$$

$$= \frac{\frac{3}{4} - 1}{2(\frac{3}{4}) - 1} + \frac{120}{[2(\frac{3}{4}) - 1](400)}$$

$$= -\frac{1}{2} + \frac{3}{5} = \frac{1}{10} = .1$$

The estimated variance of $\hat{p}$ is given in equation (11.15) as

$$\hat{V}(\hat{p}) = \frac{1}{n}\left[\frac{1}{16(\theta - \frac{1}{2})^2} - (\hat{p} - \frac{1}{2})^2\right]$$

$$= \frac{1}{400}\left[\frac{1}{16(\frac{3}{4} - \frac{1}{2})^2} - (\frac{1}{10} - \frac{1}{2})^2\right] = .0021$$

The estimate of p with a bound on the error of estimation is then
$$\hat{p} \pm 2\sqrt{\hat{V}(\hat{p})}, \quad \text{or} \quad .1 \pm 2\sqrt{.0021}, \quad \text{or} \quad .1 \pm .092$$

This method generally requires a very large sample size in order to obtain a reasonably small variance of the estimator. This is true because each response provides little information on the population proportion p.

The randomized response technique presented here is the very simplest of many such techniques. For further information on these techniques, you might like to look at the papers by Campbell and Joiner and by Leysieffer and Warner listed in the references at the end of this chapter.

Randomized response techniques can be used more widely than the simple "yes" or "no" type of response situation employed above might indicate. To see how this is developed, look at the paper by Greenberg, Kuebler, Abernathy, and Horvitz.

Randomized response techniques can be used more widely than the simple "yes" or "no" type of response situation employed above might indicate. To see how this is developed, look at the paper by Greenberg, Kuebler, Abernathy, and Horvitz.

11.5 SELECTING THE NUMBER OF CALLBACKS

As discussed earlier in the book, nonresponse is an important problem to consider in any survey. If a simple random sample of size n is employed and only n_1 $(n_1 < n)$ responses are obtained, then the two groups (response and nonresponse) can be thought of as constituting a stratified random sample with two strata. Note that this is not quite a true stratified

11. Supplemental Topics

random sampling situation since n_1 and $n_2 = n - n_1$ are random variables whose values are determined only after the initial sampling is completed. Nevertheless, thinking in terms of stratified sampling allows us to find an approximately optimal rule for allocating resources to callbacks.

Suppose that, out of the n_2 nonrespondents, we decide to make intensive callbacks on r of them, where $r = n_2/k$ for some constant $k > 1$. Also, suppose that it costs c_1 dollars for a standard response and c_2 dollars ($c_2 > c_1$) for a callback response, with c_0 denoting an overhead cost. Then the total cost is

$$c = c_0 + n_1 c_1 + r c_2$$

If $\bar{y}_1$ denotes the average of the initial responses and $\bar{y}_2$ the average of the r callback responses, then

$$\bar{y}^* = \frac{1}{n}(n_1 \bar{y}_1 + n_2 \bar{y}_2) \qquad (11.17)$$

is an unbiased estimator of the population mean μ.

A theoretical variance expression for $\bar{y}^*$ can be derived, and then we can find the values of k and n that minimize the expected cost of sampling for a desired fixed value of $V(\bar{y}^*)$, say V_0. The optimal values of k and n are, for large N,

$$k = \sqrt{\frac{c_2(\sigma^2 - W_2 \sigma_2^2)}{\sigma_2^2(c_0 + c_2 W_1)}} \qquad (11.18)$$

$$n = \frac{N[\sigma^2 + (k-1)W_2 \sigma_2^2]}{NV_0 + \sigma^2} \qquad (11.19)$$

where W_2 is the nonresponse rate for the population, $W_1 = 1 - W_2$, and σ^2 and σ_2^2 are the variances for the entire population and the nonresponse group, respectively. The variance of $\bar{y}^*$ can be estimated by

$$\hat{V}(\bar{y}^*) = \frac{k-1}{n} W_2 s_2^2 + \left(\frac{N-n}{Nn}\right) s^2$$

where s_2^2 estimates the variance of the nonresponse group and s^2 estimates the overall population variance.

Example 11.6
A mailed questionnaire is to be used to collect data for estimating the average amount per week that a certain group of 1000 college males spends on entertainment. From past experience the response rate is anticipated to be about 60%. It is thought that $\sigma^2 \approx 120$ and $\sigma_2^2 \approx 80$. (The nonresponse group tends to be those not interested in entertainment and hence spend less and have less variation in spending habits.) If $c_0 = 0$, $c_1 =$

11.6 Summary

1, and $c_2 = 4$ and a simple random sample is to be used initially, find n and k so that the variance of the resulting estimator is approximately 5 units.

Solution
Observing that $W_2 = 1 - W_1 = .4$, it follows from the equations above that

$$k = \sqrt{\frac{4[120 - .4(80)]}{80(4)(.6)}} = 1.35$$

$$n = \frac{1000[120 + (.35)(.4)(80)]}{1000(5) + 120} = 25.6 \text{ or } 26$$

Since $E(n_2) = nW_2 = 26(.4) = 10.4$ we can expect that approximately 16 persons will respond initially, and

$$r = \frac{n_2}{k} \approx \frac{10.4}{1.35} = 7.7 \text{ or } 8$$

callbacks will have to be made.

11.6 SUMMARY

This chapter presents three useful techniques for estimating population parameters when the assumptions underlying the elementary sample survey designs are not valid.

The effect of interviewer bias can be reduced by using interpenetrating subsamples. The estimator of the population mean in this case is given by equation (11.2) and the estimated variance of this estimator is given by equation (11.3).

An adequate frame generates the problem of estimating means and totals over subpopulations. The estimator of the subpopulation mean is given by equation (11.5) and estimators of the subpopulation total are given by equations (11.8) and (11.11).

When persons being interviewed will not give correct answers to sensitive questions, a random response technique can sometimes be used. The method for estimating a population proportion p using this procedure is explained in section 11.4.

Sometimes it is possible to treat the nonrespondents as a separate stratum, for purposes of choosing an optimal number of callbacks, as shown in section 11.5.

REFERENCES

Campbell, C., and Joiner, B. "How to Get the Answer Without Being Sure You Asked the Question." *American Statistician*, vol. 27 (1973), pp. 229–31.

11. Supplemental Topics

Cochran, W. G. *Sampling Techniques.* 3rd ed. New York: Wiley, 1977.

Deming, W. E. *Sample Design in Business Research.* New York: Wiley, 1960.

Greenberg, B. G.; Kuebler, R. R.; Abernathy, J. R.; and Horvitz, D. G. "Application of Randomized Response Technique in Obtaining Quantitative Data." *Journal of the American Statistical Association,* vol. 66 (1971), pp. 245–50.

Leysieffer, F., and Warner, S. "Respondent Jeopardy and Optimal Designs in Randomized Response Models." *Journal of the American Statistical Association,* vol. 71 (1976), pp. 649–56.

Warner, S. L. "Randomized Response: A Survey Technique for Eliminating Evasive Answer Bias." *Journal of the American Statistical Association,* vol. 60 (1965), pp. 63–69.

EXERCISES

11.1 A researcher is interested in estimating the average yearly medical expense per family in a community of 545 families. The researcher has eight assistants available to do the field work. Skill is required to obtain accurate information on medical expenses because some respondents are reluctant to give detailed information on their health. Since the assistants differ in their interviewing abilities, the researcher decides to use 8 interpenetrating subsamples of 5 families each, with one assistant assigned to each subsample. Hence a simple random sample of 40 families is selected and divided into 8 random subsamples. The interviews are conducted and

Subsample	Amount (in dollars) of Medical Expenses for Past Year				
1	101	95	310	427	680
2	157	192	108	960	312
3	689	432	187	512	649
4	322	48	93	162	495
5	837	649	152	175	210
6	1015	864	325	470	295
7	837	249	1127	493	218
8	327	419	291	114	287

yield the results shown in the table. Estimate the average medical expense per family for the past year, and place a bound on the error of estimation.

11.2 An experiment is designed to gauge the emotional reaction to a city's decision on school desegregation. A simple random sample of 50 people is interviewed and the emotional reactions are given a score from 1 to 10. The scale on which scores are assigned runs from extreme anger to extreme joy. Ten interviewers do the questioning and scoring, with each interviewer working on a random subsample (interpenetrating subsample) of 5 people. Interpenetrating subsamples are used because of the flexible nature of the scoring. The results are given in the table. Estimate the

Exercises

Subsample	Scores				
1	5	4	6	1	8
2	4	6	5	2	7
3	9	8	9	7	5
4	8	5	4	6	3
5	6	4	5	7	9
6	1	5	6	4	7
7	6	4	3	5	2
8	5	6	7	3	4
9	2	4	4	5	3
10	9	7	8	6	4

average score for people in the city, and place a bound on the error of estimation.

11.3 A retail store wants to estimate the average amount of all past-due accounts. The available list of past-due accounts is outdated because some accounts have since been paid. Because drawing up a new list would be expensive, the store uses the outdated list. A simple random sample of 20 accounts is selected from the list, which contains 95 accounts. Of the 20 sampled accounts, 4 have been paid. The 16 past-due accounts contain the following amounts (in dollars): 3.65, 15.98, 40.70, 2.98, 50.00, 60.31, 67.21, 14.98, 10.20, 14.32, 1.87, 32.60, 19.80, 15.98, 12.20, 15.00. Estimate the average amount of past-due accounts for the store, and place a bound on the error of estimation.

11.4 For exercise 11.3, estimate the total amount of past-due accounts for the store, and place a bound on the error of estimation.

11.5 An employee of the store in the exercise 11.3 decides to look through the list of past-due accounts and mark those that have been paid. He finds that only 83 of the 95 accounts are past due. Estimate the total amount of past-due accounts using this additional information and the data of exercise 11.3. Place a bound on the error of estimation.

11.6 A study is conducted to estimate the average number of miles from home to place of employment for household heads living in a certain suburban area. A simple random sample of 30 people is selected from the 493 heads of households in the area. While conducting interviews, the experimenter finds some household heads are not appropriate for the study because they are retired or do not go to a place of employment for various reasons. Of the 30 sampled household heads, 24 are appropriate for the study, and the data on miles to place of employment are as follows:

8.5	10.2	25.1	5.0	6.3	7.9	15.8	2.1
9.2	4.2	8.3	4.2	6.7	10.1	15.6	22.1
10.0	6.1	7.9	1.5	8.0	11.0	20.2	9.3

Estimate the average distance between home and place of employment for household heads who commute to a place of employment. Place a bound on the error of estimation.

11. Supplemental Topics

11.7 For the data of exercise 11.6 estimate the total travel distance between home and place of employment for all household heads in the suburban area. Place a bound on the error of estimation.

11.8 It is known that 420 out of the 493 household heads (exercise 11.6) commute to a place of employment. Estimate the total travel distance for all household heads in the suburban area making use of this additional information. Place a bound on the error of estimation.

11.9 A public health official wants to estimate the proportion of dog owners in a city who have had their dogs vaccinated against rabies. He knows that a dog owner often gives incorrect information about rabies shots out of fear something might happen to his dog if it has not had the shots. Thus the official decides to use a randomized response technique. He has a stack of cards with .8 of the cards marked A for the group having the shots and .2 marked B for the group not having the shots. A simple random sample of 200 dog owners is selected. Each sampled owner is interviewed and asked to draw a card and to respond with "yes" if the letter on the card agrees with the group he is in. The official obtained 145 "yes" responses. Estimate the proportion of dog owners who have had their dogs vaccinated, and place a bound on the error of estimation. Assume that the number of dog owners in the city is very large.

11.10 A corporation executive wants to estimate the proportion of corporation employees who have been convicted of a misdemeanor. Since the employees would not want to answer the question directly, the executive uses a randomized response technique. A simple random sample of 300 people is selected from a large number of corporation employees. In separate interviews each employee draws a card from a deck that has .7 of the cards marked "convicted" and .3 marked "not convicted." The employee responds "yes" if the card agrees with his or her category and "no" otherwise. The executive obtains 105 "yes" responses. Estimate the proportion of employees who have been convicted of a misdemeanor and place a bound on the error of estimation.

EXPERIENCES WITH REAL DATA

Select a simple random sample from the appropriate population in at least one of the situations outlined below. Estimate the indicated proportion or average and place a bound on the error by using the appropriate results from section 11.3 on subpopulations. In each case it is assumed that the items in the subpopulation cannot be classified as such until after they are observed.

1. Estimate the proportion of voters favoring a certain local governmental proposal from among those who voted in the most recent election.
2. Estimate the proportion of students on your campus favoring the quarter system from among those who have been college students on the quarter system and at least one other system.
3. Estimate the average amount spent for utilities in the past month for *homeowners* in a certain neighborhood.
4. Estimate the average number of words per page among pages that contain no boxed formulas or tables in this book.

12.

Summary

You will recall that the objective of statistics is to make inferences about a population based on information contained in a sample. This text discusses the design of sample surveys and associated methods of inference for populations containing a finite number of elements. Practical examples have been selected primarily from the fields of business and the social sciences where finite populations of human responses are frequently the target of surveys. Natural resource management examples are also included.

The method of inference employed for most sample surveys is estimation. Thus we consider appropriate estimators for population parameters and the associated two-standard-deviation bound on the error of estimation. In repeated sampling the error of estimation will be less than its bound with probability approximately equal to .95. Equivalently, we construct confidence intervals which, in repeated sampling, enclose the true population parameter approximately 95 times out of 100. The quantity of information pertinent to a given parameter is measured by the bound on the error of estimation.

The material in this text falls naturally into five segments. The first is a review of elementary concepts, the second contains useful sample survey designs, the third considers an estimator that utilizes information obtained on an auxiliary variable, the fourth gives methods of estimating the size of wildlife populations, and the fifth considers methods for making inferences when one or more of the basic assumptions with the standard techniques are not satisfied.

12. Summary

The first segment, presented in chapters 1, 2, and 3, reviews the objective of statistics and points to the peculiarities of problems arising in the social sciences, business, and natural resource management that make them different from the traditional type of experiment conducted in the laboratory. These peculiarities primarily involve sampling from finite populations along with a number of difficulties that occur in drawing samples from human populations. The former requires modification of the formulas for the bounds on the error of estimation that are encountered in an introductory course in statistics. The difficulties associated with sampling from human populations suggest specific sample survey designs that reduce the cost of acquiring a specified quantity of information.

In chapters 4, 5, 7, 8, and 9 we consider specific sample survey designs and their associated methods of estimation. The basic sample survey design, simple random sampling, is presented in chapter 4. For this design the sample is selected so that every sample of size n in the population has an equal chance of being chosen. The design does not make a specific attempt to reduce the cost of the desired quantity of information. It is the most basic type of sample survey design and all other designs are compared to it.

The second type of design, stratified random sampling (chapter 5), divides the population into homogeneous groups called strata. This usually produces an estimator that possesses a smaller variance than can be acquired by simple random sampling. Thus the cost of the survey can be reduced by selecting fewer elements to achieve an equivalent bound on the error of estimation.

The third type of sample survey design is cluster sampling, which is presented in chapters 7 and 9. Cluster sampling may reduce cost because each sampling unit is a collection of elements usually selected so as to be physically close together. Cluster sampling is most often used when a frame that lists all population elements is not available or when travel costs from element to element are considerable. Cluster sampling reduces the cost of the survey primarily by reducing the cost of collecting the data.

The fourth type of experimental design is systematic sampling (chapter 8), which is usually applied to population elements that are available in a list or line, such as names on file cards in a drawer or people coming out of a factory. A random starting point is selected and then every kth element thereafter is sampled. Systematic sampling is frequently conducted when it is extremely costly or impossible to collect a simple random or a stratified random sample. Once again, the reduction in survey cost is primarily associated with the cost of collecting the sample.

A discussion of ratio and regression estimators, which utilize information on an auxiliary variable, is covered in the third segment of

12. Summary

material, chapter 6. The ratio estimator illustrates how additional information, frequently acquired at little cost, can be used to reduce the variance of the estimator and, consequently, reduce the overall cost of a survey. It also suggests the possibility of acquiring more sophisticated estimators using information on more than one auxiliary variable. This chapter on ratio estimation follows naturally the discussion on simple random sampling contained in chapter 4. This is because you could take a measurement on y, the response of interest, for each element of the simple random sample and utilize the traditional estimators of chapter 4. Or, as suggested in chapter 6, you might take a measurement on both y and an auxiliary variable x for each element and utilize the additional information contributed by the auxiliary variable to acquire a better estimator of the parameter of interest. Thus, although it was not particularly stressed, ratio estimators could be employed with any of the designs discussed in the text. Because these topics are of a more advanced nature, they are omitted from the text.

Chapter 10 deals with the specific problems of estimating the size of wildlife populations. The estimators employed use recapture data, which requires that the sampling be done in at least two stages.

The fifth and final segment of material is contained in chapter 11, which deals with four situations in which some of the basic assumptions of the standard procedures cannot be satisfied. The situations are (1) interviewer biases, which can sometimes be minimized by using interpenetrating subsamples, (2) an inadequate frame, which can sometimes be accounted for by using an estimator for subpopulations of the sampled population, (3) information on sensitive questions, which can be obtained by using a randomized response model, and (4) nonresponse, which can be planned for and designed into the survey by treating nonrespondents as a separate stratum.

To summarize, we have presented various elementary sample survey designs along with their associated methods of inference. Treatment of the topics has been directed toward practical applications so that you can see how sample survey design can be employed to make inferences at minimum cost when sampling from finite social, business, or natural resource populations.

Appendix

Appendix

Table 1/*Normal curve areas*

z	.00	.01	.02	.03	.04	.05	.06	.07	.08	.09
0.0	.0000	.0040	.0080	.0120	.0160	.0199	.0239	.0279	.0319	.0359
0.1	.0398	.0438	.0478	.0517	.0557	.0596	.0636	.0675	.0714	.0753
0.2	.0793	.0832	.0871	.0910	.0948	.0987	.1026	.1064	.1103	.1141
0.3	.1179	.1217	.1255	.1293	.1331	.1368	.1406	.1443	.1480	.1517
0.4	.1554	.1591	.1628	.1664	.1700	.1736	.1772	.1808	.1844	.1879
0.5	.1915	.1950	.1985	.2019	.2054	.2088	.2123	.2157	.2190	.2224
0.6	.2257	.2291	.2324	.2357	.2389	.2422	.2454	.2486	.2517	.2549
0.7	.2580	.2611	.2642	.2673	.2704	.2734	.2764	.2794	.2823	.2852
0.8	.2881	.2910	.2939	.2967	.2995	.3023	.3051	.3078	.3106	.3133
0.9	.3159	.3186	.3212	.3238	.3264	.3289	.3315	.3340	.3365	.3389
1.0	.3413	.3438	.3461	.3485	.3508	.3531	.3554	.3577	.3599	.3621
1.1	.3643	.3665	.3686	.3708	.3729	.3749	.3770	.3790	.3810	.3830
1.2	.3849	.3869	.3888	.3907	.3925	.3944	.3962	.3980	.3997	.4015
1.3	.4032	.4049	.4066	.4082	.4099	.4115	.4131	.4147	.4162	.4177
1.4	.4192	.4207	.4222	.4236	.4251	.4265	.4279	.4292	.4306	.4319
1.5	.4332	.4345	.4357	.4370	.4382	.4394	.4406	.4418	.4429	.4441
1.6	.4452	.4463	.4474	.4484	.4495	.4505	.4515	.4525	.4535	.4545
1.7	.4554	.4564	.4573	.4582	.4591	.4599	.4608	.4616	.4625	.4633
1.8	.4641	.4649	.4656	.4664	.4671	.4678	.4686	.4693	.4699	.4706
1.9	.4713	.4719	.4726	.4732	.4738	.4744	.4750	.4756	.4761	.4767
2.0	.4772	.4778	.4783	.4788	.4793	.4798	.4803	.4808	.4812	.4817
2.1	.4821	.4826	.4830	.4834	.4838	.4842	.4846	.4850	.4854	.4857
2.2	.4861	.4864	.4868	.4871	.4875	.4878	.4881	.4884	.4887	.4890
2.3	.4893	.4896	.4898	.4901	.4904	.4906	.4909	.4911	.4913	.4916
2.4	.4918	.4920	.4922	.4925	.4927	.4929	.4931	.4932	.4934	.4936
2.5	.4938	.4940	.4941	.4943	.4945	.4946	.4948	.4949	.4951	.4952
2.6	.4953	.4955	.4956	.4957	.4959	.4960	.4961	.4962	.4963	.4964
2.7	.4965	.4966	.4967	.4968	.4969	.4970	.4971	.4972	.4973	.4974
2.8	.4974	.4975	.4976	.4977	.4977	.4978	.4979	.4979	.4980	.4981
2.9	.4981	.4982	.4982	.4982	.4984	.4984	.4985	.4985	.4986	.4986
3.0	.4987	.4987	.4987	.4988	.4988	.4989	.4989	.4989	.4990	.4990

Abridged from Table I of *Statistical Tables and Formulas* by A. Hald (New York: John Wiley & Sons, Inc., 1952). Reproduced by permission of A. Hald and the publishers, John Wiley & Sons, Inc.

Appendix

Table 2/*Squares and square roots*

n	n^2	$\sqrt{n}$	$\sqrt{10n}$	n	n^2	$\sqrt{n}$	$\sqrt{10n}$
				25	625	5.000 000	15.81139
1	1	1.000 000	3.162 278	26	676	5.099 020	16.12452
2	4	1.414 214	4.472 136	27	729	5.196 152	16.43168
3	9	1.732 051	5.477 226	28	784	5.291 503	16.73320
4	16	2.000 000	6.324 555	29	841	5.385 165	17.02939
5	25	2.236 068	7.071 068	30	900	5.477 226	17.32051
6	36	2.449 490	7.745 967	31	961	5.567 764	17.60682
7	49	2.645 751	8.366 600	32	1 024	5.656 854	17.88854
8	64	2.828 427	8.944 272	33	1 089	5.744 563	18.16590
9	81	3.000 000	9.486 833	34	1 156	5.830 952	18.43909
10	100	3.162 278	10.00000	35	1 225	5.916 080	18.70829
11	121	3.316 625	10.48809	36	1 296	6.000 000	18.97367
12	144	3.464 102	10.95445	37	1 369	6.082 763	19.23538
13	169	3.605 551	11.40175	38	1 444	6.164 414	19.49359
14	196	3.741 657	11.83216	39	1 521	6.244 998	19.74842
15	225	3.872 983	12.24745	40	1 600	6.324 555	20.00000
16	256	4.000 000	12.64911	41	1 681	6.403 124	20.24846
17	289	4.123 106	13.03840	42	1 764	6.480 741	20.49390
18	324	4.242 641	13.41641	43	1 849	6.557 439	20.73644
19	361	4.358 899	13.78405	44	1 936	6.633 250	20.97618
20	400	4.472 136	14.14214	45	2 025	6.708 204	21.21320
21	441	4.582 576	14.49138	46	2 116	6.782 330	21.44761
22	484	4.690 416	14.83240	47	2 209	6.855 655	21.67948
23	529	4.795 832	15.16575	48	2 304	6.928 203	21.90890
24	576	4.898 979	15.49193	49	2 401	7.000 000	22.13594

From *Handbook of Tables for Probability and Statistics,* Second Edition, edited by William H. Beyer (Cleveland: The Chemical Rubber Company, 1968). Reproduced by permission of the publishers, The Chemical Rubber Company.

Appendix

Table 2/(continued)

n	n^2	$\sqrt{n}$	$\sqrt{10n}$	n	n^2	$\sqrt{n}$	$\sqrt{10n}$
50	2 500	7.071 068	22.36068	90	8 100	9.486 833	30.00000
51	2 601	7.141 428	22.58318	91	8 281	9.539 392	30.16621
52	2 704	7.211 103	22.80351	92	8 464	9.591 663	30.33150
53	2 809	7.280 110	23.02173	93	8 649	9.643 651	30.49590
54	2 916	7.348 469	23.23790	94	8 836	9.695 360	30.65942
55	3 025	7.416 198	23.45208	95	9 025	9.746 794	30.82207
56	3 136	7.483 315	23.66432	96	9 216	9.797 959	30.98387
57	3 249	7.549 834	23.87467	97	9 409	9.848 858	31.14482
58	3 364	7.615 773	24.08319	98	9 604	9.899 495	31.30495
59	3 481	7.681 146	24.28992	99	9 801	9.949 874	31.46427
60	3 600	7.745 967	24.49490	100	10 000	10.00000	31.62278
61	3 721	7.810 250	24.69818	101	10 201	10.04988	31.78050
62	3 844	7.874 008	24.89980	102	10 404	10.09950	31.93744
63	3 969	7.937 254	25.09980	103	10 609	10.14889	32.09361
64	4 096	8.000 000	25.29822	104	10 816	10.19804	32.24903
65	4 225	8.062 258	25.49510	105	11 025	10.24695	32.40370
66	4 356	8.124 038	25.69047	106	11 236	10.29563	32.55764
67	4 489	8.185 353	25.88436	107	11 449	10.34408	32.71085
68	4 624	8.246 211	26.07681	108	11 664	10.39230	32.86335
69	4 761	8.306 624	26.26785	109	11 881	10.44031	33.01515
70	4 900	8.366 600	26.45751	110	12 100	10.48809	33.16625
71	5 041	8.426 150	26.64583	111	12 321	10.53565	33.31666
72	5 184	8.485 281	26.83282	112	12 544	10.58301	33.46640
73	5 329	8.544 004	27.01851	113	12 769	10.63015	33.61547
74	5 476	8.602 325	27.20294	114	12 996	10.67708	33.76389
75	5 625	8.660 254	27.38613	115	13 225	10.72381	33.91165
76	5 776	8.717 798	27.56810	116	13 456	10.77033	34.05877
77	5 929	8.774 964	27.74887	117	13 689	10.81665	34.20526
78	6 084	8.831 761	27.92848	118	13 924	10.86278	34.35113
79	6 241	8.888 194	28.10694	119	14 161	10.90871	34.49638
80	6 400	8.944 272	28.28427	120	14 400	10.95445	34.64102
81	6 561	9.000 000	28.46050	121	14 641	11.00000	34.78505
82	6 724	9.055 385	28.63564	122	14 884	11.04536	34.92850
83	6 889	9.110 434	28.80972	123	15 129	11.09054	35.07136
84	7 056	9.165 151	28.98275	124	15 376	11.13553	35.21363
85	7 225	9.219 544	29.15476	125	15 625	11.18034	35.35534
86	7 396	9.273 618	29.32576	126	15 876	11.22497	35.49648
87	7 569	9.327 379	29.49576	127	16 129	11.26943	35.63706
88	7 744	9.380 832	29.66479	128	16 384	11.31371	35.77709
89	7 921	9.433 981	29.83287	129	16 641	11.35782	35.91657

Appendix

Table 2/(*continued*)

n	n^2	$\sqrt{n}$	$\sqrt{10n}$	n	n^2	$\sqrt{n}$	$\sqrt{10n}$
130	16 900	11.40175	36.05551	170	28 900	13.03840	41.23106
131	17 161	11.44552	36.19392	171	29 241	13.07670	41.35215
132	17 424	11.48913	36.33180	172	29 584	13.11488	41.47288
133	17 689	11.53256	36.46917	173	29 929	13.15295	41.59327
134	17 956	11.57584	36.60601	174	30 276	13.19091	41.71331
135	18 225	11.61895	36.74235	175	30 625	13.22876	41.83300
136	18 496	11.66190	36.87818	176	30 976	13.26650	41.95235
137	18 769	11.70470	37.01351	177	31 329	13.30413	42.07137
138	19 044	11.74734	37.14835	178	31 684	13.34166	42.19005
139	19 321	11.78983	37.28270	179	32 041	13.37909	42.30839
140	19 600	11.83216	37.41657	180	32 400	13.41641	42.42641
141	19 881	11.87434	37.54997	181	32 761	13.45362	42.54409
142	20 164	11.91638	37.68289	182	33 124	13.49074	42.66146
143	20 449	11.95826	37.81534	183	33 489	13.52775	42.77850
144	20 736	12.00000	37.94733	184	33 856	13.56466	42.89522
145	21 025	12.04159	38.07887	185	34 225	13.60147	43.01163
146	21 316	12.08305	38.20995	186	34 596	13.63818	43.12772
147	21 609	12.12436	38.34058	187	34 969	13.67479	43.24350
148	21 904	12.16553	38.47077	188	35 344	13.71131	43.35897
149	22 201	12.20656	38.60052	189	35 721	13.74773	43.47413
150	22 500	12.24745	38.72983	190	36 100	13.78405	43.58899
151	22 801	12.28821	38.85872	191	36 481	13.82027	43.70355
152	23 104	12.32883	38.98718	192	36 864	13.85641	43.81780
153	23 409	12.36932	39.11521	193	37 249	13.89244	43.93177
154	23 716	12.40967	39.24283	194	37 636	13.92839	44.04543
155	24 025	12.44990	39.37004	195	38 025	13.96424	44.15880
156	24 336	12.49000	39.49684	196	38 416	14.00000	44.27189
157	24 649	12.52996	39.62323	197	38 809	14.03567	44.38468
158	24 964	12.56981	39.74921	198	39 204	14.07125	44.49719
159	25 281	12.60952	39.87480	199	39 601	14.10674	44.60942
160	25 600	12.64911	40.00000	200	40 000	14.14214	44.72136
161	25 921	12.68858	40.12481	201	40 401	14.17745	44.83302
162	26 244	12.72792	40.24922	202	40 804	14.21267	44.94441
163	26 569	12.76715	40.37326	203	41 209	14.24781	45.05552
164	26 896	12.80625	40.49691	204	41 616	14.28286	45.16636
165	27 225	12.84523	40.62019	205	42 025	14.31782	45.27693
166	27 556	12.88410	40.74310	206	42 436	14.35270	45.38722
167	27 889	12.92285	40.86563	207	42 849	14.38749	45.49725
168	28 224	12.96148	40.98780	208	43 264	14.42221	45.60702
169	28 561	13.00000	41.10961	209	43 681	14.45683	45.71652

Appendix

Table 2/(continued)

n	n^2	$\sqrt{n}$	$\sqrt{10n}$	n	n^2	$\sqrt{n}$	$\sqrt{10n}$
210	44 100	14.49138	45.82576	250	62 500	15.81139	50.00000
211	44 521	14.52584	45.93474	251	63 001	15.84298	50.09990
212	44 944	14.56022	46.04346	252	63 504	15.87451	50.19960
213	45 369	14.59452	46.15192	253	64 009	15.90597	50.29911
214	45 796	14.62874	46.26013	254	64 516	15.93738	50.39841
215	46 225	14.66288	46.36809	255	65 025	15.96872	50.49752
216	46 656	14.69694	46.47580	256	65 536	16.00000	50.59644
217	47 089	14.73092	46.58326	257	66 049	16.03122	50.69517
218	47 524	14.76482	46.69047	258	66 564	16.06238	50.79370
219	47 961	14.79865	46.79744	259	67 081	16.09348	50.89204
220	48 400	14.83240	46.90416	260	67 600	16.12452	50.99020
221	48 841	14.86607	47.01064	261	68 121	16.15549	51.08816
222	49 284	14.89966	47.11688	262	68 644	16.18641	51.18594
223	49 729	14.93318	47.22288	263	69 169	16.21727	51.28353
224	50 176	14.96663	47.32864	264	69 696	16.24808	51.38093
225	50 625	15.00000	47.43416	265	70 225	16.27882	51.47815
226	51 076	15.03330	47.53946	266	70 756	16.30951	51.57519
227	51 529	15.06652	47.64452	267	71 289	16.34013	51.67204
228	51 984	15.09967	47.74935	268	71 824	16.37071	51.76872
229	52 441	15.13275	47.85394	269	72 361	16.40122	51.86521
230	52 900	15.16575	47.95832	270	72 900	16.43168	51.96152
231	53 361	15.19868	48.06246	271	73 441	16.46208	52.05766
232	53 824	15.23155	48.16638	272	73 984	16.49242	52.15362
233	54 289	15.26434	48.27007	273	74 529	16.52271	52.24940
234	54 756	15.29706	48.37355	274	75 076	16.55295	52.34501
235	55 225	15.32971	48.47680	275	75 625	16.58312	52.44044
236	55 696	15.36229	48.57983	276	76 176	16.61325	52.53570
237	56 169	15.39480	48.68265	277	76 729	16.64332	52.63079
238	56 644	15.42725	48.78524	278	77 284	16.67333	52.72571
239	57 121	15.45962	48.88763	279	77 841	16.70329	52.82045
240	57 600	15.49193	48.98979	280	78 400	16.73320	52.91503
241	58 081	15.52417	49.09175	281	78 961	16.76305	53.00943
242	58 564	15.55635	49.19350	282	79 524	16.79286	53.10367
243	59 049	15.58846	49.29503	283	80 089	16.82260	53.19774
244	59 536	15.62050	49.39636	284	80 656	16.85230	53.29165
245	60 025	15.65248	49.49747	285	81 225	16.88194	53.38539
246	60 516	15.68439	49.59839	286	81 796	16.91153	53.47897
247	61 009	15.71623	49.69909	287	82 369	16.94107	53.57238
248	61 504	15.74802	49.79960	288	82 944	16.97056	53.66563
249	62 001	15.77973	49.89990	289	83 521	17.00000	53.75872

Appendix

Table 2/(*continued*)

n	n^2	$\sqrt{n}$	$\sqrt{10n}$	n	n^2	$\sqrt{n}$	$\sqrt{10n}$
290	84 100	17.02939	53.85165	330	108 900	18.16590	57.44563
291	84 681	17.05872	53.94442	331	109 561	18.19341	57.53260
292	85 264	17.08801	54.03702	332	110 224	18.22087	57.61944
293	85 849	17.11724	54.12947	333	110 889	18.24829	57.70615
294	86 436	17.14643	54.22177	334	111 556	18.27567	57.79273
295	87 025	17.17556	54.31390	335	112 225	18.30301	57.87918
296	87 616	17.20465	54.40588	336	112 896	18.33030	57.96551
297	88 209	17.23369	54.49771	337	113 569	18.35756	58.05170
298	88 804	17.26268	54.58938	338	114 244	18.38478	58.13777
299	89 401	17.29162	54.68089	339	114 921	18.41195	58.22371
300	90 000	17.32051	54.77226	340	115 600	18.43909	58.30952
301	90 601	17.34935	54.86347	341	116 281	18.46619	58.39521
302	91 204	17.37815	54.95453	342	116 964	18.49324	58.48077
303	91 809	17.40690	55.04544	343	117 649	18.52026	58.56620
304	92 416	17.43560	55.13620	344	118 336	18.54724	58.65151
305	93 025	17.46425	55.22681	345	119 025	18.57418	58.73670
306	93 636	17.49286	55.31727	346	119 716	18.60108	58.82176
307	94 249	17.52142	55.40758	347	120 409	18.62794	58.90671
308	94 864	17.54993	55.49775	348	121 104	18.65476	58.99152
309	95 481	17.57840	55.58777	349	121 801	18.68154	59.07622
310	96 100	17.60682	55.67764	350	122 500	18.70829	59.16080
311	96 721	17.63519	55.76737	351	123 201	18.73499	59.24525
312	97 344	17.66352	55.85696	352	123 904	18.76166	59.32959
313	97 969	17.69181	55.94640	353	124 609	18.78829	59.41380
314	98 596	17.72005	56.03570	354	125 316	18.81489	59.40790
315	99 225	17.74824	56.12486	355	126 025	18.84144	59.58188
316	99 856	17.77639	56.21388	356	126 736	18.86796	59.66574
317	100 489	17.80449	56.30275	357	127 449	18.89444	59.74948
318	101 124	17.83255	56.39149	358	128 164	18.92089	59.83310
319	101 761	17.86057	56.48008	359	128 881	18.94730	59.91661
320	102 400	17.88854	56.56854	360	129 600	18.97367	60.00000
321	103 041	17.91647	56.65686	361	130 321	19.00000	60.08328
322	103 684	17.94436	56.74504	362	131 044	19.02630	60.16644
323	104 329	17.97220	56.83309	363	131 769	19.05256	60.24948
324	104 976	18.00000	56.92100	364	132 496	19.07878	60.33241
325	105 625	18.02776	57.00877	365	133 225	19.10497	60.41523
326	106 276	18.05547	57.09641	366	133 956	19.13113	60.49793
327	106 929	18.08314	57.18391	367	134 689	19.15724	60.58052
328	107 584	18.11077	57.27128	368	135 424	19.18333	60.66300
329	108 241	18.13836	57.35852	369	136 161	19.20937	60.74537

Appendix

Table 2/(*continued*)

n	n^2	$\sqrt{n}$	$\sqrt{10n}$	n	n^2	$\sqrt{n}$	$\sqrt{10n}$
370	136 900	19.23538	60.82763	410	168 100	20.24846	64.03124
371	137 641	19.26136	60.90977	411	168 921	20.27313	64.10928
372	138 384	19.28730	60.99180	412	169 744	20.29778	64.18723
373	139 129	19.31321	61.07373	413	170 569	20.32240	64.26508
374	139 876	19.33908	61.15554	414	171 396	20.34699	64.34283
375	140 625	19.36492	61.23724	415	172 225	20.37155	64.42049
376	141 376	19.39072	61.31884	416	173 056	20.39608	64.49806
377	142 129	19.41649	61.40033	417	173 889	20.42058	64.57554
378	142 184	19.44222	61.48170	418	174 724	20.44505	64.65292
379	143 641	19.46792	61.56298	419	175 561	20.46949	64.73021
380	144 400	19.49359	61.64414	420	176 400	20.49390	64.80741
381	145 161	19.51922	61.72520	421	177 241	20.51828	64.88451
382	145 924	19.54482	61.80615	422	178 084	20.54264	64.96153
383	146 689	19.57039	61.88699	423	178 929	20.56696	65.03845
384	147 456	19.59592	61.96773	424	179 776	20.59126	65.11528
385	148 225	19.62142	62.04837	425	180 625	20.61553	65.19202
386	148 996	19.64688	62.12890	426	181 476	20.63977	65.26868
387	149 769	19.67232	62.20932	427	182 329	20.66398	65.34524
388	150 544	19.69772	62.28965	428	183 184	20.68816	65.42171
389	151 321	19.72308	62.36986	429	184 041	20.71232	65.49809
390	152 100	19.74842	62.44998	430	184 900	20.73644	65.57439
391	152 881	19.77372	62.52999	431	185 761	20.76054	65.65059
392	153 664	19.79899	62.60990	432	186 624	20.78461	65.72671
393	154 449	19.82423	62.68971	433	187 489	20.80865	65.80274
394	155 236	19.84943	62.76942	434	188 356	20.83267	65.87868
395	156 025	19.87461	62.84903	435	189 225	20.85665	65.95453
396	156 816	19.89975	62.92853	436	190 096	20.88061	66.03030
397	157 609	19.92486	63.00794	437	190 969	20.90454	66.10598
398	158 404	19.94994	63.08724	438	191 844	20.92845	66.18157
399	159 201	19.97498	63.16645	439	192 721	20.95233	66.25708
400	160 000	20.00000	63.24555	440	193 600	20.97618	66.33250
401	160 801	20.02498	63.32456	441	194 481	21.00000	66.40783
402	161 604	20.04994	63.40347	442	195 224	21.02380	66.48308
403	162 409	20.07486	63.48228	443	196 249	21.04757	66.55825
404	163 216	20.09975	63.56099	444	197 136	21.07131	66.63332
405	164 025	20.12461	63.63961	445	198 025	21.09502	66.70832
406	164 836	20.14944	63.71813	446	198 916	21.11871	66.78323
407	165 649	20.17424	63.79655	447	199·809	21.14237	66.85806
408	166 464	20.19901	63.87488	448	200 704	21.16601	66.93280
409	167 281	20.22375	63.95311	449	201 601	21.18962	67.00746

Table 2/(continued)

n	n^2	$\sqrt{n}$	$\sqrt{10n}$	n	n^2	$\sqrt{n}$	$\sqrt{10n}$
450	202 500	21.21320	67.08204	490	240 100	22.13594	70.00000
451	203 401	21.23676	67.15653	491	241 081	22.15852	70.07139
452	204 304	21.26029	67.23095	492	242 064	22.18107	70.14271
453	205 209	21.28380	67.30527	493	243 049	22.20360	70.21396
454	206 116	21.30728	67.37952	494	244 036	22.22611	70.28513
455	207 025	21.33073	67.45369	495	245 025	22.24860	70.35624
456	207 936	21.35416	67.52777	496	246 016	22.27106	70.42727
457	208 849	21.37756	67.60178	497	247 009	22.29350	70.49823
458	209 764	21.40093	67.67570	498	248 004	22.31591	70.56912
459	210 681	21.42429	67.74954	499	249 001	22.33831	70.63993
460	211 600	21.44761	67.82330	500	250 000	22.36068	70.71068
461	212 521	21.47091	67.89698	501	251 001	22.38303	70.78135
462	213 444	21.49419	67.97058	502	252 004	22.40536	70.85196
463	214 369	21.51743	68.04410	503	253 009	22.42766	70.92249
464	215 296	21.54066	68.11755	504	254 016	22.44994	70.99296
465	216 225	21.56386	68.19091	505	255 025	22.47221	71.06335
466	217 156	21.58703	68.26419	506	256 036	22.49444	71.13368
467	218 089	21.61018	68.33740	507	257 049	22.51666	71.20393
468	219 024	21.63331	68.41053	508	258 064	22.53886	71.27412
469	219 961	21.45641	68.48357	509	259 081	22.56103	71.34424
470	220 900	21.67948	68.55655	510	260 100	22.58318	71.41428
471	221 841	21.70253	68.62944	511	261 121	22.60531	71.48426
472	222 784	21.72556	68.70226	512	262 144	22.62742	71.55418
473	223 729	21.74856	68.77500	513	263 169	22.64950	71.62402
474	224 676	21.77154	68.84766	514	264 196	22.67157	71.69379
475	225 625	21.79449	68.92024	515	265 225	22.69861	71.76350
476	226 576	21.81742	68.99275	516	266 256	22.71563	71.83314
477	227 529	21.84033	69.06519	517	267 289	22.73763	71.90271
478	228 484	21.86321	69.13754	518	268 324	22.75961	71.97222
479	229 441	21.88607	69.20983	519	269 361	22.78157	72.04165
480	230 400	21.90890	69.28203	520	270 400	22.80351	72.11103
481	213 361	21.93171	69.35416	521	271 441	22.82542	72.18033
482	232 324	21.95450	69.42622	522	272 484	22.84732	72.24957
483	233 289	21.97726	69.49820	523	273 529	22.86919	72.31874
484	234 256	22.00000	69.57011	524	274 576	22.89105	72.38784
485	235 225	22.02272	69.64194	525	275 625	22.91288	72.45688
486	236 196	22.04541	69.71370	526	276 676	22.93469	72.52586
487	237 169	22.06808	69.78539	527	277 729	22.95648	72.59477
488	238 144	22.09072	69.85700	528	278 784	22.97825	72.66361
489	239 121	22.11334	69.92853	529	279 841	23.00000	72.73239

Appendix

Table 2/(*continued*)

n	n^2	$\sqrt{n}$	$\sqrt{10n}$	n	n^2	$\sqrt{n}$	$\sqrt{10n}$
530	280 900	23.02173	72.80110	570	324 900	23.87467	75.49834
531	281 961	23.04344	72.86075	571	326 041	23.89561	75.56454
532	283 024	23.06513	72.93833	572	327 184	23.91652	75.63068
533	284 089	23.08679	73.00685	573	328 329	23.93742	75.69676
534	185 156	23.10844	73.07530	574	329 476	23.95830	75.76279
535	286 225	23.13007	73.14369	575	330 625	23.97916	75.82875
536	287 296	23.15167	73.21202	576	331 776	24.00000	75.89466
537	288 369	23.17326	73.28028	577	332 929	24.02082	75.96052
538	289 444	23.19483	73.34848	578	334 084	24.04163	76.02631
539	290 521	23.21637	73.41662	579	335 241	24.06242	76.09205
540	291 600	23.23790	73.48469	580	336 400	24.08319	76.15773
541	292 681	23.25941	73.55270	581	337 561	24.10394	76.22336
542	293 764	23.28089	73.62065	582	338 724	24.12468	76.28892
543	294 849	23.30236	73.68853	583	339 889	24.14539	76.35444
544	295 936	23.32381	73.75636	584	341 056	24.16609	76.41989
545	297 025	23.34524	73.82412	585	342 225	24.18677	76.48529
546	298 116	23.36664	73.89181	586	343 396	24.20744	76.55064
547	299 209	23.38803	73.95945	587	344 569	24.22808	76.61593
548	300 304	23.40940	74.02702	588	345 744	24.24871	76.68116
549	301 401	23.43075	74.09453	589	346 921	24.26932	76.74634
550	302 500	23.45208	74.16198	590	348 100	24.28992	76.81146
551	303 601	23.47339	74.22937	591	349 281	24.31049	76.87652
552	304 704	23.49468	74.29670	592	350 464	24.33105	76.94154
553	305 809	23.51595	74.36397	593	351 649	24.35159	77.00649
554	306 916	23.53720	74.43118	594	352 836	24.37212	77.07140
555	308 025	23.55844	74.49832	595	354 025	24.39262	77.13624
556	309 136	23.57965	74.56541	596	355 216	24.41311	77.20104
557	310 249	23.60085	74.63243	597	356 409	24.43358	77.26578
558	311 364	23.62202	74.69940	598	357 604	24.45404	77.33046
559	312 481	23.64318	74.76630	599	358 801	24.47448	77.39509
560	313 600	23.66432	74.83315	600	360 000	24.49490	77.45967
561	314 721	23.68544	74.89993	601	361 201	24.51530	77.52419
562	315 844	23.70654	74.96666	602	362 404	24.53569	77.58866
563	316 969	23.72762	75.03333	603	363 609	24.55606	77.65307
564	318 096	23.74868	75.09993	604	364 816	24.57641	77.71744
565	319 225	23.76973	75.16648	605	366 025	24.59675	77.78175
566	320 356	23.79075	75.23297	606	367 236	24.61707	77.84600
567	321 489	23.81176	75.29940	607	368 449	24.63737	77.91020
568	322 624	23.83275	75.36577	608	369 664	24.65766	77.97435
569	323 761	23.85372	75.43209	609	370 881	24.67793	78.03845

Appendix

Table 2/(continued)

n	n²	√n	√10n	n	n²	√n	√10n
610	372 100	24.69818	78.10250	650	422 500	25.49510	80.62258
611	373 321	24.71841	78.16649	651	423 801	25.51470	80.68457
612	374 544	24.73863	78.23043	652	425 104	25.53429	80.74652
613	375 769	24.75884	78.29432	653	426 409	25.55386	80.80842
614	376 996	24.77902	78.35815	654	427 716	25.57342	80.87027
615	378 225	24.79919	78.42194	655	429 025	25.59297	80.93207
616	379 456	24.81935	78.48567	656	430 336	25.61250	80.00383
617	380 689	24.83948	78.54935	657	431 649	25.63201	81.05554
618	381 924	24.85961	78.61298	658	432 964	25.65151	81.11720
619	383· 161	24.87971	78.67655	659	434 281	35.67100	81.17881
620	384 400	24.89980	78.74008	660	435 600	25.69047	81.24038
621	385 641	24.91987	78.80355	661	436 921	25.70992	81.30191
622	386 884	24.93993	78.86698	662	438 244	25.72936	81.36338
623	388 129	24.95997	78.93035	663	439 569	25.74879	81.42481
624	389 376	24.97999	78.99367	664	440 896	25.76820	81.48620
625	390 625	25.00000	79.05694	665	442 225	25.78759	81.54753
626	391 876	25.01999	79.12016	666	443 556	25.80698	81.60882
627	393 129	25.03997	79.18333	667	444 889	25.82634	81.67007
628	394 384	25.05993	79.24645	668	446 224	25.84570	81.73127
629	395 641	25.07987	79.30952	669	447 561	25.86503	81.79242
630	396 900	25.09980	79.37254	670	448 900	25.88436	81.85353
631	398 161	25.11971	79.43551	671	450 241	25.90367	81.91459
632	399 424	25.13961	79.49843	672	451 584	25.92296	81.97561
633	400 689	25.15949	79.56130	673	452 929	25.94224	82.03658
634	401 956	25.17936	79.62412	674	454 276	25.96151	82.09750
635	403 225	25.19921	79.68689	675	455 625	25.98076	82.15838
636	404 496	25.21904	79.74961	676	456 976	26.00000	82.21922
637	405 769	25.23886	79.81228	677	458 329	26.01922	82.28001
638	407 044	25.25866	79.87490	678	459 684	26.03843	82.34076
639	408 321	25.27845	79.93748	679	461 041	26.05763	82.40146
640	409 600	25.29822	80.00000	680	462 400	26.07681	82.46211
641	410 881	25.31798	80.06248	681	463 761	26.09598	82.52272
642	412 164	25.33772	80.12490	682	465 124	26.11513	82.58329
643	413 449	25.35744	80.18728	683	466 489	26.13427	82.64381
644	414 736	25.37716	80.24961	684	467 856	26.15339	82.70429
645	416 025	25.39685	80.31189	685	469 225	26.17250	82.76473
646	417 316	25.41653	80.37413	686	470 596	26.19160	82.82512
647	418 609	25.43619	80.43631	687	471 969	26.21068	82.88546
648	419 904	25.45584	80.49845	688	473 344	26.22975	82.94577
649	421 201	25.47548	80.56054	689	474 721	26.24881	83.00602

Appendix

Table 2/(*continued*)

n	n^2	$\sqrt{n}$	$\sqrt{10n}$	n	n^2	$\sqrt{n}$	$\sqrt{10n}$
690	476 100	26.26785	83.06624	730	532 900	27.01851	85.44004
691	477 481	26.28688	83.12641	731	534 361	27.03701	85.49854
692	478 864	26.30589	83.18654	732	535 824	27.05550	85.55700
693	480 249	26.32489	83.24662	733	537 289	27.07397	85.61542
694	481 636	26.34388	83.30666	734	538 756	27.09243	85.67380
695	483 025	26.36285	83.36666	735	540 225	27.11088	85.73214
696	484 416	26.38181	83.42661	736	541 696	27.12932	85.79044
697	485 809	26.40076	83.48653	737	543 169	27.14774	85.84870
698	487 204	26.41969	83.54639	738	544 644	27.16616	85.90693
699	488 601	26.43861	83.60622	739	546 121	27.18455	85.96511
700	490 000	26.45751	83.66600	740	547 600	27.20294	86.02325
701	491 401	26.47640	83.72574	741	549 081	27.22132	86.08136
702	492 804	26.49528	83.78544	742	550 564	27.23968	86.13942
703	494 209	26.51415	83.84510	743	552 049	27.25803	86.19745
704	495 616	26.53300	83.90471	744	553 536	27.27636	86.25543
705	497 025	26.55184	83.96428	745	555 025	27.29469	86.31338
706	498 436	26.57066	84.02381	746	556 516	27.31300	86.37129
707	499 849	26.58947	84.08329	747	558 009	27.33130	86.42916
708	501 264	26.60827	84.14274	748	559 504	27.34959	86.48699
709	502 681	26.62705	84.20214	749	561 001	27.36786	86.54479
710	504 100	26.64583	84.26150	750	562 500	27.38613	86.60254
711	505 521	26.66458	84.32082	751	564 001	27.40438	86.66026
712	506 944	26.68333	84.38009	752	565 504	27.42262	86.71793
713	508 369	26.70206	84.43933	753	567 009	27.44085	86.77557
714	509 796	26.72078	84.49852	754	568 516	27.45906	86.83317
715	511 225	26.73948	84.55767	755	570 025	27.47726	86.89074
716	512 656	26.75818	84.61678	756	571 536	27.49545	86.94826
717	514 089	26.77686	84.67585	757	573 049	27.51363	87.00575
718	515 524	26.79552	84.73488	758	574 564	27.53180	87.06320
719	516 961	26.81418	84.79387	759	576 081	27.54995	87.12061
720	518 400	26.83282	84.85281	760	577 600	27.56810	87.17798
721	519 841	26.85144	84.91172	761	579 121	27.58623	87.23531
722	521 284	26.87006	84.97058	762	580 644	27.60435	87.29261
723	522 729	26.88866	85.02941	763	582 169	27.62245	87.34987
724	524 176	26.90725	85.08819	764	583 696	27.64055	87.40709
725	525 625	26.92582	85.14693	765	585 225	27.65863	87.46428
726	527 076	26.94439	85.20563	766	586 756	27.67671	87.52143
727	528 529	26.96294	85.26429	767	588 289	27.69476	87.57854
728	529 984	26.98148	85.32292	768	589 824	27.71281	87.63561
729	531 441	27.00000	85.38150	769	591 361	27.73085	87.69265

Appendix

Table 2/(*continued*)

n	n^2	$\sqrt{n}$	$\sqrt{10n}$	n	n^2	$\sqrt{n}$	$\sqrt{10n}$
770	592 900	27.74887	87.74964	810	656 100	28.46050	90.00000
771	594 441	27.76689	87.80661	811	657 721	28.47806	90.05554
772	595 984	27.78489	87.86353	812	659 344	28.49561	90.11104
773	597 529	27.80288	87.92042	813	660 969	28.51315	90.16651
774	599 076	27.82086	87.97727	814	662 596	28.53069	90.22195
775	600 625	27.83882	88.03408	815	664 225	28.54820	90.27735
776	602 176	27.85678	88.09086	816	665 856	28.56571	90.33272
777	603 729	27.87472	88.14760	817	667 489	28.58321	90.38805
778	605 284	27.89265	88.20431	818	669 124	28.60070	90.44335
779	606 841	27.91057	88.26098	819	670 761	28.61818	90.49862
780	608 400	27.92848	88.31761	820	672 400	28.63564	90.55385
781	609 961	27.94638	88.37420	821	674 041	28.65310	90.60905
782	611 524	27.96426	88.43076	822	675 684	28.67054	90.66422
783	613 089	27.98214	88.48729	823	677 329	28.68798	90.71935
784	614 656	28.00000	88.54377	824	678 976	28.70540	90.77445
785	616 225	28.01785	88.60023	825	680 625	28.72281	90.82951
786	617 796	28.03569	88.65664	826	682 276	28.74022	90.88354
787	619 369	28.05352	88.71302	827	683 929	28.75761	90.93954
788	620 944	28.07134	88.76936	828	685 584	28.77499	90.99451
789	622 521	28.08914	88.82567	829	687 241	28.79236	91.04944
790	624 100	28.10694	88.88194	830	688 900	28.80972	91.10434
791	625 681	28.12472	88.93818	831	690 561	28.82707	91.15920
792	627 264	28.14249	88.99438	832	692 224	28.84441	91.21403
793	628 849	28.16026	89.05055	833	693 889	28.86174	91.26883
794	630 436	28.17801	89.10668	834	695 556	28.87906	91.32360
795	632 025	28.19574	89.16277	835	697 225	28.89637	91.37833
796	633 616	28.21347	89.21883	836	698 896	28.91366	91.43304
797	635 209	28.23119	89.27486	837	700 569	28.93095	91.48770
798	636 804	28.24889	89.33085	838	702 244	28.94823	91.54234
799	638 401	28.26659	89.38680	839	703 921	28.96550	91.59694
800	640 000	28.28427	89.44272	840	705 600	28.98275	91.65151
801	641 601	28.30194	89.49860	841	707 281	29.00000	91.70605
802	643 204	28.31960	89.55445	842	708 964	29.01724	91.76056
803	644 809	28.33725	89.61027	843	710 649	29.03446	91.81503
804	646 416	28.35489	89.66605	844	712 336	29.05168	91.86947
805	648 025	28.37252	89.72179	345	714 025	29.06888	91.92388
806	649 636	28.39014	89.77750	846	715 716	29.08608	91.97826
807	651 249	28.40775	89.83318	847	717 409	29.10326	92.03260
808	652 864	28.42534	89.88882	848	719 104	29.12044	92.08692
809	654 481	28.44293	89.94443	849	720 801	29.13760	92.14120

Appendix

Table 2/(*continued*)

n	n^2	$\sqrt{n}$	$\sqrt{10n}$	n	n^2	$\sqrt{n}$	$\sqrt{10n}$
850	722 500	29.15476	92.19544	890	792 100	29.83287	94.33981
851	724 201	29.17190	92.24966	891	793 881	29.84962	94.39280
852	725 904	29.18904	92.30385	892	795 664	29.86637	94.44575
853	727 609	29.20616	92.35800	893	797 449	29.88311	94.49868
854	729 316	29.22328	92.41212	894	799 236	29.89983	94.55157
855	731 025	29.24038	92.46621	895	801 025	29.91655	94.60444
856	732 736	29.25748	92.52027	896	802 816	29.93326	94.65728
857	734 449	29.27456	92.57429	897	804 609	29.94996	94.71008
858	736 164	29.29164	92.62829	898	806 404	29.96665	94.76286
859	737 881	29.30870	92.68225	899	808 201	29.98333	94.81561
860	739 600	29.32576	92.73618	900	810 000	30.00000	94.86833
861	741 321	29.34280	92.79009	901	811 801	30.01666	94.92102
862	743 044	29.35984	92.84396	902	813 604	30.03331	94.97368
863	744 769	29.37686	92.89779	903	815 409	30.04996	95.02631
864	746 496	29.39388	92.95160	904	817 216	30.06659	95.07891
865	748 225	29.41088	93.00538	905	819 025	30.08322	95.13149
866	749 956	29.42788	93.05912	906	820 836	30.09983	95.18403
867	751 689	29.44486	93.11283	907	822 649	30.11644	95.23655
868	753 424	29.46184	93.16652	908	824 464	30.13304	95.28903
869	755 161	29.47881	93.22017	909	826 281	30.14963	95.34149
870	756 900	29.49576	93.27379	910	828 100	30.16621	95.39392
871	758 641	29.51271	93.32738	911	829 921	30.18278	95.44632
872	760 384	29.52965	93.38094	912	831 744	30.19934	95.49869
873	762 129	29.54657	93.43447	913	833 569	30.21589	95.55103
874	763 876	29.56349	93.48797	914	835 396	30.23243	95.60335
875	765 625	29.58040	93.54143	915	837 225	30.24897	95.65563
876	767 376	29.59730	93.59487	916	839 056	30.26549	95.70789
877	769 129	29.61419	93.64828	917	840 889	30.28201	95.76012
878	770 884	29.63106	93.70165	918	842 724	30.29851	95.81232
879	772 641	29.64793	93.75500	919	844 561	30.31501	95.86449
880	774 400	29.66479	93.80832	920	846 400	30.33150	95.91663
881	776 161	29.68164	93.86160	921	848 241	30.34798	95.96874
882	777 924	29.69848	93.91486	922	850 084	30.36445	96.02083
883	779 689	29.71532	93.96808	923	851 929	30.38092	96.07289
884	781 456	29.73214	94.02127	924	853 776	30.39737	96.12492
885	783 225	29.74895	94.07444	925	855 625	30.41381	96.17692
886	784 996	29.76575	94.12757	926	857 476	30.43025	96.22889
887	786 769	29.78255	94.18068	927	859 329	30.44667	96.28084
888	788 544	29.79933	94.23375	928	861 184	30.46309	96.33276
889	790 321	29.81610	94.28680	929	863 041	30.47950	96.38465

Appendix

Table 2/(*continued*)

n	n^2	$\sqrt{n}$	$\sqrt{10n}$	n	n^2	$\sqrt{n}$	$\sqrt{10n}$
930	864 900	30.49590	96.43651	965	931 225	31.06445	98.23441
931	866 761	30.51229	96.48834	966	933 156	31.08054	98.28530
932	868 624	30.52868	96.54015	967	935 089	31.09662	98.33616
933	870 489	30.54505	96.59193	968	937 024	31.11270	98.38699
934	872 356	30.56141	96.64368	969	938 961	31.12876	98.43780
935	874 225	30.57777	96.69540	970	940 900	31.14482	98.48858
936	876 096	30.59412	96.74709	971	942 841	31.16087	98.53933
937	877 969	30.61046	96.79876	972	944 784	31.17691	98.59006
938	879 844	30.62679	96.85040	973	946 729	31.19295	98.64076
939	881 721	30.64311	96.90201	974	948 676	31.20897	98.69144
940	883 600	30.65942	96.95360	975	950 625	31.22499	98.74209
941	885 481	30.67572	97.00515	976	952 576	31.24100	98.79271
942	887 364	30.69202	97.05668	977	954 529	31.25700	98.84331
943	889 249	30.70831	97.10819	978	956 484	31.27299	98.89388
944	891 136	30.72458	97.15966	979	958 441	31.28898	98.94443
945	893 025	30.74085	97.21111	980	960 400	31.30495	98.99495
946	894 916	30.75711	97.26253	981	962 361	31.32092	99.04544
947	896 809	30.77337	97.31393	982	964 324	31.33688	99.09591
948	898 704	30.78961	97.36529	983	966 289	31.35283	99.14636
949	900 601	30.80584	97.41663	984	968 256	31.36877	99.19677
950	902 500	30.82207	97.46794	985	970 225	31.38471	99.24717
951	904 401	30.83829	97.51923	986	972 196	31.40064	99.29753
952	906 304	30.85450	97.57049	987	974 169	31.41656	99.34787
953	908 200	30.87070	97.62172	988	976 144	31.43247	99.39819
954	910 116	30.88689	97.67292	989	978 121	31.44837	99.44848
955	912 025	30.90307	97.72410	990	980 100	31.46427	99.49874
956	913 936	30.91925	97.77525	991	982 081	31.48015	99.54898
957	915 849	30.93542	97.82638	992	984 064	31.49603	99.59920
958	917 764	30.95158	97.87747	993	986 049	31.51190	99.64939
959	919 681	30.96773	97.92855	994	988 036	31.52777	99.69955
960	921 600	30.98387	97.97959	995	990 025	31.54362	99.74969
961	923 521	31.00000	98.03061	996	992 016	31.55947	99.79980
962	925 444	31.01612	98.08160	997	994 009	31.57531	99.84989
963	927 369	31.03224	98.13256	998	996 004	31.59114	99.89995
964	929 296	31.04835	98.18350	999	998 001	31.60966	99.94999
				1000	1000 000	31.62278	100.00000

Appendix

Table 3 / Random numbers

Line/Col.	(1)	(2)	(3)	(4)	(5)	(6)	(7)	(8)	(9)	(10)	(11)	(12)	(13)	(14)
1	10480	15011	01536	02011	81647	91646	69179	14194	62590	36207	20969	99570	91291	90700
2	22368	46573	25595	85393	30995	89198	27982	53402	93965	34095	52666	19174	39615	99505
3	24130	48360	22527	97265	76393	64809	15179	24830	49340	32081	30680	19655	63348	58629
4	42167	93093	06243	61680	07856	16376	39440	53537	71341	57004	00849	74917	97758	16379
5	37570	39975	81837	16656	06121	91782	60468	81305	49684	60672	14110	06927	01263	54613
6	77921	06907	11008	42751	27756	53498	18602	70659	90655	15053	21916	81825	44394	42880
7	99562	72905	56420	69994	98872	31016	71194	18738	44013	48840	63213	21069	10634	12952
8	96301	91977	05463	07972	18876	20922	94595	56869	69014	60045	18425	84903	42508	32307
9	89579	14342	63661	10281	17453	18103	57740	84378	25331	12566	58678	44947	05585	56941
10	85475	36857	53342	53988	53060	59533	38867	62300	08158	17983	16439	11458	18593	64952
11	28918	69578	88231	33276	70997	79936	56865	05859	90106	31595	01547	85590	91610	78188
12	63553	40961	48235	03427	49626	69445	18663	72695	52180	20847	12234	90511	33703	90322
13	09429	93969	52636	92737	88974	33488	36320	17617	30015	08272	84115	27156	30613	74952
14	10365	61129	87529	85689	48237	52267	67689	93394	01511	26358	85104	20285	29975	89868
15	07119	97336	71048	08178	77233	13916	47564	81056	97735	85977	29372	74461	28551	90707
16	51085	12765	51821	51259	77452	16308	60756	92144	49442	53900	70960	63990	75601	40719
17	02368	21382	52404	60268	89368	19885	55322	44819	01188	65255	64835	44919	05944	55157
18	01011	54092	33362	94904	31273	04146	18594	29852	71585	85030	51132	01915	92747	64951
19	52162	53916	46369	58586	23216	14513	83149	98736	23495	64350	94738	17752	35156	35749
20	07056	97628	33787	09998	42698	06691	76988	13602	51851	46104	88916	19509	25625	58104
21	48663	91245	85828	14346	09172	30168	90229	04734	59193	22178	30421	61666	99904	32812
22	54164	58492	22421	74103	47070	25306	76468	26384	58151	06646	21524	15227	96909	44592
23	32639	32363	05597	24200	13363	38005	94342	28728	35806	06912	17012	64161	18296	22851
24	29334	27001	87637	87308	58731	00256	45834	15398	46557	41135	10367	07684	36188	18510
25	02488	33062	28834	07351	19731	92420	60952	61280	50001	67658	32586	86679	50720	94953

Abridged from *Handbook of Tables for Probability and Statistics*, Second Edition, edited by William H. Beyer (Cleveland: The Chemical Rubber Company, 1968). Reproduced by permission of the publishers, The Chemical Rubber Company.

Appendix

26	81525	72295	04839	96423	24878	82651	66566	14778	76797	14780	13300	87074	79666	95725
27	29676	20591	68086	26432	46901	20849	89768	81536	86645	12659	92259	57102	80428	25280
28	00742	57392	39064	66432	84673	40027	32832	61362	98947	96067	64760	64584	96096	98253
29	05366	04213	25669	26422	44407	44048	37937	63904	45766	66134	75470	66520	34693	90449
30	91921	26418	64117	94305	26766	25940	39972	22209	71500	64568	91402	42416	07844	69618
31	00582	04711	87917	77341	42206	35126	74087	99547	81817	42607	43808	76655	62028	76630
32	00725	69884	62797	56170	86324	88072	76222	36086	84637	93161	76038	65855	77919	88006
33	69011	65795	95876	55293	18988	27354	26575	08625	40801	59920	29841	80150	12777	48501
34	25976	57948	39888	88604	67917	48708	18912	82271	65424	69774	33611	54262	85963	03547
35	09763	83473	73577	12908	30883	18317	28290	35797	05998	41688	34952	37888	38917	88050
36	91567	42595	27958	30134	04024	86385	29880	99730	55536	84855	29080	09250	79656	73211
37	17955	56349	90999	49127	20044	59931	06115	20542	18059	02008	73708	83517	36103	42791
38	46503	18584	18845	49618	02304	51038	20655	58727	28168	15475	56942	53389	20562	87338
39	92157	89634	94824	78171	84610	82834	09922	25417	44137	48413	25555	21246	35509	20468
40	14577	62765	35605	81263	39667	47358	56873	56307	61607	49518	89656	20103	77490	18062
41	98427	07523	33362	64270	01638	92477	66969	98420	04880	45585	46565	04102	46880	45709
42	34914	63976	88720	82765	34476	17032	87589	40836	32427	70002	70663	88863	77775	69348
43	70060	28277	39475	46473	23219	53416	94970	25832	69975	94884	19661	72828	00102	66794
44	53976	54914	06990	67245	68350	82948	11398	42878	80287	88267	47363	46634	06541	97809
45	76072	29515	40980	07391	58745	25774	22987	80059	39911	96189	41151	14222	60697	59583
46	90725	52210	83974	29992	65831	38857	50490	83765	55657	14361	31720	57375	56228	41546
47	64364	67412	33339	31926	14883	24413	59744	92351	97473	89286	35931	04110	23726	51900
48	08962	00358	31662	25388	61642	34072	81249	35648	56891	69352	48373	45578	78547	81788
49	95012	68379	93526	70765	10592	04542	76463	54328	02349	17247	28865	14777	62730	92277
50	15664	10493	20492	38391	91132	21999	59516	81652	27195	48223	46751	22923	32261	85653
51	16408	81899	04153	53381	79401	21438	83035	92350	36693	31238	59649	91754	72772	02338
52	18629	81953	05520	91962	04739	13092	97662	24822	94730	06496	35090	04822	86774	98289
53	73115	35101	47498	87637	99016	71060	88824	71013	18735	20286	23153	72924	35165	43040
54	57491	16703	23167	49325	45021	33132	12544	41035	80780	45393	44812	12515	98931	91202
55	30405	83946	23792	14422	15059	45799	22716	19792	09983	74353	68668	30429	70735	25499

Appendix

Table 3/(continued)

Line/Col.	(1)	(2)	(3)	(4)	(5)	(6)	(7)	(8)	(9)	(10)	(11)	(12)	(13)	(14)
56	16631	35006	85900	98275	32388	52390	16815	69298	82732	38480	73817	32523	41961	44437
57	96773	20206	42559	78985	05300	22164	24369	54224	35083	19687	11052	91491	60383	19746
58	38935	64202	14349	82674	66523	44133	00697	35552	35970	19124	63318	29686	03387	59846
59	31624	76384	17403	53363	44167	64486	64758	75366	76554	31601	12614	33072	60332	92325
60	78919	19474	23632	27889	47914	02584	37680	20801	72152	39339	34806	08930	85001	87820
61	03931	33309	57047	74211	63445	17361	62825	39908	05607	91284	68833	25570	38818	46920
62	74426	33278	43972	10119	89917	15665	52872	73823	73144	88662	88970	74492	51805	99378
63	09066	00903	20795	95452	92648	45454	09552	88815	16553	51125	79375	97596	16296	66092
64	42238	12426	87025	14267	20979	04508	64535	31355	86064	29472	47689	05974	52468	16834
65	16153	08002	26504	41744	81959	65642	74240	56302	00033	67107	77510	70625	28725	34191
66	21457	40742	29820	96783	29400	21840	15035	34537	33310	06116	95240	15957	16572	06004
67	21581	57802	02050	89728	17937	37621	47075	42080	97403	48626	68995	43805	33386	21597
68	55612	78095	83197	33732	05810	24813	86902	60397	16489	03264	88525	42786	05269	92532
69	44657	66999	99324	51281	84463	60563	79312	93454	68876	25471	93911	25650	12682	73572
70	91340	84979	46949	81973	37949	61023	43997	15263	80644	43942	89203	71795	99533	50501
71	91227	21199	31935	27022	84067	05462	35216	14486	29891	68607	41867	14951	91696	85065
72	50001	38140	66321	19924	72163	09538	12151	06878	91903	18749	34405	56087	82790	70925
73	65390	05224	72958	28609	81406	39147	25549	48542	42627	45233	57202	94617	23772	07896
74	27504	96131	83944	41575	10573	08619	64482	73923	36152	05184	94142	25299	84387	34925
75	37169	94851	39117	89632	00959	16487	65536	49071	39782	17095	02330	74301	00275	48280
76	11508	70225	51111	38351	19444	66499	71945	05422	13442	78675	84081	66938	93654	59894
77	37449	30362	06694	54690	04052	53115	62757	95348	78662	11163	81651	50245	34971	52924
78	46515	70331	85922	38329	57015	15765	97161	17869	45349	61796	66345	81073	49106	79860
79	30986	81223	42416	58353	21532	30502	32305	86482	05174	07901	54339	58861	74818	46942
80	63798	64995	46583	09785	44160	78128	83991	42865	92520	83531	80377	35909	81250	54238

Appendix

81	82486	84846	99254	67632	43218	50076	21361	64816	51202	88124	41870	52689	51275	83556
82	21885	32906	92431	09060	64297	51674	64126	62570	26123	05155	59194	52799	28225	85762
83	60336	98782	07408	53458	13564	59089	26445	29789	85205	41001	12535	12133	14645	23541
84	43937	46891	24010	25560	86355	33941	25786	54990	71899	15475	95434	98227	21824	19585
85	97656	63175	89303	16275	07100	92063	21942	18611	47348	20203	18534	03862	78095	50136
86	03299	01221	05418	38982	55758	92237	26759	86367	21216	98442	08303	56613	91511	75928
87	79626	06486	03574	17668	07785	76020	79924	25651	83325	88428	85076	72811	22717	50585
88	85636	68335	47539	03129	65651	11977	02510	26113	99447	68645	34327	15152	55230	93448
89	18039	14367	61337	06177	12143	46609	32989	74014	64708	00533	35398	58408	13261	47908
90	08362	15656	60627	36478	65648	16764	53412	09013	07832	41574	17639	82163	60859	75567
91	79556	29068	04142	16268	15387	12856	66227	38358	22478	73373	88732	09443	82558	05250
92	92608	82674	27072	32534	17075	27698	98204	63863	11951	34648	88022	56148	34925	57031
93	23982	25835	40055	67006	12293	02753	14827	23235	35071	99704	37543	11601	35503	85171
94	09915	96306	05908	97901	28395	14186	00821	80703	70426	75647	76310	88717	37890	40129
95	59037	33300	26695	62247	69927	76123	50842	43834	86654	70959	79725	93872	28117	19233
96	42488	78077	69882	61657	34136	79180	97526	43092	04098	73571	80799	76536	71255	64239
97	46764	86273	63003	93017	31204	36692	40202	35275	57306	55543	53203	18098	47625	88684
98	03237	45430	55417	63282	90816	17349	88298	90183	36600	78406	06216	95787	42579	90730
99	86591	81482	52667	61582	14972	90053	89534	76036	49199	43716	97548	04379	46370	28672
100	38534	01715	94964	87288	65680	43772	39560	12918	86537	62738	19636	51132	25739	56947

Appendix

Table 4/ *A population of 100 measurements*

67.772	47.688	89.117	74.758	90.005
7.114	91.808	65.951	39.132	30.040
26.738	21.662	93.652	61.973	70.194
5.401	3.697	68.350	19.649	50.807
91.762	27.227	67.228	60.140	73.098
1.962	30.085	88.224	83.998	81.321
85.912	35.467	24.289	62.734	30.045
97.815	42.035	51.714	20.419	48.379
13.682	33.011	91.687	57.910	19.866
1.754	19.752	84.696	63.687	83.783
87.389	21.411	82.991	60.930	23.903
8.546	50.698	35.682	92.400	89.376
64.769	11.491	67.175	6.030	21.128
11.706	12.662	81.911	4.580	22.384
87.312	72.554	86.893	73.210	44.152
18.518	21.364	84.156	98.038	63.452
25.301	75.197	22.901	29.341	83.346
85.146	58.908	79.995	93.703	29.009
83.169	76.672	73.872	98.147	23.938
32.702	29.861	23.268	45.554	82.547

$\mu = 52.575 \qquad \sigma^2 = 886.847$

Table 5/ *A population of 20 measurements*

13.554	17.478
1.223	1.709
5.348	12.954
1.080	2.341
18.352	17.482
.392	3.704
17.182	4.060
19.583	17.029
2.736	16.634
.351	6.540

$\mu = 9.035 \qquad \sigma^2 = 52.019$

Appendix

THE COVARIANCE AND VARIANCE OF $\bar{y}$ IN SIMPLE RANDOM SAMPLING

For a simple random sample $(y_1, \ldots, y_n)$ from a population of size N, consider

$$\text{Cov}(y_i, y_j) = E[(y_i - \mu)(y_j - \mu)] = E(y_i y_j) - \mu^2$$

$$= \sum_{i \neq j}^{N} u_i u_j \left[\frac{1}{N(N-1)}\right] - \frac{1}{N^2}\left(\sum_{i=1}^{N} u_i\right)^2$$

$$= \frac{1}{N}\left[\sum_{i \neq j}^{N} \frac{u_i u_j}{N-1} - \frac{1}{N}\left(\sum_{i=1}^{N} u_i\right)^2\right]$$

$$= \frac{1}{N}\left[\frac{\left(\sum_{i=1}^{N} u_i\right)^2 - \sum_{i=1}^{N} u_i^2}{N-1} - \frac{1}{N}\left(\sum_{i=1}^{N} u_i\right)^2\right]$$

$$= -\frac{1}{N}\left[\frac{1}{N-1}\sum_{i=1}^{N} u_i^2 - \frac{1}{N(N-1)}\left(\sum_{i=1}^{N} u_i\right)^2\right]$$

$$= -\frac{1}{N(N-1)}\sum_{i=1}^{N}(u_i - \mu)^2 = -\frac{1}{N-1}\sigma^2$$

Using this fact and a result from section 2.6, we can find the variance of $\bar{y}$. We have

$$V(\bar{y}) = V\left(\frac{1}{n}\sum_{i=1}^{n} y_i\right) = \frac{1}{n^2}\left[\sum_{i=1}^{n} \sigma^2 + 2\sum\sum_{i<j} \text{Cov}(y_i, y_j)\right]$$

$$= \frac{1}{n^2}\left[\sum_{i=1}^{n} \sigma^2 + 2\sum\sum_{i<j} \frac{-\sigma^2}{N-1}\right]$$

$$= \frac{1}{n^2}\left\{n\sigma^2 - \frac{2\sigma^2}{N-1}\left[\frac{n(n-1)}{2}\right]\right\}$$

since there are $n(n-1)/2$ pairs (i, j) selected from the integers $1, \ldots, n$ so that $i < j$. It follows that

$$V(\bar{y}) = \frac{\sigma^2}{n}\left(\frac{N-n}{N-1}\right)$$

Answers

Chapter 4

4.5. $\hat{p} = 5/6, B = .1313$

4.6. $n = 128$

4.7. $\bar{y} = 12.5, B = 7.0412$

4.8. $\hat{\tau} = 125{,}000, B = 70{,}412.4989$

4.9. $\hat{\mu}_1 = 2.30, \hat{\mu}_2 = 4.52, B = .0703, B = .0858$

4.10. $\hat{p} = .625, B = .1535$

4.11. $\hat{\mu} = 2.0, B = .9381$

4.12. $\hat{p} = .43, B = .0312$

4.13. $n = 2392$

4.14. $\hat{\tau} = 100, B = 31.29$

4.15. $\hat{\mu} = 2.1, B = .1697$

4.16. $n = 4$

4.17. $\hat{\mu} = 5.0125, B = .8711$

4.18. $\hat{p} = 11/60, B = .0958$

4.19. $n = 87$

4.20. $\hat{\tau} = 37{,}800, B = 3{,}379.94$

4.21. $n = 400$

4.22. $\hat{\tau} = 1{,}498{,}000, B = 263{,}920$

Answers

Chapter 5

5.1. $\hat{p}_{st} = .3004$, $B = .1160$

5.2. $n_1 = 18$, $n_2 = 10$, $n_3 = 2$

5.3. $\hat{\tau} = 1903.90$, $B = 676.80$

5.4. $\bar{y}_{st} = 13{,}208.63$, $B = 560.485$

5.5. $n = 27$, $n_1 = 16$, $n_2 = 7$, $n_3 = 4$

5.6. $\bar{y}_{st} = 59.99$, $B = 3.032$

5.7. $n_1 = 11$, $n_2 = 21$, $n_3 = 18$

5.8. $n = 33$

5.9. $n = 32$

5.10. $\hat{\tau} = 50{,}505.60$, $B = 8{,}663.124$

5.11. $n = 156$

5.12. $n = 29$

5.13. $n = 158$, $n_1 = 39$, $n_2 = 17$, $n_3 = 69$, $n_4 = 33$

5.14. $\hat{p}_{st} = .701$, $B = .0503$

5.15. $n = 62$, $n_1 = 17$, $n_2 = 6$, $n_3 = 26$, $n_4 = 13$

5.16. (a) $\bar{y}_{st} = 251.07$, $\hat{V}(\bar{y}_{st}) = 141.81$
  (b) $\bar{y}_{st} = 250.05$, $\hat{V}(\bar{y}_{st}) = 181.25$

5.17. dividing points: 40, 70, 90

Chapter 6

6.1. $\hat{\tau}_y = 1589.5522$, $B = 186.3176$

6.2. $\hat{\tau}_y = 2958.3333$, $B = 730.13697$

6.3. $r = .2113$, $B = .0126$

6.4. $\hat{\tau}_y = 145{,}943.7809$, $B = 7{,}353.67$

6.5. $\hat{\mu}_y = 1186.5348$, $B = 59.79$

6.6. $\hat{\mu}_y = 17.5892$, $B = .2710$

6.7. $\hat{\mu}_y = 4.1646$, $B = .0847$

6.8. $r = .283$, $B = .0616$

6.9. $\hat{\tau}_y = 5492.3077$, $B = 428.4381$

6.10. $r = 1.037$, $B = .001391$

6.11. $\hat{\mu}_y = 1061.0376$, $B = 139.9468$

Answers

6.12. $\hat{\tau}_y = 231{,}611.86$, $B = 3{,}073.83$

6.13. $n = 14$

6.14. $\hat{\mu}_{yL} = 1186.5457$, $B - 61.35$

6.16. $\hat{\tau}_y = 5515.48$, $B = 448.40$

6.17. $r = .835$, $B = .012$

6.18. $\hat{\tau}_{yRS} = 48{,}205$, $\hat{V}(\hat{\tau}_{yRS}) = 564{,}742.1$

Chapter 7

7.2. $\bar{y} = 19.73077$, $B = 1.78$

7.3. $\hat{\tau} = N\bar{y}_t = 12{,}312$, $B = 3{,}175.067$

7.4. $\hat{\tau} = M\bar{y} = 14{,}008.846$, $B = 1{,}110.7845$

7.5. $n = 14$

7.6. $\bar{y} = 51.56$, $B = 1.344$

7.7. $n = 13$

7.8. $\hat{p} = .709$, $B = .048$

7.9. $n = 7$

7.10. $\bar{y} = 40.1688$, $B = .6406$

7.11. $\hat{\tau} = 157{,}020$, $B = 6{,}927.875$

7.12. $n = 30$

7.13. $\bar{y} = 16.005$, $B = .0215$

7.14. $\hat{p} = .57$, $B = .0307$

7.15. $n = 21$

7.16. $\bar{y} = 5.91$, $B = .3224$

7.17. $\hat{p} = .4$, $B = .1165$

7.18. $N\bar{y}_t = 3532.80$, $B = 539.50$

7.19. $\bar{y}^* = 2.68$, $\hat{V}(\bar{y}^*) = .06$

Chapter 8

8.3. (a) .1275   (b) .009

8.4. $\hat{p}_{sy} = .66$, $B = .0637$

8.5. $n = 1636$

8.6. $\bar{y}_{sy} = 11.9447, B = .0259$

8.7. $n = 27$

8.8. $\bar{y}_{sy} = 2007.1111, B = 151.028$

8.9. $\hat{p} = .81, B = .0363$

8.10. $n = 1432$

8.11. $\hat{\tau} = 127{,}500, B = 30{,}137.0593$

8.12. $n = 259$

8.13. $\bar{y}_{sy} = 3.54, B = .406$

8.14. $\bar{y}_{sy} = 225.4717, B = 6.7524$

8.15. $\hat{\tau} = 48{,}680, B = 1{,}370.3446$

8.16. $\bar{y}_{sy} = 7038.0952, B = 108.7363$

8.17. $\hat{p}_{sy} = .738, B = .1041$

8.18. $\hat{\tau} = 4400, B = 784.079$

Chapter 9

9.2. $\hat{\mu}_r = 9.3789, B = 1.4536$

9.3. $\hat{\mu} = 9.5593, B = 1.3672$

9.4. $\hat{p} = .2865, B = .1116$

9.5. $\hat{p} = .351, B = .1767$

9.6. $\hat{\tau} = 3980.7, B = 274.7317$

9.7. $\hat{p} = .1200, B = .0667$

9.8. $\hat{\tau} = 1276.2425, B = 333.4435$

9.9. $\hat{\mu} = 7.9333, B = .0924$

Chapter 10

10.4. $N = 444.444 \approx 445, B = 150.596$

10.5. $\hat{N} = 1811, B = 344.512$

10.6. $\hat{N} = 10{,}868, B = 715.82086$

10.7. $\hat{N} = 3348.2143, B = 445.10$

10.8. $\hat{N} = 200, B = 78.88$

10.9. $\hat{V}(\hat{N})/N = 12.67$ or $t \approx 625, n \approx 625$

10.10. $\hat{N} = 1067, B = 507.7182$

Answers

10.11. $\hat{N} = 750, B = 441.588$

10.13. $\hat{N} = 250, B = 52.04$

Chapter 11

11.1. $\bar{y} = 407.125, B = 93.703$

11.2. $\bar{y} = 5.26, B = .7889$

11.3. $\bar{y} = 23.6113, B = 9.0972$

11.4. $\hat{\tau} = 1794.455, B = 778.1539$

11.5. $\hat{\tau}_1 = 1959.7338, B = 763.5104$

11.6. $\bar{y} = 9.8042, B = 2.3758$

11.7. $\hat{\tau} = 3866.7633, B = 1171.2750$

11.8. $\hat{\tau}_1 = 4117.764, B = 999.8094$

11.9. $\hat{p} = .875, B = .1052$

11.10. $\hat{p} = .125, B = .1377$

Index

Allocation of the sample, 68, 78
  Neyman, 71
  optimum, 69
  proportional, 74, 83
Animal populations, 217
Average cluster size, 144

Biased estimator, 12
Bound on the error of estimation, 14

Callbacks, 24, 239
Cluster sampling, 23, 141, 201
  estimator of a mean, 144, 203
  estimator of a proportion, 155, 209
  estimator of a total, 144, 203
Coefficient of linear correlation, 11, 177
Confidence coefficient, 15
Confidence interval, 15
Correlation, 11, 177
Cost, 60, 69
Covariance, 11

Design of the sample survey, 21
Difference estimator, 125

Element, 20
Error of estimation, 14, 22
Estimation, 12
  interval, 15

Estimator, 12
  of population mean, 36, 62, 107, 123, 125, 144, 176, 188, 204, 208
  of population proportion, 46, 77, 155, 183, 210
  of population ratio, 102
  of population size, 218, 220
  of population total, 41, 64, 104, 147, 148, 181, 189, 206
Expected value, 9
Experiment, 2

Finite population correction, 36
Frame, 21

Independence, 8, 12
Inference, 1, 3
Interpenetrating subsamples, 229
  estimator of a mean, 230
Interval estimation, 15
Interviews, 24
  personal, 25
  telephone, 25

Linear functions, 11
Lower confidence limit, 15

Mean,
  estimator of, *see* Estimator
  population, 6
  sample, 6

Index

Neyman allocation, 71
Nonresponse, 23, 24
Normal distribution, 13

Optimal stratification, 88
Optimum allocation, 69
Ordered population, 177, 178

Parameters, 12
Periodic population, 177, 178
Personal interview, 25
Population, 1, 20
Population, types of
 ordered, 177, 178
 periodic, 177, 178
 random, 177
Probability, 7
Probability distribution, 7, 8
Proportion,
 estimator of, 46, 77, 155, 183, 210
Proportional allocation, 74, 83

Questionnaire, 26
 dichotomous, 26
 mail, 25
 multiple-choice, 26
 open-end, 27
 self-administered, 25

Random number tables, 32, 33, 264
Random population, 177
Random response, 237
Random sampling, 22, 31
Random variable, 7
Ratio estimation, 22, 99
 mean, 107
 ratio, 102
 total, 104
Regression estimator, 123
Repeated systematic sampling, 187
 estimating a mean, 188

Sample, 1, 21
Sample, allocation of, 68, 69, 71, 74, 78, 83

Sample size, 43, 48, 66, 79, 111, 152, 158, 185, 186, 221
Sample standard deviation, 7
Sample survey design, 31
Sampling unit, 20
Sample variance, 6
Simple random sampling, 22, 31
 estimator of a mean, 36
 estimator of a proportion, 46
 estimator of a total, 41
Standard deviation, 7
Stratified random sampling, 22, 59
 estimator of a mean, 62
 estimator of a proportion, 77
 estimator of a total, 64
Stratum, 59
Subpopulation, 232
 estimator of a mean, 200
 estimator of a total, 234
Subsidiary variable, 99
Survey, 2
Systematic sampling, 23, 173
 estimator of a mean, 176
 estimator of a proportion, 183
 estimator of a total, 181

Tchebysheff's Theorem, 7, 15
Telephone interview, 25
Total, estimator of, *see* Estimator
Two-stage cluster sampling, 201
 estimator of a mean, 204. 208
 estimator of a proportion, 210
 estimator of a total, 206

Unbiased estimator, 12
Upper confidence limit, 15

Variance, 6, 9, 12
 population, 6
 sample, 6

Wildlife population, 217
 estimator of population size, 218, 220